Over the Mountains

OVER THE MOUNTAINS

More Thoughts
on Things That Matter

Rafe Mair

with a foreword by Stevie Cameron

HARBOUR PUBLISHING

HARBOUR PUBLISHING CO. LTD.
P.O. Box 219
Madeira Park, BC V0N 2H0
www.harbourpublishing.com

"What I Told the Gomery Commission" and "An Act of Plunder" reprinted with the kind consent of *thetyee.ca*.
Cover illustration by Peter Lynde.
Printed and bound in Canada.

Harbour Publishing acknowledges financial support from the Government of Canada through the Book Publishing Industry Development Program and the Canada Council for the Arts, and from the Province of British Columbia through the BC Arts Council and the Book Publishing Tax Credit.

LIBRARY AND ARCHIVES CANADA CATALOGUING IN PUBLICATION

Mair, Rafe, 1931–
        Over the mountains : more thoughts on things that matter / Rafe Mair.

Includes index.
ISBN 1-55017-371-5

        I. Title.

AC8.M315 2006   081   C2006-903313-7

To the long-suffering environmentalist who must keep up the fight knowing that there's no one in any government in the country who gives a damn.

Contents

Foreword   *Stevie Cameron*   9
Preface   11

PART ONE   **The State of the Union**

Am I a Canadian or a British Columbian?   15
What Is a Nation?   27
How Energy May Divide Us   30
Do We Need a New Policy Vis-à-Vis Our Neighbours?   33
The War to Come   39
A Loathsome Libel   48

PART TWO   **Putting It on Record**

A Presentation to the Kirby Commission on Mental Health   55
What I Told the Gomery Commission   62
A Letter to Former Premier Bill Bennett   70

PART THREE   **Foreign Affairs**

The European Community: An Exercise in Deception   81
The EC and Racism   94
The Forgotten Player   96
The Muddle East   101
Terrorism: What Is It?   105
Do We Have to Be Stupid
    When We Deal With Terrorism?   115

PART FOUR   **The Free Press and Other Myths**

The Rear-View Mirror   121
The Journalist's Duty   125
The Modern Media and What to Do About It   129

PART FIVE   **Some Thoughts on Religions**

The Christian Right   147
The Catholic Church   155
A Thought on Sin   159

PART SIX   Idle and Not-So-Idle Thoughts

Small Can Be Beautiful   163
Things I Can Do Without   168
Help for Stats Canada   172
The Longest Year   177
Dogs and a Couple of Cats I've Known   180
Tiger's the Best, Period   194
On Writing and Language   197

PART SEVEN   Collecting

Whither Books and Other Good Things?   205
On Parting with Old Friends   209
Rattling Records with Rafe   211

PART EIGHT   Troubling Times, Troubling Questions

The Welfare State—The Philosophy   223
Corporations or Countries?   232
Supply Needs More Than Demand   241
The Time Has Come   245
Is Churchill Still Relevant?   249
Who's to Blame?   253
An Act of Plunder   257

PART NINE   Still Travelling

In Which the World Traveller
    Goes to the Big Apple—Finally   263
Travel Vignettes   268
 Some Thoughts of London on August 25, 2005   279

PART TEN   Mortal Thoughts

The Good Old Days   285
Growing Old Is Not for the Faint of Heart   288
On Staying Alive   293
Why Me?   295

Index   297

Foreword

Sometimes Rafe irritates the hell out of me. For years I've had this great idea of writing an essay on how poorly people speak these days—you know, how grammar has gone to the bow-wows and kids use "like" to start every thought and "goes" instead of "says" and "me and him" instead of "he and I," and … well, you get the idea. Rafe has not only scooped me in this book, he has ranted up a perfect storm of examples of how we fail our lovely language every day, even hauling out his knowledge of arcane grammatical rules, ones I obey but have forgotten why. Rafe remembers why. He even manages to be funny. What a show-off. Language and grammar are just two of Rafe's passions; others you'll enjoy reading about in this collection of essays are Canadian history, fly fishing, good clothes and fine hotels, international politics, his chocolate Lab Chauncey; his beautiful wife Wendy. You will not be surprised to find a diatribe about the Charlottetown Accord in his run through Canadian constitutional arguments (a subject more interesting, I think, to Rafe than to his readers); nor will you wonder why he raves on against corruption in politics. That's a constant concern to him. But you will always understand that this is a man who is crazy about his country and his province and it drives him nuts when they don't work the way they should.

One of the reasons I have always loved Rafe so much, aside from the fact that for many years he has cared so much for me and my work, my well-being and the well-being of my family, is that he wears his heart on his sleeve. He isn't afraid to say he loves. He isn't afraid to say he has suffered from severe depression and has to take medication to manage it. In fact, that's a subject he discussed in a piece he wrote for me several years ago when I was editing *Elm Street* magazine. His story generated more mail than anything else we ever published during my years as editor. He isn't afraid to write about his own suffering and failures: the embarrassment of going broke, for example, or the indignities of aging or worst of all, the humiliation of being fired in a brutal and public way from his job as the province's most influential radio host.

And it was when he was in that job that we met. For many years Rafe, along with the CBC's Peter Gzowski, was a major supporter of Canadian writers. You were out on a book flog? He would work to get you on his show, get his open lines ringing, get those listeners into the bookstores to buy it. (He'd even read it first, a nice change from most press interviews.) Hundreds of Canadian writers know what they owe this curious and intelligent man who talked to them about their books. He's slaved on enough of his own to know the feeling; this volume is his sixth collection of essays. Rafe can't stop buying books and he can't stop writing them. Lucky for us.

— STEVIE CAMERON
August, 2006

Preface

This is my seventh book and like many of the others it is really a book of essays, though because I hated reading essays in school, I hesitate to use that word.

I come from Scottish/English heritage but consider myself of Scots ancestry. My surname is Scots from Aberdeenshire, and through my grandmother, née Jane Macdonald, I descend, as hundreds of millions do and have, from the great Somerled, the first Lord of the Isles. My mom always told me I should think more of my English roots, and indeed I should since through my maternal side I am a Leigh and thus related to the Drakes, the Spencers and the Churchills. One of my great-great-grandfathers, Sir Percival Leigh, was the editor of *Punch* magazine and I have seen his name where he carved it—in the magazine's tradition—in the oak round table in the Punch Tavern on Fleet Street.

Through my father I have New Zealand citizenship, and I have visited New Zealand over twenty-five times. Ours was a pioneer European family in New Zealand and much written about in New Zealand history. My great-great-grandparents, Gilbert and Elizabeth, and their eldest son, Gilbert II, were present at the signing of the Treaty of Waitangi in 1840, and it was noted that "Mrs. Mair entertained the ladies at tea." I've often wondered what would make a man like Gilbert, aged eighteen, leave his homeland forever to settle in a place literally halfway around the world, a home that still harboured angry aboriginals. Was he in trouble with the law? Did he need work? Was he simply adventuresome? Judging from the presents he and Elizabeth received on their wedding day, including a lovely sonnet, they must have come from reasonably well-off people, so this remains a mystery.

I was born in Vancouver and have spent all but six months of my life in British Columbia. I have lived in two communities outside Vancouver: Kamloops, where I became an MLA in 1975, and Victoria for the five years I was in the BC cabinet under Bill Bennett. Because of my service under the Social Credit flag I'm sometimes described as "right wing," but I contend that my record in cabinet, the legislation and policy I put forward and my record generally would indicate I'm centre-left. I have voted Green in the past three elections.

My first career was law, which I practised for fifteen years in Vancouver and Kamloops. My second was politics, which had my serious attention from 1973 until I left the legislature and cabinet in 1981. Since then I've been in the media. My last career started when I was in my fiftieth year and during that span I've been BC Broadcast Performer of the Year, won the prestigious Michener Award and been shortlisted twice, was awarded the Bruce Hutchison Lifetime Achievement Award and have been inducted into the Canadian Association of Broadcasters Hall of Fame.

That I write from a British Columbia perspective should come as no surprise, but I have also travelled a great deal and am blessed to have a wonderful wife, Wendy, who shares that love.

I hope that the reader will be challenged by some of what follows, amused by some it, and indeed both for much of it.

PART ONE

The State of the Union

Am I a Canadian
or a British Columbian?

One night many years ago when I was doing an open-line segment on my midnight-until-two radio show on CKNW, I was confronted by a question I had constantly debated unto myself but on which I had never really made a public commitment. "Rafe," the caller asked bluntly (as I am also wont to do), "are you a Canadian or a British Columbian first?"

I paused . . . for quite a time. I knew that the quick, easy answer was "Of course I'm a Canadian first . . . how dare you question that?" But my temerity cost me the advantage of a quick assertive answer. I fumbled then blurted out, "I think I'm a British Columbian first." I don't remember what the reaction from the audience was, if any, but I do know that I'm still working through what the real answer to that basic of all basic questions is. It's not easy for there are times I feel very Canadian and others where I'm anything but. The proper answer is, of course, "I'm a Canadian, damn it! How dare you challenge my patriotism?" But I'm not noted for always having the proper answer.

I was born in Vancouver of a New Zealand father of Scots descent and a Canadian mother. My mother's English father was by accident of birth born in Minneapolis, Minnesota. Her mother, Jane Macdonald, was born on Cape Breton Island, Nova Scotia, her ancestors having fled the Scottish clearances to go to "New Scotland." I am, then, a Canadian with a mixed background but one whose Canadian lineage on one side of the family goes back several generations. Leaving aside the fact that I also carry New Zealand citizenship, the question is: If I'm not a Canadian, what else could I be?

Well, I was, in fact, born English or, more correctly, a British subject. My late childhood was during World War II when "O Canada" still contained the lines "At Britain's side, whate'er betide, unflinchingly we'll stand." Our real national anthem was "God Save the King," which when played on the radio in our home, brought everyone to attention, even Mom—sorry, *Mum*—in the kitchen. The national flag was the Union Jack and the "frogs" in Quebec were cowards who wouldn't fight for King and Country. During the war years I was a student at St. George's School for Boys (a veddy British school, don't you know?). We played cricket (I loved it) and rugby, and the headmaster, John Harker, never let us forget that baseball and American—or Canadian for that matter—football were foreign games. Dreadful stuff—not British, you know. I don't want you to think that there wasn't some genuinely Canadian material thrown in because there was. We sometimes sang "The Maple Leaf Forever," especially emphasizing the part where Wolfe kicked the shit out of Montcalm.

The history of Canada we were taught came from a text published by James Dent and Sons, straight out of Toronto, and was all about eastern Canada. We learned about the Iroquois, Huron and Algonquins and nary a word about the Musqueam, Salish or Nisga'a (we're now paying for our ignorance big time). We learned about Wolfe and Montcalm, Cartier and Champlain, Radisson and Des Groseilliers and nothing about James Cook, George Vancouver,

Simon Fraser or David Thompson. We got a footnote about Alexander Mackenzie because he crossed the continent before the Americans Lewis and Clark did. We were taught nothing about "Hanging Judge" Begbie or the man named William Smith who called himself Amor De Cosmos, was BC's second premier and founded the *Colonist* newspaper, now the *Victoria Times-Colonist.*

De Cosmos was the principal force behind BC joining Canada, but whether or not that's to his credit I leave to you. British Columbia was little more than a footnote to Canadian history, evidently only included at all because the CPR had to end someplace. In fact, the second book I wrote (*Canada: Is Anyone Listening?*—to which the answer was obviously *No!*) was spawned by the realization that you could not find the name of the first premier of British Columbia in any standard history of Canada. It was not that he was any hell as a premier—he wasn't—but rather that I was appalled that no Canadian students or other researchers for that matter would ever see his name in a text. Until Google, it was an unresearchable trivia question!

I wasn't taught anything about British Columbia until I was in second year at UBC and took a History of BC course from a wonderful old prof named Dr. Walter Sage. From Sage I finally heard about our first premier and how Ottawa had bribed BC into joining Canada by promising a railway, building some docks and paying off the colony's debt. For those who don't care about that obscure first premier of BC, skip on; for those who do want to know, his name was John Foster McCreight, and after a little over a year as premier he lost a vote of confidence that brought De Cosmos to power.

When I was growing up, the part of life that was "Canadian content" (to quote a later nauseating phrase) was contained in CBC Toronto, the *Toronto Star Weekly* and Toronto's *Saturday Night.* We were expected to accept—and I exaggerate not—that we were an extension of Ontario—which was to say Toronto. The big deal was *The Happy Gang,* a purely "Torontoese" show, which the CBC delivered across the country after the 10 A.M. time signal.

It was sort of a variety show that was supposed to make us all feel at home with the centre of the Canadian universe. We got *Hockey Night in Canada* on CBC Radio but all we were permitted to hear were Toronto Maple Leaf games. Why would anyone want anything else? Weren't the Maple Leafs (the ignorant buggers didn't even know that the plural of "leaf" is "leaves") *the* Canadian team? Didn't every red-blooded Canadian lad want to don the Leaf uniform and play alongside Syl Apps, Gordie Drillon and later Ted "Teeder" Kennedy and Howie Meeker? And didn't every decent Canadian kid know that the Montreal Canadiens were French slackers with yellow streaks down their backs? And wasn't it unbelievable that Leafs owner Conn Smythe, Captain Canada himself, had actually allowed a "frog," Paul Bibeault, to play for Toronto during the war when all decent men were overseas? (It didn't happen again until the sixties when a journeyman defenceman named Marc Rheaume briefly played for them.)

It was that bad. The racism that spewed so naturally from Foster Hewitt, who was the Leafs' and CBC's broadcaster, was so endemic that it got so you hardly noticed. The Hot Stove League—the between-periods gathering of hockey writers—confirmed that the only reason there were five other teams in the league was because the Leafs had to play someone, didn't they? It wasn't until the fifties that CBC started broadcasting *some* Montreal Canadiens games for those of us who were so turned off by the public masturbation pumped out by the CBC, Toronto and the Leafs (like the Holy Trinity—all the same thing under different guises) that we became devout, in every sense of the word, Canadiens fans. I digress to say that the high point of sports life to me was 1960 when the Canadiens beat the Leafs four games straight (after doing the same to the Chicago Black Hawks) to win the Cup, the final score being 4–0 with my hero Maurice Richard scoring the last goal of the game and of his illustrious career.

You will now, I trust, understand that one reason I didn't buy entirely into the vision of Canada I was taught to believe was the *only* one came from a dislike of being told what to think plus plain and simple anti-authoritarianism—character defects, if they so be, that have accompanied me all my life.

But I haven't told the whole story. The fact is I simply didn't know anyone from east of the Rockies except for my mother's friend Constance Mackay, a snooty lady from TO who deplored my lack of interest in classical music (more later). And there was her son Pierre (imagine naming your Anglo kid Pierre!), who spent most of his time getting into accidents—a clumsier kid you never saw—and waiting for the winter snowfall that never came. If he represented Toronto kids, we were sure as hell glad we were different! There was also Sir Ernest MacMillan, a celebrated man of music also from Toronto—or so we were told when he arrived at Maple Grove Elementary School to give us the benefit of his superior breeding, knowledge and place of origin. He patronizingly assured us that there must be—as a matter of mathematics, I suppose—one or two of us with the raw talent necessary to be taken hence to the Toronto Conservatory of Music and taught properly.

At school, the only non-British Columbians I got to know were British kids sent here for the war. One of my best friends, Roger Cantrell, was just such a kid, and I can still remember his address: 1 Oldfield Close, Stanmore, Middlesex, England. A dozen years ago in a bout of nostalgia caused by seeing that wonderful movie with Anne Bancroft, *84 Charing Cross Road,* I wrote to the "occupant" at Roger's old address. They kindly replied that they could not help me a bit. I still look though, so far in vain.

For the benefit of those from eastern Canada who refer to BC as part of "the West" I must say that the occasional Prairie kid who came our way was just as foreign as the Brits. For one thing they could skate and none of us could. How could we? There was seldom any natural ice and at that time the old Forum was the only artificial ice in town. The Prairie kids spoke kind of funny too—sort of like Gary Cooper. Where British Columbians sound like Californians, these kids sounded as if they came from Topeka, Kansas. (I say that because there was a kid at school from Topeka and he sounded like the kids from the Prairies.) When I was in high school a guy named Hugh Blair arrived from Calgary wearing jeans before they were generally fashionable, and he was immediately dubbed "Tex"—which he hated. When I got to UBC I met a lot more kids from the Prairies and they still sounded different and were all crazy about hockey though more especially football, this being the time of the Western Interprovincial Football Union (now the Western Conference of the Canadian Football League), which wouldn't let Vancouver play. Understandably, our interest was more a matter of curiosity. UBC played American football in a league with western Washington colleges—and consistently lost.

French Canadian kids simply did not exist except near Maillardville, where there is a French Canadian settlement of some antiquity, though it is now pretty much anglicized. In law school we had one French Canadian, Jacques Barbeau, but he didn't have an accent and went by Jack.

Now, mind you, it wasn't that we didn't like these kids because we did. It was just that they were different. To this day you can bring up a name of a kid I knew in school or university and I can tell you whether or not he or she was a British Columbian. Even my old friend John Fraser, as devout an advocate for BC as there ever was, can never forget he was born of British Columbia parents but in Yokohama. Being a British Columbian is like membership in a Scottish clan—you must be born to it!

But there is another very important factor that led me to later confess that I am a British Columbian before I'm Canadian: this is where I was born and have lived all my life. I grew up on the evergreen West Coast at a time when it was relatively unspoiled. I cruised the waters with my dad, angled for the plentiful salmon that abounded in our waters. I played on the beaches and in later times made love on those beaches. I dug for clams and watched the eagles, gulls and herons along this coast of mine. I smelled the ocean and learned to love the sound of rain on the rooftop. (My mom told me that when I was a little boy I asked her why there was so much rain. She replied, "God gives us all this rain so we can have the big green trees," to which I evidently came back, "Couldn't we ask God for a little less rain and slightly smaller trees?") To this day, when taking our chocolate Lab Chauncey to the beach for his daily swim, I'm still enchanted by the otter family there, the ubiquitous seals, the gulls and the eagles, both golden and bald-headed.

But I was more than just a West Coaster. Because of regular summer visits I came to love the desert in BC's south central region. In fact, I loved it so much that later in life I moved to Kamloops to practise law, eventually representing that constituency in the legislature.

Thus, I am a British Columbian physically, mentally, and deep into my soul. I couldn't and wouldn't live anywhere else, though I did try. After I graduated from law school in 1956, having a wife and a baby and being unable to afford to article, I went to Edmonton and joined Imperial Oil. As our train passed Wabamun Lake on May 15 I could see that the ice was just breaking. May 15, for God's sake! And it snowed on Labour Day! I couldn't hack it. I turned tail and headed for home and the smell of the sea.

When I confess that I'm first and foremost a British Columbian, I'm often chided with the assertion that having only lived in BC I don't really understand the country—the inference being that I'm a rare beast indeed. The only people who are real Canadians, according to this theory, are those who have lived in various regions. My reply is simple: what then do we say about William Lyon Mackenzie King, Louis St. Laurent, John Diefenbaker, Lester Pearson, Pierre Trudeau, Joe Clark, Brian Mulroney, Jean Chrétien and Paul Martin? All of them have professed to understand my province, and none of them ever lived a day here. The only reason any of them bothered to visit BC was to attend party fundraisers and do the wine-and-cheese bit with local party hacks. And what about Peter Lougheed, Robert Stanfield, Rene Lévesque and Jean Charest? They never lived in BC yet are considered important and influential Canadians. On that point, why am I to be chastised for seeing myself as a British Columbian first while no one would dare criticize a Quebecker who feels a greater attachment to his province than to Canada and, indeed, calls his legislature the "National Assembly"?

In the 1970s, as the BC cabinet minister responsible for constitutional matters, I was told that once I got to know people in Central Canada I would see that they really understood us and cared about us. One constitutional conference I went to in Toronto had a large bas-relief map of Canada behind the podium. "Where are the Queen Charlotte Islands?" I asked. There was a bewildered look from the chairman, but he was silently though obviously reacting with "Who cares?" Four years later, after God only knows how many more conferences involving constitutional and other matters, I was able to reply to those who gave me such a glowing report on my eastern co-citizens, "What a crock of shit! They neither understand us nor care to learn. They see us as part of 'the West,' indistinguishable from the good citizens of The Pas, Manitoba; Swift Current, Saskatchewan; or Medicine Hat, Alberta. They believe that Canada is the ongoing struggle between Upper and Lower Canada and that our role is to get instructions from Ontario then dutifully do what we're told. We're patronized and, indeed, actively disliked." I felt this way in 1980 and if anything I would be more emphatic today.

What am I then, a "western separatist"? Apart from the fact that I'm not a "westerner," I think that those who ask that question misunderstand the political dynamics involved. First, it must be understood that there is no "West." It's a designation of convenience used by Central Canadian politicians ever since Confederation and, indeed, by "western Canadians" as well when it suited them, but it's a word without historical, political, geographical, geological or demographic meaning. It is simply a term that Ottawa politicians have used instead of "out there somewhere." It is true that the Prairie Provinces have often described themselves as "the West." However, Preston Manning, the only bright political light in the country during the last quarter of the past century, grossly erred when he said "The West wants in." The fact is that it was not until 1976 that British Columbia was finally invited to the Western Premiers' Conference and even at that we withdrew from deliberations when issues pertaining only to the Prairie Provinces were discussed. But even if one could assume that there was once a "West" between the Lakehead and the Rockies, that concept is now behind us as Alberta has unquestionably become one of Canada's regions and is quite distinct from Saskatchewan and Manitoba. Indeed, Manitoba has edged over to being rather more a Central Canadian province than a Western one.

If there is no "West," there is no basis for western separation, thus no need for a western separatist party. That is not to say that there haven't been and always will be so-called parties calling themselves western separatists under one designation or the other—there have and will be. But they represent nobody for the very good reason that there is no natural physical or political base for such a party to function.

I realize how confusing this must seem to Central Canadians. After all, wasn't there a Social Credit Party in both Alberta and BC and didn't they run those provinces for a long time? The answer is a strange sort of "No." There were parties of that name in both provinces—as there was in New Zealand—but they were as unlike as chalk and cheese. In Alberta, Social Credit started as a party of protest against the evils of Ottawa as evidenced by freight rates and agricultural policy. It had a strong Christian evangelical bent and wound up as a small-c conservative party under Ernest Manning. In British Columbia it was a flag of convenience for W.A.C. Bennett in 1952 when, as a renegade Tory MLA, he sought a vehicle for an assault on the existing Liberal-Conservative coalition. He had tried first to be elected Conservative leader but, after failing, it was a case of any old port in the storm would do—including that group of funny-money weirdos (that's how they were perceived at any rate) called the Social Credit League.

There were occasions when Bennett would pretend that there was a great Social Credit movement abroad in the land, but that was humbug and he knew it as did everyone else. No one in the entire province, let alone the Social Credit Party itself, had the faintest idea what Social Credit was all about. Put bluntly, there was no connection between Social Credit as professed in Alberta and Mr. Bennett's political philosophy and way of doing things. Bennett was a hell of a lot closer to the centre and indeed to the left than any other successful Canadian politician of the day, including Tommy Douglas. It was Bennett who brought hospital insurance then medicare to BC and it was he who pioneered groundbreaking consumer legislation. He stopped short of giving a fiddler's fart about the environment but then no one else, save for the bearded hippies, cared much about that in those days either.

Can we assume then that, apart from being a long way from Ottawa, there is virtually no common ground—other than common citizenship—uniting BC and the other western provinces, very much including Alberta, and little now connecting the so-called Prairie provinces to each other? If we can so assume, we must also agree that a "western Canada" separatist movement will always be seed sown on barren ground. That doesn't mean that there is no danger from separatism sentiments in western Canada. Far from it. The difference between that which motivates anti-national feeling west of the Lakehead and that sentiment in Quebec is only in causes and emphasis. Anyone who has had the national political experiences I have will have seen an extraordinary amount of common ground shared between BC and La Belle Province, only one of which is dislike of what Toronto and southern Ontario appear to stand for. It is true that in Quebec there is a demographic, cultural and linguistic majority that can be brought together, conditions so warranting, to take a stance against the federation of Canada. This is a majority that can always be marshalled into the game of threatening Ottawa with secession if the right amount of money or other concessions is not proffered. The alienation in western Canada (a term not to be confused with "the West") can only be made into a real separation situation if Ottawa screws up sufficiently that there seems to be no other option.

Let us at this stage make short work of what is *not* going to happen. There never will be a federation of western provinces. As I discussed in my book *Hard Talk*, if one were tried, it would fail. As BC's population nearly equals that of the other provinces combined, the good citizens of Manitoba and Saskatchewan would never consent to a "rep by pop" government where they would always be badly outnumbered. Alberta might, if there were a "Triple-E" senate, because with just a little help from her eastern colleagues she could easily dominate BC. But does anyone really suppose that in such a union either BC or Alberta, now so enthusiastic for a reformed upper house, would think a Triple-E Senate such a hot idea?

So what about Alberta and British Columbia coming together? With all those resources it would be one of the richest nations in the world! But Albertans and British Columbians are not the same people and never have been. The analogy of the Czechs and the Slovaks comes to mind—similar yet oh so different! Can you imagine Alberta agreeing to a unicameral house based on rep by pop? And can you imagine British Columbia agreeing to a Triple-E Senate giving equal representation to Alberta?

The short answer to it all is that there will be no serious and effective "western separation" movement in the foreseeable future. That is not to say that if Canada broke up, other provinces might not try to unite, but in that melancholy event any union of provinces in western Canada would surely fail. Some looser political arrangements could happen, of course, as in the United Arab Emirates.

Does that end the matter? Can Canada concentrate on Quebec certain that her flanks are secure? Not at all, and this is the part that central and Atlantic Canadians must understand. To put it in simple and graphic terms, the more Quebec is appeased, especially with powers, the less relevant Canada becomes to British Columbia.

You will note, I hope, that I'm now just talking about British

Columbia. What must be understood is that British Columbia is as natural a country as Quebec is, or as Newfoundland is. Starting over again from scratch, it would make no sense having BC as part of any country on the eastern side of the Rockies. Fly over BC. See how everything—mountains, lakes, coastal islands—slants north-south. With the obvious exception of the Peace River country, BC is a north-south place. It's that simple. And as BC becomes less and less dependant upon other parts of Canada as customers, as BC deals more and more with the Orient, as issues become more and more Pacific Coast issues, the less important Canada becomes to what is sometimes called Lotusland.

Here, in part, is why that is so. When BC gets into scraps with the United States over fish, lumber and other matters, the province is represented in the subsequent negotiations by the federal government. The trouble is that the federal government has dozens of trade issues with Washington of which British Columbia's problem of the day is but one, and this determines the degree of intensity the feds take into such disputes. Thus, if Quebec leaves Canada or, perhaps just as bad, as she becomes an even more politically favoured region—by which I mean is conceded powers not ceded to other provinces—British Columbia will become less and less interested in Canada and more and more concerned with its own interests.

What I have just said is not considered heresy in BC. Indeed, BC's finance minister, Carole Taylor—a native of Ontario thus having all the zeal of a convert—has talked about how British Columbia is leaning more and more away from the rest of Canada. Ms. Taylor, once a TV star from Toronto, and her husband, former Vancouver mayor Art Phillips, have long been interested in the notion of Cascadia, a loose federation of BC, Alaska, Washington, Oregon and California. That there is such an idea, pushed by such powerful people, tells us a lot about BC feelings.

I must confess, then, in all honesty to being a British Columbian first and a Canadian second. And it isn't really a close call and won't be until Canada becomes a nation, a notion I will examine next.

What Is a Nation?

The word "nation" has many meanings. To some, it is the ultimate statement of a country independent of any outside constraints, the ultimate declaration of an independent people. It is therefore a stronger statement of independence than the word "country." We talk about the "national" aspirations of a people, say the Jews, as expressed in a homeland controlled by "a people." The Israelis would bristle at the suggestion that they constitute a mere "country."

Paradoxically, to others the word "nation" implies a status that is less than a country, a minority group within a country. Aboriginals in Canada are called First Nations even though quite obviously they don't have all the indicia associated with an independent country. So it is with Quebec that thinks of itself as a nation though it legally resides within a country that also thinks of itself as a nation. With little if any complaint from the Canadian government, Quebec declares itself a nation, calls its legislature the "National Assembly" and flies the fleur-de-lis over it.

In Canada, Native and French Canadians get away with calling themselves "nations" because of the cowardice of the national government, which strives to be, above all else, politically correct.

Ottawa has concluded that, if you confer upon lesser groups of people (speaking politically) superior sounding names, they will be flattered into putting the limit you wish them to on their ambitions. It's rather like what Churchill said—though in a slightly different context: "Everyone feeds the crocodile in the hopes the crocodile will eat him last." Just keep flattering those "nations," ambitious for a greater share of autonomy, and they will always keep their demands "reasonable." But this is an unsustainable argument: one does not start down a road to an objective without wanting to attain that objective.

There is a lesson to be learned from Ireland's relationship with England. Britain always maintained the fiction that whatever the relationship would ultimately be, Ireland was under the British crown as a matter of divine certainty. As long as Britain could through thick and thin maintain His Majesty the King as the King of Ireland, all else would fall into place. Thus, when the negotiations for the "Irish Free State" took place in 1922, a sticking point for Britain was that the king/emperor must continue to be the head of state. But wise men such as Michael Collins—whose wisdom would cost him his life—knew that once the Irish MPs refused to take their seats in Westminster, meeting in the Dail in Dublin as their own parliament instead, time would take care of the king and country crap. Which is, of course, what happened.

Just as loyalty to the English crown was seen differently by Michael Collins than it was by de Valera and the British government, we should understand that when Quebec or aboriginal spokesmen assure us that they are really, after all is said and done, Canadians, that word has a much different meaning to them than to those of us in the rest of the country. In short, if (or should I say when?) Natives and Quebec get what they want, it will be as easy as waving a hanky of farewell from a departing ship to kiss Canada goodbye. We should read less of what politicians say and more history. Then we would understand that comforting words of love for a shared ideal become sheer horse shit once the group ambitions have been achieved and the words no longer have any real meaning.

This point segues neatly into a question usually asked about lawyers: how do you know when a politician is lying? The answer: when his lips are moving. This bit of cynicism is mostly believed to be true, but there is a time when it's not and that's when politicians are on the same side as the good guys, usually accidentally, and are making decisions that convince us, in the early going at any rate, that they are on the side of righteousness. A good Canadian example is the Meech Lake/Charlottetown mess where in the early going it seemed Brian Mulroney had convinced the entire country—with the exception of the late constitutional expert Mel Smith, policy guru Gordon Gibson and me—that he was on God's side against Beelzebub himself.

When you look back on it, it takes the breath away! Even though Quebec Premier Bourassa was setting his hair on fire at the thought of not having the words "distinct society" included, we were being told they meant nothing and that the day would never come when we rued giving Quebec 25 percent of the Commons "in perpetuity." We were told that it was quite okay for Quebec to have a veto if other regions had one too. And we were asked to believe, and for a trembling moment did believe, that it was a good idea to have a "damp squib" of a senate (to use the phrase of constitutional expert and one-time Liberal MP Dr. Edward McWhinney) that, even if elected, would be neither equal nor effective and could never be changed. Fortunately, the people were given three years to ask questions. If the provinces had been given only one year to approve Meech Lake, or even two, in my view it would unquestionably have passed. The politicians were on the side of the angels until the public had time to digest the message. Then the angels flew the coop, and it was clear the politicians had as usual lied through their teeth.

We have striven for nationhood but are far from our goal. We are, in fact, falling back at a considerable rate.

How Energy May Divide Us

You might well and accurately infer from what I've said that I have no doubt that "separatism"—or if you prefer "sovereignty sympathy"—is hardening if not significantly increasing. That is, that "soft separatists" are moving into the "hard separatist" camp. One thing not well noticed is the fact that much of the ethnic community—the so-called Allophone sector—is coming around to the sovereignist point of view. The Parti Québécois and the Bloc have worked hard on this issue ever since Jacques Parizeau blamed "ethnics" in part for the 1995 referendum loss.

In the referenda of 1980 and in 1995 western Canadians rallied around the Canadian flag and supported national unity. How much impact they had is an open question, but in a close race you might well think they were definitive of the matter. Will they be so again? Perhaps, but timing is everything and unless I miss my guess, there will be a very angry Alberta and British Columbia at that fateful hour.

Cast your mind back to 1980. The price of oil had risen 160 percent in a few short years, and industry, especially in Ontario, was hurting. The Trudeau government brought in the National

Energy Program (NEP), which by controlling the price Alberta could charge Central Canada for oil, effectively controlled a natural resource, which under the Constitution was a provincial power. Alberta, and to a slightly lesser degree BC, went ballistic. Alberta Premier Peter Lougheed cut back exploration and began a program of reducing exports to Central Canada. The popular bumper sticker in Alberta read, "Let those eastern bastards freeze in the dark." The program only came unstuck when oil prices dropped to less than $20 per barrel. When in 1984 Brian Mulroney abandoned the program, it was an empty gesture except that it pleased the Western provinces.

Oil is in the $60 range now and new Canadian discoveries are less than consumption, meaning that we have "peaked." This unquestionably means the price will increase, perhaps to $100 or even more. But the problem is worse than this because many experts doubt the accuracy of the oil reserves reported by such major producing countries as Saudi Arabia. They think these reserves have been much inflated and the world does not have anywhere near the reserves we think we do (see *Twilight in the Desert* by investment banker Matthew R. Simmons). Add to that the serious problems that will arise if Iran reduces production—a very real possibility—and without question Ottawa will trot out a new NEP to keep domestic oil prices down. There will be appeals to patriotism but they will fall on deaf ears west of the Manitoba–Saskatchewan border. All hell will break loose in Alberta and BC.

It could be argued that, if Sir John A. Macdonald and George-Étienne Cartier had been able to see the future, the Canadian constitution might look very different. But they were not clairvoyant, and at the confederation conventions in Charlottetown and Quebec City in 1864 the power over resources went to the provinces without anyone even mentioning fossil fuels. However, it should be noted that full control over natural resources by the Prairie provinces was not made final until 1930 and then only after a long, tough struggle. It also should be noted that back in the 1960s Ottawa protected

Alberta oil, thus increasing the price *above* the world market price for Central Canada, a fact conveniently forgotten by BC and Alberta. But in 1980 the Liberals were scarcely tactful about how they behaved. I don't think the word "glee" would be inappropriate given the arrogance of Pierre Trudeau and Marc Lalonde, his energy minister. Alberta and British Columbia were already unhappy about the new constitution that was being worked out, and there is no doubt in my mind (I was the BC minister responsible) that the supremely arrogant team of Trudeau and Lalonde loved jamming it to the "far west," and their attitude made the tough medicine they had administered through the NEP nigh unto impossible for the two provinces to swallow. Thus, any return to a National Energy Program approach from Ottawa will be even messier than the original program was in 1980.

But the situation is much worse yet. The next oil crisis may well happen during the lead-up to another Quebec separatist referendum, and there will not be the good feeling in the rest of the country for Quebec staying in Confederation that there was in 1980 and again in 1995. (Premier Jean Charest has already changed his "Canada First" language to words more pleasing to sovereignists—as I publicly predicted he would when he was elected.) Quebec and the Western provinces will have common arguments that, while they won't likely create a serious separatist option in the "far west," may well find many people in those provinces—for different reasons, no doubt—rather sympathetic to Quebec separation. One is reminded of the old Arab saying, "The enemy of my enemy is my friend." Thus, while it is difficult to believe that Ottawa will allow Alberta to sell oil domestically at high world prices, it is even harder to believe that it will provoke an all-out energy war at a time when Quebec separatists are saying to Quebeckers, "See, even western Canada is screwed by federalism."

If nothing else, the next few years will be very interesting.

Do We Need a New Policy Vis-à-Vis Our Neighbours?

C anada's relationship to the United States—and of course, vice versa—goes back to the beginning of the European presence in North America, and from that point on Canada has been in a subservient position—although we Canadians hate to admit it. And much of the problem comes from the fact that the United States is a country founded upon a revolutionary philosophy while Canada—to the extent we don't count Quebec, which of course we must—has evolved as the bastard son of a noble family does: with high expectations but not a few crosses, even of legitimacy, to bear. Even Quebec, with its own history, was cut off from the mother country at a very tender age and has had to muddle along as a cast-off trying not to be American and not be British in similar proportions. If either Quebec or Canada had a relationship to the United States as Britain has had to France or France to Germany, life might have been bloodier, but at least the lines of division would have been more obvious. Not, I suppose, that this would have made things much easier. Our problem as a country (whether or not we're a nation remains to be seen) is that we're really like that imitator of Neil Diamond I have often interviewed who calls himself "Nearly Neil." He is close and enjoyable for being that, but still a long way from the real thing.

There are regional differences and a dominant establishment in both Canada and the US. Indeed, with fifty states as opposed to ten provinces and some territories, there may be more obvious divisions in America than in Canada, but the difference lies in the fact that the United States has a basic creed every American buys into. They accept the concept that the American Revolution was a patriotic exercise on behalf of liberty and free speech, that George Washington was the man who kept it all together, that the Civil War (or War Between the States if you live below the Mason–Dixon line) put an end to slavery, and that two world wars put the United States in the position of being the arbiter of the world's morals. So while there no doubt are regional divisions in the United States, being American trumps all other considerations. Amazingly, former Confederate states have become Republican and make up the largest number of "hawks." For an excellent treatment of that phenomenon see *American Theocracy* by Kevin Phillips.

If the definition of a "nation" is a country like the USA, Canada simply wouldn't qualify. If you don't believe me, answer this question: How many British Columbians would flock to the colours if the United States invaded Newfoundland? What if Toronto were invaded? Ah, you are right there but that's unfair! But if Canada invaded Point Roberts, Americans from all over the country, even those who had never heard of the place, would as one throw us out and plant "Old Glory" back where it belongs. And we're probably the only country in the world where, if one of our athletes wins a bronze medal in a sport no one else has heard of, it's a headline story. Does any other government spend as much money telling its citizens what a great country they live in? Who else would have a huge scandal, one that threatened governments, over spending public money to convince one of the regions via displays of fireworks and flags that they should love their official country?

Canadians don't really share a history, at least not a version of history common to all. Part—but only part—of this is because of Quebec, but I'm almost serious when I say that if you asked someone on Granville Street what year the War of 1812 started they would probably shrug their shoulders. And not one in a hundred could tell you much about it other than, perhaps, fans of Johnny Horton who might remember the "Battle of New Orleans," the great battle fought after the Peace of Ghent had already ended the war. I daresay that not one in a thousand on Bloor Street could tell you when Captain Cook came to the West Coast or when his navigator, Captain Vancouver came back on his own, giving his name to Canada's third largest and only habitable city.

Canadians have, vis-à-vis the US, an inferiority complex that we hate to admit but that is nonetheless a reality. Of course, we're a better country to live in. Without question we are a more civil country by far and, though we're a long way from perfect, we get along with minorities much better. At least we think that and say that we do. The fact remains that we are the weak country cousin and we know it. Our relations with the United States have been as an insecure nation, as yet unsure of what it is or what it wants to be, dealing with the most powerful nation on earth, a nation brimming with confidence, full of certainty that whatever it does is right. For a considerable period of our relationship with the US we remained a British colony. In August 1914 Canada went to war as a consequence of Britain going to war. In 1939 we waited a week to declare war so as to show our "independence." But at Yalta in 1945 Franklin Roosevelt was still so convinced of our subservience to the UK that in putting together the United Nations Organization (as it was then known) he agreed with Stalin that two Soviet republics in addition to the USSR should be members to offset "Britain's" commonwealth countries being given seats in their own right.

The attitude of American presidents towards Canadian prime

ministers has been avuncular at best, if not downright patronizing
or antagonistic. Roosevelt called Mackenzie King "Mackenzie"
not knowing or probably caring that to his friends he was Billy.
John Kennedy called John Diefenbaker a "platitudinous bore" (he
was right) and Nixon called Trudeau an asshole (he too was right
but it sounds strange coming from a disgraced president). Lyndon
Johnson called Lester Pearson "Mr. Wilson."

But enough chatter. Let us get down to cases. Canadians love
to beat their breasts and claim that they're not afraid of the big bad
wolf to the south. The NDP and the CCF before them have an
ongoing dislike of Americans and America that is so deep they don't
recognize it in themselves—it's a knee-jerk reaction. The Liberals
are not usually much better, though they do have a side of the party
that can be described as pro-American most of the time. I suppose
these attitudes all go back to Thomas Chandler Haliburton's inven-
tion of the character Sam Slick, the slippery Yankee trader. But in
spite of our bravado, Canadians know one fact deep down: if they
wanted to, the Americans could take us over in an hour without a
shot being fired. We know that no matter how much we huff and
puff at illegal and immoral American attitudes on trade disputes
that we can't retaliate if only because if you get into a pissing match
with an elephant you're going to get drenched. Everyone with half
a brain knows that the softwood lumber dispute persisted, against all
law and equity, because Canada didn't support George Bush's invasion of Iraq. It's pretty simple. Since the heyday of Henry Kissinger,
the United States has been quick to link issues that have nothing
in common except that they are in dispute. And we know this is
true, however much we don't like to admit it. (Let me say by way of
aside that I don't like knuckling under to American foreign policy
any more than anyone else does. I simply recognize that if we piss
off the Americans there will be retaliation and there isn't much we
can do about that.)

There is another factor that the US understands perfectly while
we try to pretend otherwise: if a dispute with Canada involves

mainly Ontario or Quebec, it will be very important to the Canadian government. If it involves provinces such as BC on issues such as softwood lumber or Pacific salmon quotas, Ottawa's concern will be mild and mostly pro forma. The importance of each dispute is in direct proportion to its impact on Ontario and Quebec, and the US knows this. The name of the game is not trade but politics—raw, simple and pure. The very last thing BC needed with the softwood lumber dispute was to have it also a minor issue for the lumber industries of Ontario and Quebec because that meant Ottawa saw and continues to see the dispute as it relates to those provinces, not as it affects British Columbia where the issue is of huge importance. And we have seen over the years the negligence that Ottawa brought to the problems in the West Coast salmon industry—a story too long and lamentable to be dealt with here—even though the salmon fishing industry is part of the soul of British Columbia, more important than just the dollars it represents.

If the problem facing Canada was simply how to deal with a big bully, daunting though that task might be, it's nothing as compared to the real problem. Our national unity and the continuation of the Great Canadian Experiment depends on what we do next. Because the answer to the softwood lumber dispute—the one just settled is not likely to be the last—is British Columbia doing a better job of refining its wood products and developing new markets. This idea is late in coming but coming it is. I remember about fifteen years ago putting it to one of BC's lumber barons that soon we'd be competing, especially in the Asia market, with Russia, which has the largest untouched forests in the world and which doesn't give a fiddler's fart about spotted owls, worker safety or selling raw logs into the market. He pooh-poohed my suggestions, saying that Russia would never have the infrastructure to compete. He was wrong.

The British Columbia forest industry has huge challenges quite apart from the softwood lumber dispute with the United States but that dispute has, in Dr. Johnson's phrase, "concentrated the mind wonderfully." An unintended consequence is that British Columbia will have more and more dealings in resources with the Orient than with the rest of Canada and the United States. Whether that is a good thing or not remains to be seen, but it will mean that to some extent British Columbia will be a British Columbian trader, not a Canadian trader.

The War to Come

One thing is very sure: our trade relationship with America is changing and changing rapidly as the huge Asian market continues to increase by leaps and bounds. But this doesn't mean that the points of friction with our neighbour to the south will diminish. *Au contraire*, they will greatly be magnified because the friction points have their roots in energy supplies.

Anyone who isn't self-delusional realizes that energy is the big problem of this century—assuming we don't blow ourselves to smithereens in the meantime—and we're facing it as humans always do—badly, if at all. Experts differ but only slightly as to whether or not oil production has "peaked," meaning that we are consuming more than we are discovering. Some say this has already happened. Indeed, some (see *The End of Oil* by Paul Roberts) say that our present oil reserves are far lower than we think they are, notably because Saudi Arabia has deliberately overestimated its oil reserves. For the George W. Bushes of the world this news has provoked a scramble to bring more expensive oil from far away while doing little about finding and bringing alternative energy supplies on stream and virtually nothing about conservation. As in so many things, oilman George Bush, surrounded by other oilmen, talks a great game but does nothing to mitigate his country's difficulties.

The Canadian and British Columbia governments are no better. As time marches inexorably on, they plan a new pipeline from the hugely expensive Alberta tar sands, which only makes sense if oil prices go over $100 a barrel, and another pipeline to bring oil from discoveries we hope to make in the Peace River plus liquefied natural gas to a new port in Prince Rupert. And, of course, we mustn't forget the right wingers drooling at the prospect of oil and gas off the shores of the Queen Charlotte Islands. At the same time both governments continue to subsidize fossil fuel producers. Those who think a gas price of $1.25 or more a litre is too much should look at Europe where the prices are twice that or more. There, people drive small cars just as we should and indeed did for a while after the oil crisis of the seventies. Government policies in Europe and the UK have forced car manufacturers to meet consumer demands for less wasteful cars. In the meantime General Motors in North America wallows in deep trouble because they vastly overproduced SUVs for a public that could once easily afford their gasoline bills. In short, Canada and the United States have done nothing to temper demands for fossil fuels and have, indeed, done the reverse.

Would that the problem ended there but it doesn't. Canada has the most accessible fresh water supply in the world and the United States has the biggest thirst. Canada is also part of NAFTA, which means that once we supply these commodities—oil, gas and water—to the US, we can't reduce the amount of those supplies unless we proportionally reduce our own consumption. Although just how that would work with fresh water is not clear. At least not to me.

The big Canadian challenge, then, is much more difficult to solve than just trade disputes over trees and fish. Simply stated it is this: how do we protect our resources—or more broadly stated, our environment—when shortages of oil, gas and water are felt so acutely in the United States that it would be perilous for us to refuse them our products in the quantity they demand? How do we develop (because we haven't got one) a Canadian foreign policy when to do so might invite—as it already has—American retaliation? The Chrétien government's response to the mainly American assault on Iraq may have been the correct one, but since we don't know why it was taken, it's tough to tell. With hindsight it's easy to say that President Bush, his senior advisers and UK Prime Minister Blair lied, but Chrétien didn't base Canada's policy on knowing that they were lying because no one knew that yet.

The problem of arriving at a consistent policy is also much aggravated by the fact that in Canada, while over-the-border trade is a federal matter, the provinces control the natural resources. And Albertans and British Columbians are likely to look at federal interference with their rights to control natural resources as a call to constitutional arms. That fight, if it comes and if it comes during a period of increasing unrest in Quebec, could be just too much for this country to handle.

The question is: why have we gone in a few short years from peace and quiet on the trading front, especially in the case of resources, to where we have, at the very best, uncertainty about our trading partners? To answer that, you must ask where the United States has gone wrong. And the answer to that one is more than just George W. Bush—though, God knows, he's been a large part. The United States' sin is not that the country dominates the world but that its government has been unable to understand that being powerful must mean more than the chest-thumping, self-serving notion that "we know what's right." From the outset, certainly since the Louisiana Purchase in 1803, Americans have been deeply convinced that they had God's own chosen political system and that it should therefore be exported, much as one once took the Bible to aboriginal peoples. This is a concept that, needless to say, has not been universally accepted.

Now, like Br'er Rabbit and the Tar Baby, the United States is helplessly stuck to the Middle East. The nation's finances are in a parlous state and it stands on the brink of a huge economic meltdown. Don't be fooled by the Dow Jones or the TSX—with the American deficit and foreign trade deficit both around the US$700 billion range something bad about to happen is far more likely than something good. The United States is the modern version Lemuel Gulliver—huge and powerful but impotent in many of the situations it has got into. Theirs is a wartime economy, more self-centred than ever before. Thus, George Bush needs a helpful Congress or at least one that is not unhelpful. But when Canadians ask themselves about the softwood lumber dispute, they still don't understand that the US is refusing to obey all those rulings because a) they're mad at us and b) they are short of money—a bad combination. A better question for us to ask is: How long will the American manufacturers and farmers be able to use their support of the Republicans and George Bush's war aims to trump any NAFTA or other rulings? And the answer to that is: Probably for a very long time. The United States has a history of ignoring the rulings of courts and tribunals when they don't like them.

So what about expanding our trade into, say, the European Union? The EU has horrible political and economic problems of its own. On the economic side, the Community Agriculture Policy has reached the point that British dollars going into the EU are subsidizing French farmers so that British farmers can't compete in their own country! Moreover, the EU has become sort of a large "Ponzi" scheme where new countries are added in order to sustain an unworkable scheme. It was doomed not from the start but from the time Britain entered. Churchill and de Gaulle were right—Churchill for seeing that Britain's better course of action was to stay with the English-speaking peoples and de Gaulle for deciding, perhaps more from passion than reason, that creating a group with three major nations in it would derogate from the power to be shared by Germany and France. Besides, de Gaulle never for a moment thought that the UK could be suckered into a Community

Agriculture Policy that subsidizes the hell out of French agriculture. He was wrong.

Anyone who has watched the shadowboxing over the last five decades could see that the Brits are hopelessly divided on the question of surrendering political power to another constitutional entity, especially one where France plays a major role. And those who opposed the expansion of the Union rightly saw that there was insufficient political unity to maintain an economic union, which is why Britain has so far refused to yield power over its own fiscal and foreign affairs to a central government. The big trouble is that the British people were told at each stage of EU development that it wouldn't cost them a soupçon of sovereignty. That, of course, was untrue, was known to be untrue by those saying it, and is untrue today. There may be some trading light for Canada at the end of this tunnel, however. If the EU does come apart at the seams—I don't mean folds but loses the means to enforce Brussels authority—there's reason to hope that the UK might follow Churchill's advice and look elsewhere for trading partners.

What about Asia as a trading partner for Canada? There are prospects there, of course, but assessing this market discloses that there are at least two stumbling blocks. First off, the Chinese tradition is concrete buildings, not wooden. Second, the sleepy Russian bear is awakening and when it comes to BC's major export, forest products, they're becoming a major factor, a nasty one, too, since they don't have the environmental and safety restraints we place upon our industry, and they are happy to send raw logs abroad to supply their customers' lumber mills.

However, it's not all doom and gloom. Canada, the United States and the European Union have the potential to trade with each other in spite of other formal trading relationships because they have the most elements in common. They share histories, cultures and peoples. All have English as the major trading language. Canadians are, for the most part, culturally Europeans, notwithstanding the huge new and increasing Asian element in this country. We have many of the same values and national goals. Even though sometimes the common thread is that we have from time to time hated each other almost enough to go to war with one another, we still feel comfortable in each other's company. Not always, of course—such as when George W. Bush was slavering to go to war with Iraq—and probably not enough to face the common enemy: globalization.

For into the international power game has entered a new kid: the large corporation. We've always had big companies on the international playing fields, but until the last twenty-five years they have always been companies with specific nationalities playing in a game that had government rules that could be and often were enforced. The silicon chip changed all that because it effectively removed the national government's ability to control the use, flow and exchange of money. And it happened so quickly many didn't notice.

When, back in 1978, Noranda threatened to take over MacMillan and Bloedel, which at that time was our very own mega forest power and seen by British Columbians as an icon, BC Premier Bill Bennett announced that BC was not for sale! "That's telling 'em, Bill!" was the reaction of most British Columbians. But look what happened. When eventually MacMillan Bloedel was taken over by Weyerhaeuser, to the surprise of all of us who considered Mac-Blo ours, the biggest shareholder was now an American pension fund! We now see the British Columbia government eliminating the Canadian-content rule on the sale of Terasen (formerly BC Gas) so it can be controlled by an American company. It was an unpopular move—and it still is with me—but the government was probably right in assuming that in the long run it was powerless to stop it.

During the run-up to the formation of the North American Free Trade Agreement the cry from the left was that the maquiladoras, the Mexican border towns, would vacuum up all our jobs. (In fact, it was that fear that gave rise to the strange political career of Ross Perot, scarcely a "leftie.") Subsequently, the maquiladoras did suck up our jobs, but over the past couple of years those jobs have been unceremoniously sucked from Mexico by Thailand, India and

China! What has happened is simple. Communication technology now allows virtually every service to be sent for action to the cheapest bidder, no matter where situated, which usually means somewhere else.

The secondary yet vitally important factor to know in this equation is that poor countries are finding it easier and easier to export their economic problems to better-off countries. The problems that France, for example, sees with the expansion of the EU is that the poor and the Muslims—the latter being a greater problem to French conservatives—can come into France as of right and that, even if they get in illegally, it is all but impossible to evict them because the French, like the British, gave residents of conquered lands, citizenship. Now they see that not only are major French companies "outsourcing," meaning many French jobs lost, but that the remaining jobs are going to newcomers who will work for less. Similarly the loss of Mexican jobs to Asia has created huge demographic and political problems in the United States, problems that will not easily be solved, if they ever can be. In recent years Hispanics have become the second-largest minority in the US, and they are moving African-Americans out of the market for cruddy jobs. (To see what that has meant, even some of the San Francisco Giants' jerseys read *Gigantes*.)

Thomas L. Friedman, in his classic *The Lexus and the Olive Tree*, used the term the "electronic herd" to describe the massive international speculation that has hit different European currencies at various times. In 1992 it forced Britain to leave the Exchange Rate Mechanism (ERM) that had been designed to keep EU currencies within a tight range and thus promote monetary stability. Black Wednesday, September 16, 1992, also showed that a single individual, George Soros, could take on the government of the UK and win. Individual wealth met national currency and individual wealth won hands down.

I suppose the worst part of all this is that while the future is always murky, at least in past years young people could make reasonable guesses as to what would and would not be good career paths. This is now impossible. Youngsters see the student loans they took on to train for their future careers becoming huge millstones around their necks as they try to find careers in areas they didn't train for or that no longer exist.

Are there solutions? Certainly there are no magic bullets or anything close. But because governments can no longer contain the flow of *all* funds doesn't mean they can't control some and influence some. The G8 and other similar organizations must learn to use the clout that's available to them by acting in concert. They may not be able to control Wal-Mart's outsourcing and other "anti-labour" moves, but they can collectively agree to link Wal-Mart's behaviour to other matters and put on pressure accordingly. It's the old Henry Kissinger knack of "linking"—you will not get anywhere on problem A unless you make the solution of problem B contingent upon settling A.

How does all this globalization and distortion of trading patterns impact on Canada? What does it mean to Canadian unity? Free trade and globalization has meant that our government is considerably more restricted in what it can do. Tariffs sheltering our industries probably had to go anyway, but the result has been trading decisions made in the corporate boardrooms that show less concern, if any at all, for the rules of the country in which they do business. The MacMillan Bloedel case I noted above shows just how ineffective governments have become. Another example is the auto industry in Central Canada where governments don't dare use muscle lest what they have left goes elsewhere.

As oil prices shoot up, the federal government will be under terrific stress from Ontario and Quebec to come up with a new sort of National Energy Program that forces resource-based companies to give them preference. When the world market price of fossil fuels hits Ontario and Quebec, there will be great pressure on the federal government to return to something like the NEP and all hell will break out in Alberta and BC. Governments, which are now unable to influence the oil company boardrooms, will have to rearrange the *Titanic*'s constitutional deck chairs against constitutional rules, thus creating substantial unity problems, because the international situation gives them little choice.

There is something we can do. The softwood lumber dispute did not become Ottawa's concern until it was seen that not only BC, an electorally unimportant province, was heavily impacted but that Ontario and Quebec had a stake in the problem too. We also learned that the dispute resolution process of NAFTA is toothless at best. Canada must have in place its own ongoing federal-provincial dispute assessment mechanism so that problems can be diagnosed early (the softwood lumber dispute started in 1981!) and strategies developed. Facing the problems I have outlined and with many more to come, Canada cannot remain a nation of dissidents trying to deal with international trade matters on their own. The impacts on our various economies are too large.

If we don't get our warring tribes together on trade issues, it's hard to imagine how we'll deal successfully with the strains that threaten us politically.

A Loathsome Libel

The cynic would observe that the bigger the lie, the greater its acceptance—provided it is repeated often enough and long enough. One of the reasons is that the attention span of the average citizen is that of an absent-minded gnat. As time passes, there being no exposition of the truth, the lie flourishes. Such lies often do great injustices, and as Peter C. Newman's best-selling book, *The Secret Mulroney Tapes: Unguarded Confessions of a Prime Minister*, demonstrates, so it is with the Honourable Clyde Wells, former premier of Newfoundland and Labrador and now chief justice of its Court of Appeal.

A little history: in 1987, then Prime Minister Brian Mulroney, after getting large support from Quebec in the 1984 election on his promise to appease that province's constitutional complaints, chaired a first ministers meeting at Meech Lake in Quebec. Out of that meeting came the Meech Lake Accord, which among other things promised Quebec a veto over any future constitutional changes and a special designation as a "distinct society." The premiers outside Quebec didn't seem to understand that their own constitutional ambitions would thus be subject to a Quebec veto and that Quebec would use that veto if anything that was proposed even appeared to impinge on her powers. It's a tribute to Mulroney's persuasive powers that he managed to gloss over that critical point.

To the best of my knowledge no one in the mainstream media except me questioned this deal, and I railed against it and its successor deal, the Charlottetown Accord, from beginning to end. The governments were given three years to ratify the deal. By the final day, June 23, 1990, all provinces but two—Manitoba and Newfoundland and Labrador—were on board. In fact, Newfoundland and Labrador, under the Conservative government of Brian Peckford, had ratified the deal, but when the Liberals under Clyde Wells took office, that ratification was rescinded and a new vote was set for the last day, June 23.

Clyde Wells had made no secret of his opposition to Meech Lake either in opposition or as premier. His objections were the same as those of constitutional experts Mel Smith and Senator Eugene Forsey, BC Liberal Leader Gordon Wilson, public affairs commentator Gordon Gibson, former Court of Appeal judge Ron Cheffins and, for all that it mattered, me. We all asked what "distinct society" meant and opposed giving anyone, much less Quebec, a veto over constitutional change.

Let me digress for a moment and deal with this question of a veto. The issue of bringing the Constitution (the British North America Act of 1867, a British Statute) home to Canada had been bedeviled by one question—how do you amend it? There were many formulas suggested over the years, and the one proposed by first ministers in Victoria in 1970, which would have given Atlantic Canada, Ontario, Quebec and "the West" vetoes, failed because Quebec Premier Bourassa backed out. I'm glad he did for it was a lousy solution. During the years of the run-up to the patriation of the constitution in 1982, the question of a veto for Quebec was the major sticking point. Eventually, an amending formula acceptable to all the parties was adopted and, instead of vetoes, it was based upon a formula that effectively meant that an amendment could pass with seven out of ten of the provinces containing 50 percent of the population. You'll note I said "all" of the parties because, despite his later tantrums, Rene Lévesque did sign a memorandum agreeing to the amending formula. This may seem like arcane, dusty stuff, but the effect of any province having a veto over constitutional change, no matter how many others also do, is that you can never change the constitution because anything proposed that impinges even a teeny little bit upon the powers of Quebec—or Ontario, for that matter—will be vetoed unless that province is given something in exchange.

Mulroney told Quebeckers that the term "distinct society" meant a great deal but told the rest of Canada the term was meaningless. Some sharp-eared folks detected a bit of inconsistency there and demanded a straight answer to the obvious question: if the words "distinct society" mean nothing, why does Quebec set its collective hair on fire at the thought of its removal from the Accord? And if the phrase does mean something, what is that meaning?

Back to business: the final date for approval came on June 23, 1990. I spoke to Clyde Wells a lot during the days prior to that deadline and asked him what he would do. He said that it would be a "free vote" and that his reading of it, after talking to the opposition leader, was that the motion would fail. But *before* the Newfoundland vote was to be taken, Premier Filmon of Manitoba brought the motion forward in the Manitoba legislature. For procedural reasons he needed unanimous consent to hold the vote on short notice. NDP backbencher Elijah Harper, a Native, refused to give the necessary consent so the Meech Lake Accord was killed. Dead. Done. It no longer mattered what Newfoundland and Labrador did.

When Premier Wells heard the news, he stated that there was no point in Newfoundland and Labrador voting. And there wasn't. He told me that if he called a vote and it was "yes," he felt that this would have brought no end of disapprobation on the Native community who would be accused of killing the Canadian Constitution. If the vote was no, it would bring revenge from the federal government, bearing in mind that Newfoundland and Labrador was, in those days especially, an economic basket case. However, immediately after the failure of Meech Lake, Brian Mulroney and his political sidekick Senator Lowell Murray started dumping all over Clyde Wells, calling him, in their moderate moments, a traitor to his country. And they kept it up. Indeed, in his interviews with Peter C. Newman, as revealed in *The Secret Mulroney Tapes*, Brian Mulroney repeated his charges against Wells in hyperbolic pungent terms. Thus a base canard has been permitted to become, in the minds of many Canadians, an accepted "fact."

Why would Mulroney do this? I'm sad to say that the reason is simple: Brian Mulroney thought that in making his excuses for a bad idea gone badly wrong, it was much safer politically to crap all over a Liberal premier in a vassal province than a Native Indian. Whether or not this chapter will form part of the historical record I cannot say. But herewith let it be known that Martin Brian Mulroney, with the concurrence of the establishment and its controlled media, has badly defamed Clyde Wells, a decent man and a fine Canadian.

PART TWO

Putting It on Record

A Presentation to the Kirby Commission on Mental Health

I have been treated for depression for nearly twenty years. I was fortunate that when I finally sought medical help—and it was hell on wheels for me to break past my self-imposed barriers against seeking advice—I got the right guy, Dr. Mel Bruchet in North Vancouver. I have told that story in my book *Rafe: A Memoir* (2004), but the point I wish to make here is that since that time I have been pleading with governments to make some simple but critical changes to the process and let hundreds of thousands of depressed people and other mentally ill folks into the system.

Then on October 7, 2004, Senator Michael Kirby moved that the Senate committee on Social Affairs, Science and Technology's study of Canada's health care system be expanded to include "issues concerning mental health and mental illness." I knew Senator Kirby from another movie: he had authored the Machiavellian memo leaked just before the First Ministers Constitutional Conference of September 1980 that destroyed the conference before it began.

Thus, I did not have kind thoughts about the good senator. However, I was delighted that the Senate was going down this road and, while I had my doubts about the committee's chair and although I had been consulted before by governments and not too much had happened, I agreed to appear before the Commission.

Here is the presentation I made:

Members of the Senate:

I am what is called a consumer of mental health services, having been diagnosed with depression/anxiety in about 1988. It happened this way. It was not without its moments of humour.

I had a pain in my right side that, after consulting the *Columbia Medical Encyclopedia*, I diagnosed as liver cancer. After getting more and more anxious, unto being unable to do my job properly, I phoned my doctor and demanded of the receptionist that I see him, Dr. Mel Bruchet of North Vancouver, immediately. When she asked why, and I told her it was liver cancer, she paused perceptibly and said he could see me the following afternoon. That wasn't good enough so I went to his office and waited him out. He examined me and said, "You dumb bugger (we're good friends!), you haven't got liver cancer. You have gallstones." I told him he was wrong and asked why he was lying to me. He got me an appointment for ultrasound the next day. The doctor who watched the instrument pass over the area of my liver frowned, whereupon I said, "It's cancer, isn't it? Tell me the truth—I can take it!" which I certainly could not. The doctor had me turn on my side, whereupon he gave me a couple of chops with his hands over the affected area, looked up at the screen and said, "There! You had a gallstone lodged in the entrance to the gall bladder."

I said, "You mean after all of this I only needed a *&^%# chiropractor?"

When I saw Dr. Bruchet a day or two later, he went over the results of the ultrasound and talked to me about dealing with gallstones. I called him a liar and accused him of hiding the truth from me. Then out of the blue he asked, "How long ago was it that your daughter was killed?" prompting me to ask, "What the hell has that to do with liver cancer?"

He said, "Just answer a few questions for me," and by about number three I broke into uncontrollable sobbing. He consoled me and told me that in his opinion I was depressed and it was manifesting itself in bouts of extreme anxiety. He explained about "serotonin" and how I should not in any way feel ashamed. We quickly and luckily found the right medicine and for the most part it has worked. I literally owe my life to Mel Bruchet for I know I wouldn't have been able to carry on were it not my great good fortune to have a doctor who knew something about depression. Just before I talk about my recommendations, let me say that some years later, against Dr. Bruchet's advice, I insisted on trying a new medicine. It meant I had to go without any medicine for two weeks—two weeks I spent, on what was meant to be a vacation, sobbing uncontrollably in my wife's arms.

Some years later while interviewing a marvellous doctor named Teresa Hogarth and taking calls on air, I heard one man describe how he felt, how his wife was telling him he should just put his chin to the wind and be like a man, and how he didn't know what to do, I found myself telling him, and some one hundred thousand other people, that I too was depressed and how the good news was that help, often spectacular help, was available. I wasn't telling that man the whole truth, which is that there is help available if you happen to be lucky enough to have a doctor who knows something about depression.

Over the years I have hosted an annual Depression Screening Show in conjunction with the BC Branch of the Canadian Mental Health Association. We have a dozen mental health counsellors taking calls off-air as I do my show on the subject. They take hundreds of calls and could take hundreds more if time permitted. These callers are people who have got up the nerve to admit they have a mental health problem and have screwed up their courage to seek help.

And what can these volunteers tell them? Basically, call your doctor and pray to God that he/she knows something about mental health.

Here are some recommendations:

1. Every medical doctor, as a condition of a certificate to practise, must have passed a course in diagnosing and, in appropriate cases, dealing with mental illness. Can you imagine if a woman went to see her doctor with a lump on her breast being told, "Sorry, madam, I don't do lumps but I can get you in to see a specialist in six months to a year's time." Yet the equivalent of that happens regularly to people who finally overcome the stigma attached to mental health and go to their doctors. This is not rocket science. It's a matter that the medical schools and College of Physicians and Surgeons can deal with immediately. Although all suicides are tragic, the most tragic of all are young people whose deaths come because symptoms were not recognized and properly, medically treated. Doctors must know about the signs of teenage depression and be able to advise parents and kids alike.

2. It follows that general practitioners must be appropriately compensated for the time it takes to deal with mentally ill people. Unfortunately, for mental illness, the substitute for X-rays and other diagnostic tools is time; the evidence does not come from diagnostic tools but careful and understanding questions and advice from the doctor.

3. Every medical association in the country must be encouraged to keep a list of general practitioners who are equipped to take mentally ill people on as patients. It is preposterous, indeed highly dangerous, to turn away a mentally ill person either with some recommendation to "keep a stiff upper lip, old chap" or with an appointment many months later with a psychiatrist. This is a crucial point. *People, men especially, are afraid to let anyone know about their problem, feel sure that no one can help anyway, avoid the doctor and self-medicate with alcohol or other drugs.* I am convinced that a huge part of alcoholism is self-medication, and I'm fortified in this opinion by every expert in the field of mental health I've spoken to.

4. The notion of a separate government ministry for mental health, however well intentioned, is not the way to go. Such a ministry becomes a backwater, with the minister's job being a sort of a training spot for promotion. The mentally ill must have the same access to power as all other ill people do.

5. There must be an independent mental health advocate, selected much as other servants of the legislature are. Mental health advocates become unpopular with the government because they look for and find people who need help, thus cost the treasury money. Which point segues into:

6. A proper analysis of the cost of mental illness is long overdue so that ministers of finance and treasury boards can see that money spent upfront in diagnosis and treatment can be demonstrated to bring substantial cost reductions to the social ministries.

7. There must be made available immediately to all who deal with young people, especially school counsellors, education in the field of mental illness.

These are but a few recommendations. I have not dealt with the need for proper funding for organizations like the Canadian Mental Health Association or the many community drop-in centres that take so much pressure off the government because I assume that others will make those presentations. My presentation is simply that of a consumer who, by nature of what he does, sees the mental health picture as it is, not as well meaning politicians and civil servants see it or wish it to be.

I close with this harsh but accurate assessment. To the extent that governments do not deal with mental illness as they do physical illness, they are financing other government programs on the backs of the mentally ill. One doesn't have to go too far to see the truth of this—any walk down Granville Street will show you some of the 1,500 homeless of Vancouver, many of whom are mentally ill, and all of whom now run the risk, thanks to the BC government's Safe Streets Act, of going to jail for begging. All across this country we deinstitutionalized the mentally ill so that, a cynic might say, instead of these patients living in expensive institutions, they can live off paltry sums from begging and sleep under bridges and in doorways. I realize this is an extreme view but you couldn't blame those on the street and the workers who try to help them from seeing it that way.

Yours sincerely,

Rafe Mair

The Kirby Commission tabled its report in May 2006, and I must say it is thorough, though perhaps too thorough to be widely enough read. The report does deal with the issues and I am pleased to say it actually quotes from my presentation. The suggestion that ongoing federal/provincial cooperative processes be started is perhaps the key one. For those of us in the field either as consumers or caregivers or both, this report, if it is indeed a harbinger of things to come, is a very good start indeed.

What I Told the Gomery Commission

So neither Jean Chrétien nor Paul Martin knew about the sponsorship caper? Let's see what else these guys didn't know anything about. There's the Business Development Bank fiasco (that's the one in which Chrétien denies putting pressure on the federal crown corporation to make a dubious loan to a pal). There's the Human Resources Ministry scandal, which golly gee whiz you can't expect then Finance Minister Paul Martin to know anything about. Then there are the Shawinigan golf course shenanigans that the MP and part owner of the golf club, one Jean Chrétien, knew nothing about.

BC, too, has experienced some of this amnesia at the top. In the amazing Doug Walls case of 2004, Premier Campbell had never heard of the man to whom he gave $600,000 tax dollars to administer. He didn't know this man even though Mrs. Walls and Mrs. Campbell are cousins and despite the fact that Campbell went all the way to Prince George to lease a car from Walls and stayed at his house. And it goes without saying that he knew nothing about what every living, breathing Liberal in Prince George knew: namely, that Mr. Walls was an undischarged bankrupt who was under active investigation for a million bucks worth of fraud (he has since been charged).

All this is by way of saying that the Gomery Commission was a glorious waste of money. The latest media estimate of the cost of the inquiry after the second leg is complete is upwards of $80 million. This second leg calls upon the Commission to make recommendations to the Government of Canada, based upon its findings of fact, to prevent mismanagement of sponsorship programs and advertising activities in the future.

And this is where I came in. In October 2005, I received a call from the Commission asking if, in a week's time, I could appear before it and help them with stage two of the mandate. I was not happy with the idea because, while I was certain I could help, it looked much like they wanted my presence but not my opinion. And so it proved to be.

Three days before I was to appear I received the "briefing book," which delegated to me the responsibility of enlightening the judge on access to information laws in BC. I phoned the lady in charge and told her I knew very little about the subject since I was the mouthpiece and someone else did the research. I told her that my appearance on that issue would be a waste of everyone's time.

The next day I received a call from the Commission telling me that there had been a change and now I was to advise Justice Gomery about the pros and cons of "whistleblower" legislation. I got quite angry and told her that while I had a lot of knowledge about politics and the media, I had nothing to say on the question posed. I told her I wasn't going to attend.

That evening, I received a call from John Fraser, former speaker of the House of Commons, a permanent member of the Commission and a lifelong friend. He begged me to appear. I told him what I wanted to say and that there was no place on the agenda for me to say it. John assured me that I would have the opportunity to say what I wished, that it was important that Justice Gomery hear it. I reluctantly agreed to go.

I duly attended and listened as various experts told us how what was needed was a better code of ethics and stuff like that. Senator Pat Carney from BC, giving an oral sketch of her time in government, opined that the rules were all there so they only needed to be enforced. I could see that my tummy feeling was right—I should have stayed home.

When my turn came, I used the opportunity to tell Justice Gomery of the slipshod way I had been approached and how I had protested that neither of the subjects chosen for me were suitable. Judge Gomery hemmed and hawed and said he understood that I did have an opinion and would I like to summarize it? I said I preferred to read my brief, which I did. (I am attaching a copy of this brief at the end.) In essence, I said that this and other similar shenanigans were bound to recur unless there were watchmen and that the natural watchmen were MPs and the media, both of which, as things are, are woefully ill-equipped to perform these tasks. When I finished, you would have thought I was some wild-eyed radical who had just demanded the overthrow of the system. Unlike other statements, my presentation drew no comment.

Now there's always a good chance that someone who thinks he knows something, in fact, does not. So perhaps my conclusions were all wet. That, however, doesn't alter the fact that I was invited and therefore there must have been a reason. If they wanted to know what I thought, you'd think they would have asked before they made the agenda and then, seeing I was a square peg for a round hole, withdrawn the invitation.

I end with an opinion: if Justice Gomery doesn't think our mild-mannered media and neutered MPs contributed to this scandal, I believe his second report will be useless. I came away from this meeting, one of five regional hearings across Canada, feeling it was window-dressing and that Justice Gomery didn't want to hear anything that might make him exercise his mind and ask himself questions that establishment people such as him don't like to ask.

Here is the tabled report I read into the record.

I frankly don't know much about federal access rules and can only say that the information received in the limited number of releases I've seen look more like a fan dancer than the real thing—tantalizing but hardly fully exposed.

Access to information is an essential tool to finding the truth, but my concern is down a slightly different road; what is the effect of massive scandals on the citizens? Is Access to Information, however helpful, a constant searchlight into public affairs or is it a tool requiring use by ever-vigilant snoops who may be in very short supply indeed? Do we have the machinery without the workers? Have Canadians, suckled on the notion of peace, order and good government, been anaesthetized such that they really don't much care what goes on in Ottawa?

I say it's critical to our national unity that we find the means and determination to root out and punish wrongdoing and prevent it occurring in the future. That we may deal with it, as this Commission indicates, is a good thing, but is it enough that we wait for wrongdoing to become scandalous rather than, by constant vigilance, deter it? And is the rot one infers is in government harmful to our national unity?

Why do I bring national unity into this?

Because in this province, from what I've been able to glean, the reaction to federal scandals ranges from boredom to "what else would you expect?" Their MPs answer their concerns, if they answer them at all, with a patronizing "there, there, we're getting to the bottom of this just as quickly as we can." There is such a strong sense of disconnect between British Columbians and Ottawa that no one expects much more from their MPs.

This raises two issues that may or may not be within this Commission's terms of reference. First is the fact that the concentration and convergence of media ownership has, to all intents and purposes, eliminated the muckraker. Thus it is that questions are just not being asked or, if asked, lightly pursued. That is not to say there aren't good writers in the national papers because there are. What there is not is a media culture of holding governments' feet firmly to the fire. We have good writers, some able electronic reporters, who take a poke here, a funny little aside there, perhaps laced with criticism but always suitably polite and deferential. The fact that active journalists reporting on the national government have been awarded and have accepted Orders of Canada speaks volumes for the coziness of the relationship.

Every once in a while there is a discovery of chicanery, but it seems that the media involved are often unwilling to follow through. One example is the story on the front page of the *Globe and Mail* some time ago that told of Brian Mulroney getting shopping bags full of money from the Airbus fixer, Karl-Heinz Schreiber. It was the editor's front page editorial and Mr. Greenspon also told us that Mr. Mulroney tried to get him not to print the story and if he agreed, he, Mulroney, would give the editor another even better story! Given Stevie Cameron's book on the Airbus scandal—which spawned no libel suits, incidentally—one would have thought that a skeptical media would pounce on this story and follow it through. Nothing of the sort happened and we're left as it was when Sherlock Holmes asked why the dog wasn't barking.

Of even more importance—and the issues are linked—is the concentration of all power in the Prime Minister's Office. Pierre Trudeau once said that fifty yards off the Hill, the MP was a nobody, and I always wondered why the geographical limitation. MPs individually and in committees with real power to investigate should hold the Prime Minister's Office and the various ministries to close account; they don't because they can't. There is talk of the "democracy deficit," but when the political culture is based on the myth that Parliament controls the executive (which on paper it does, but the reality is that the PMO is all powerful), there is very limited surveillance indeed. That so much power could be cornered by the prime minister is scary, especially when you consider that the superintendent of the RCMP is no longer an independent officer but a deputy minister to the solicitor-general and picked/appointed by the prime minister.

I may seem to be drifting off the point but I'm not. I hope I'm demonstrating that it is not just the scandal that is weakening the nation but the reasons it was possible in the first place. Canada has an establishment that runs the show. There can be dissent but only within reasonable, to them, boundaries. A quick example would be the Charlottetown Accord where the establishment got its backside kicked. Every segment—political, management, labour, the artsy-fartsy set and with one exception I won't bore you with, the media—decided to ask no questions. One powerful media member, Maclean-Hunter, actually signed onto the "yes" side without raising an eyebrow! You would now think that there never had been a Meech Lake/Charlottetown issue that gripped the nation for six years; it has been airbrushed out of history by the media and politicians alike. It didn't happen.

I raise that issue because it makes this point: all those set in authority over us are secretive by nature. That not only means that they hide things but that they resist every effort by MPs or anyone else to find out what they're doing, and when bad things happen, they all become as the inkfish. I've been there. For the politician and too many bureaucrats, the only passion greater than hiding things is the compulsion to cover up and distract.

The sponsorship scandals and all your work, with respect, will just be matters to airbrush from the scene, too, once enough time passes if this Commission doesn't recognize that the scandal itself is secondary to the public cynicism it fuels and doesn't see clearly that, for all the sins committed, the greater sins may be the system itself and the passiveness of the national media.

You can have, Mr. Commissioner, the best access to information laws and procedures in the world, but if neither our elected members nor the national media have both the means and the motive to use that access vigorously and often, we might just as well not have it. If we the people cannot have a constant bright light looking into the goings-on of the government, there is no democracy. Since there's little enough democracy in the system itself we are in grave danger of losing our country unless those we vote into power and the free press, so essential to a free people, start doing their jobs properly.

That, sir, is how important your deliberations and recommendations are to all who love their country and want to revive it and keep it.

My remarks were met with a brief thanks and no discussion ensued. I stayed until lunch and went home.

The point of this is not that I am right—I think I am, of course—but that they wanted to bag a "western name" to show that the entire country had been consulted. It was crap. The Commission had no intention of dealing with the tough bits like the accretion of all power to the Prime Ministers' Office and the tame pro-Liberal press. They were content to stir around and ladle out some warm porridge and hope that no one noticed that they had avoided the main issues.

At the time I felt my appearance at the hearings was an utter waste of my time and effort, but much, much more than that it demonstrated that part two of the Gomery Commission hearings were a mindless sham. But perhaps Mr. Justice Gomery did listen after all because in his final report he did deal with the necessity of giving more money and powers to parliamentary committees. And he did recommend that the House Public Accounts Committee be beefed up and properly funded.

A Letter to Former Premier
Bill Bennett

Dear Bill,

I have to tell you that the tremendous welcome you got, with three standing ovations at the Board of Trade luncheon on May 2, 2006, was very much deserved.

And this also seems as good a time as any to tell you how much I admire you and to say what great times they were when we were colleagues. We travelled quite a bit together to various conferences and you get to know a man that way. In every case I witnessed, and they were many, you always represented our province superbly. That the media didn't seem to grasp what the politicians and bureaucrats knew, namely that you were a force from the west coast to be reckoned with, is too bad. The British Columbia position on the patriation exercise and the many serious issues it raised was first class all the way and that very much redounds to your credit.

On a personal note, you entrusted me with a number of tasks and you supported me, even when I was wrong—which is when one needs support most. It's easy as hell to support success! I am also reminded of a time in 1979 when you had to forgive me, big time, and I'm extremely grateful that you did. As environment minister I was the chairman of the Environmental and Land Use Committee (ELUC), which among other things heard appeals by those who had been given second prize when they applied to the Land Commission to have land removed from the Agricultural Land Reserve.

One morning, at a badly attended meeting, the Gloucester land group, a Chilean outfit, had their application before us. They had been awarded second prize when they asked to have their extensive acreage in Langley released. As I recall that meeting, besides Dennis O'Gorman, the bureaucratic head of ELUC, and myself, there were only Tom Waterland and Alex Fraser present. Alex relayed to me that Bob McClelland, who couldn't be there and in whose constituency the land was located, wanted the Gloucester matter not formalized until he had a chance to see the decision, as did Bill Vander Zalm from neighbouring Surrey.

A few days later I arrived in my office at 8 A.M. to find it full of media all asking me in one way or another how come I let that Gloucester property, owned by those terrible Chileans, out of the ALR. At first I didn't know what they were talking about, then it dawned on me—when O'Gorman had brought me all those ELUC papers to sign, Gloucester's application had been among them. I took full responsibility. I simply had not read the papers carefully, if at all. To make matters worse, these were the bad days of General Pinochet in Chile so that the left within the media, especially my friend Allen Garr, frowned upon Chileans with money.

So it hit the fan. What could I do but admit it was my fault, apologize, and hope for forgiveness? You and my colleagues extended that to me although it cost all of us a couple of long, tiresome cabinet meetings to finally agree we had to let the order stand. And I embarrassed you and my colleagues.

This incident spawned another issue where I didn't get quite the same forgiveness from my colleagues nor should I have. As a

result of the Gloucester matter, you may remember, Bill, I suggested that we find a better way to handle appeals from Land
Commission decisions. Since every time an appeal was brought
forward it seemed the media had produced pictures of Socred signs
all over the property during the previous election, I suggested that
an independent board (appointed by us, of course) be set up to hear
appeals. You agreed and I was permitted to second a very able young
lawyer named Norman Prelypchan to help me. Making this change
was not as easy as it looked—it never is in government—because
a number of statutes had to be repealed at least in part, and there
were other bureaucratic cobwebs to sweep away. Finally Norm and
I came up with just the appeal board we wanted and hoped our
cabinet colleagues would approve, but when it came to cabinet,
some colleagues, especially Jim Nielsen who hated the entire ALR
system, and Don Phillips (ditto) started throwing sand in the gears.
You, uncharacteristically I thought, decided to refer the entire matter to the big caucus meeting in November, which was a couple of
months hence. I was pretty pissed off but had no recourse but to
accept your position.

But when the matter came up at that caucus meeting, which
was held in a large meeting room of a Delta hotel, the late Jack
Kempf (who was so far right his colleagues called him "Mein"
Kempf), Nielsen and others dumped on it. I was so goddamned mad
I hurled some expletives at all and sundry. I was sitting with Grace
McCarthy on my right, as I remember it, with Brian Smith, not
yet in cabinet, to her right. I leaned over Grace and said to Brian,
"You're a lawyer, Brian. Is there any law that says I must sit here and
listen to this shit?" And I stormed out of the meeting. Colleague
after colleague came up to my room to get me to return and I used
on every one of them the international words for "go away."

My behaviour was inexcusable though it was explainable. I was
becoming very tired of the right wing of the party. I had worked very
hard to get a good political solution to a nasty political problem.
If the government was going to abandon the ALR and the Land

Commission, so be it, but if we were going to keep them, they should be administered fairly and properly. But more than anything else, I was dead tired having just arrived from Japan that morning. Of course, these are reasons but not excuses.

That night when my wife and I returned from dinner, there was a note on the door inviting "the Member from Kamloops" to have breakfast with "the Member from South Okanagan." I had just finished telling the president of my constituency organization over dinner that when the expected cabinet shuffle came in a couple of weeks, I would be on the backbench. And although I didn't want that to happen, by the time I got to your room the next morning I was resigned to the fact that I was a goner.

In fact, I wasn't. I have to say you were far more understanding of me than I might have been of you had the roles been reversed. But my actions did have some ramifications. At this late date I think I can disclose that you had wanted to make me the new Minister of Intergovernmental Affairs, thus legitimizing what I had been doing in the constitutional arena. But as you rightly said to me that morning, "I can hardly make you that minister, which requires the ongoing cooperation of many other ministers, when you and your colleagues aren't on speaking terms." Then you very kindly offered me several options including the Health portfolio—which did interest me because of the way Bob McClelland had handled this most difficult of tasks—and the meeting was adjourned. You know, Bill, I've always had doubts about that "forgiveness is sweeter than revenge" bit—rather liking revenge myself. I'm glad to say, however, that this aphorism guided your handling of me.

In a couple of weeks I became Minister of Health, and Garde Gardom was appointed the new minister for Intergovernmental Affairs. I continued on as one of Prime Minister Trudeau's Cabinet Committee on the Constitution, but I was now under Gardom, whom I had always regarded as an amiable windbag—indeed, he was born to be a lieutenant-governor with a grand house, an ornate uniform, medals unearned and plenty of speaking engagements that required hot air and nothing else. Had I not lost my temper, I would have continued doing what I loved and who knows how the patriation exercise—or my political career—would have ended. In due course, this decision persuaded me to consider leaving politics, though in the event, the famous broadcaster, Jack Webster, was the active catalyst that had me leave your government for the airwaves. However, I can say in all honesty that my main concern was protecting BC's place in the patriation exercise, and when I lost that, my interest in government faded. At the same time, I had left you no other option but to ease me out.

Sadly, I must comment upon Bob Plecas's biography of you where he fantasizes as to how I left government. As you know, within hours of receiving an offer from CJOR I phoned you at your home in Westbank. We met in my office. (Out of deference to your dad you didn't have a liquor cabinet; I did.) You were very concerned about losing an MLA because of our party's five-seat majority, and I told you it was my intention to stay on as an MLA. A few days later it became clear to me that I couldn't remain as an MLA and still do a show that would likely be critical of the government from time to time. I advised you that I would have to resign and you asked me to talk with Hugh Harris first. Hugh was a great guy and I was happy to. He came to my house and was, in fact, going to stay the night. I told him that there was really no way I could be part of the "political media" and sit as a government MLA. I also pointed out that since I would be broadcasting in the mornings, I would miss every Friday session. When I got up in the morning, I found a note from Hugh saying he was going home but also telling me that he agreed with me and would so tell you. In short, Bill, while you may not have liked what I was doing, you were always kept up to date.

Plecas, however—and this surprises me as he was once a high level deputy minister—says in his book that I forced a by-election in six months. That is, of course, simply not so. You had six months within which to announce the day for a by-election, so in effect you had eight or nine months. Plecas simply got it wrong. And I must say that in his lengthy interview with me the subject didn't come up.

I think that another anecdote—this time from my time as health minister—shows what kind of a guy you are. Near Victoria was a drying-out clinic for the wealthy called Gullane Manor. It had a very good record—in fact a close relative of mine is a graduate—but it was losing money badly and looked as if it would close down. I had a number of meetings with its board and had to tell them that there simply wasn't any money in my budget and that my priorities, if I did have money, were elsewhere.

However, Hugh Curtis was both MLA for that area and minister of finance, and one day in cabinet he announced that he had a million dollars for the minister of health to use to get Gullane Manor back on its feet. I told Curtis and my other colleagues that if he had an extra million for me it would go to Vancouver's Downtown Eastside and Bella Coola, where drying-out centres were lacking and badly needed, and that if Gullane Manor needed money it should get it from the people it served, namely, the well-off. You agreed, Bill, and I've never forgotten you showing where a government's priorities ought to be.

I must tell one more anecdote. The Sunday before the 1980 Conference on the Constitution in Ottawa, you called me about 11 P.M. to tell me that the federal government had leaked a memo (the infamous Kirby memo) and to advise me that a copy of it was being delivered to my room. Would I please read it and give my thoughts to you at breakfast? Of course, I did as you asked, but what you didn't know was that I had fallen in with evil companions the night before and could hardly keep my eyes open! However, it all turned out just as we thought it would—the conference was utterly poisoned by what the feds had done.

It wasn't all peaches and cream, of course. Although I and—I think—all your colleagues in cabinet would have crawled a mile on our hands and knees over broken glass for you, I feel there were two serious policy errors, both of which remind me of the problems Premier Glen Clark got into over fast ferries.

The first was the British Columbia Resources Investment Corporation (BCRIC), which took over many crown assets and became a publicly traded corporation in which every British Columbian got five shares. I believe that the reason the BCRIC didn't work is that you didn't sufficiently consult your cabinet colleagues. I don't know who you did consult, but it seems to me that the reasons it failed were pretty easy to see in hindsight and probably would have been seen with the foresight of collective wisdom. In the event, the government lost nothing because the corporations weren't profitable, but there were many, of course, who bought shares on their own, thinking that it must be a good thing if the government was behind it

The other was North-East Coal, which from the beginning was Don Phillips' project, with very little time given to cabinet as a whole to look at it. In my brief time on the Economic Development Committee I remember asking one question of Don Phillips, namely: "If this is such a good deal, why are we putting public money into it? Why isn't the private sector falling all over itself to get in on the deal?" Don answered to the effect that I was so new to the project that there simply wasn't time to give me the full facts. I'm certainly not suggesting that I would have necessarily been opposed to the scheme or if I had been opposed that it would have made any difference. I just think that, if full cabinet including people like Grace McCarthy and Allan Williams had been on top of it the whole way, it would not have turned out to be the disaster it did. Not only was it unprofitable, it competed with South-West Coal to the latter's considerable disadvantage.

Bill, the purpose of this letter is not to point out your government's shortcomings because they pale in comparison to your strengths, which carried you and the province through some very difficult times. I believe that you were a better premier than your dad was for a simple reason—W.A.C. Bennett was in power during a very long spell of economic growth. He was able to get the money he needed to do what he thought he should and he did his developments before environmentalism was very fashionable. You had some terrible messes to clean up in 1975 and you did it with boldness. You foresaw the slump of the mid-1980s and dealt with it in a manner that cost you your popularity. Expo 86 may not have been your idea but it was your baby. It took a hell of a lot of courage to see that project through from start to finish, but Expo did for BC everything you said it would and more. It was your steadfastness on many Expo issues—not the least of which was the position of organized labour—that saw the whole thing through to such a marvellous conclusion.

There has always been one sad thing about you as premier, Bill—people outside of government didn't see your humour and they didn't know about your dedication to the welfare of ordinary British Columbians. Of course, there is also the stock market fiasco long after you left office, but I know and I hope others know that the mischief was caused by Herb Doman and your brother Russ and that you simply refused to shirk your technical responsibility and stayed with the ship as it when down. I, for one, would have said the hell with it and abandoned ship.

Bill, you were one-of-a-kind, a fact that can be easily demonstrated by the calibre of leadership we've had since you left. I'm proud to have worked for you and to be able to call you a friend.

Yours truly,
Rafe Mair

PART THREE

Foreign Affairs

The European Community:
An Exercise in Deception

This essay is not meant to be a political science examination of the European Community but more like an impressionist painting.

Perhaps the most famous efforts to bring peace to Europe were the Treaty of Westphalia in 1648, which settled the religious problems arising out of the Reformation, and the Congress of Vienna in 1814–15, which set boundaries and put the appropriate rulers in place after the fall of Napoleon. What was noteworthy about the Congress of Vienna and what made it so different from the Treaty of Versailles that was to come in 1919 was the treatment of the loser, in that case France, which had savaged virtually all of Europe. Instead of taking territory away from France, she was restored to her former boundaries and not forced to make crippling reparations.

Thus, peace lasted until the 1860s when Bismarck consolidated his new Reich with wars against Austria and Denmark, then took advantage of a foolish declaration of war by Napoleon III to humble France. At the same time he made the critical long-term mistake of annexing Alsace and Lorraine to the new German Empire. While it was true that these provinces, especially Alsace with its capital at Strasbourg, were more German than French in language and descent, they were still very much a part of France. The result was that the desire for "revanche" went deep into the heart and soul of France; as a constant reminder of the humiliation the Chamber of Deputies covered the seats of representatives from the lost provinces with black crepe. In the Pax Britannica that followed, Britain acted as the balancer in Europe, and this period of relative stability lasted until 1914 (with the exception of the Boer War).

World War I, which saw the Allies win a brutally costly victory, was ended by the Treaty of Versailles. (The United States, which refused to join the League of Nations, made a separate peace.) This treaty not only radically altered the map of Europe, it assessed huge reparations on the fallen Germany. It also messed around with geography, approving the already penciled-in Kingdom of the South Slavs (Yugoslavia), creating new states out of the old Austro-Hungarian Empire, and re-creating Poland at the expense of Russia and Germany. Thus, after the Versailles Treaty, the political landscape of Europe was settled yet unsettled.

Europe was devastated once again during World War II, but for the first time Germany herself experienced mortal combat on her own soil and saw many of her cities flattened. While after World War I she could claim, since she sustained no physical damage, that she hadn't really lost the war but had been betrayed by the Jews, among others, this time there was no such excuse or scapegoats available. (Interestingly, the man whose financial genius had kept Germany afloat in World War I, Walther Rathenau, was a Jew.) After World War II, there was no doubt that Germany was badly beaten. The country was divided into four occupation zones that morphed into West Germany, a parliamentary democracy, and East Germany, a communist dictatorship. But given that all things change and that Germany would sooner or later revive, the critical question was how to keep peace between the Teuton and the Gaul?

On September 20, 1946, at Zurich, Winston Churchill said this:

> I am now going to say something that will astonish you. The first step in the recreation of the European family must be a partnership between France and Germany. In this way only can France recover the moral and cultural leadership of Europe. There can be no revival of Europe without a spiritually great France and a spiritually great Germany.
>
> The structure of the United States of Europe will be such as to make the material strength of a single State less important. Small nations will count as much as large ones and gain their honour by a contribution to the common cause. The ancient states and principalities of Germany, freely joined for mutual convenience in a federal system, might take their individual places among the United States of Europe.

Out of this speech came the inspiration for France and Germany's Coal and Steel Pact, and from there on the momentum was unstoppable. What also must be noted is that, contrary to popular myth, Churchill did not see the UK as part of this United States of Europe but as remaining in a "special relationship" with its traditional trading partners, America and the Commonwealth, while maintaining good political and trading relations with the "new" Europe. This is a critical point because the Europhiles—those people committed to the UK being a full member of whatever Europe turned out to be—often claim Churchill as their spiritual leader. In fairness to the Europhiles, Churchill's "special relationship" was pretty one-sided. As a later US secretary of state, Dean Acheson, would say about post-war Britain, "England has lost an empire and is looking for a role." Certainly the Truman administration was not high on the notion of special relationships, especially when in 1947 it had to bail out Greece because Britain could no longer afford to finance her defence.

In 1950, in a speech inspired by Jean Monnet—who by any definition is the father of the European Union—the French foreign minister, Robert Schuman, proposed integrating the coal and steel industries of Western Europe. As a result, the European Coal and Steel Community (ECSC) was set up the following year with six members: Belgium, West Germany, Luxembourg, France, Italy and the Netherlands. The power to make decisions about the coal and steel industry in these countries was placed in the hands of an independent, supranational body called the "High Authority." Jean Monnet—no surprise here—was its first president.

The ECSC was such a success that, within a few years, these same six countries decided to go further and integrate other sectors of their economies. In 1957 they signed the Treaties of Rome, creating the European Atomic Energy Community (EURATOM) and the European Economic Community (EEC). The member states set about removing trade barriers between them and forming a "common market." In 1967 the institutions of the three European communities Benelux, France and Germany were merged. From this point on, there was a single commission and a single Council of Ministers as well as the European Parliament, although individual countries retained power over their own money, foreign affairs and armed forces.

Originally, the national parliaments chose the members of the European Parliament, but in 1979 the first direct elections were held, allowing the citizens of the member states to vote for the candidates of their choice. Since then, direct elections have been held every five years, though I'm bound to say that since the bureaucrats controlled Brussels, the European Parliament was (and mostly remains) little more than a talk shop. The Treaty of Maastricht (1992) introduced new forms of cooperation between the member state governments—for example, on defence and in the area of "justice and home affairs"—and by adding this intergovernmental cooperation to the existing "community" system, the Treaty created the European Union (EU). It must be noted that it took two tries for Denmark to vote "yes," and Prime Minister Major got some significant concessions as a condition of the UK signing on.

Throughout this long process, there was more and more "Europization" eating away at the various national sovereignties, all of which was denied or explained away as trivial by those who wanted "progress" to continue. The crunch came with the push for a single currency. In 1992 the EU decided to go for economic and monetary union (EMU), involving the introduction of a single European currency managed by a European Central Bank. The single currency—the Euro—became a reality on January 1, 2002, when Euro notes and coins replaced national currencies in twelve of the fifteen countries of the European Union (Belgium, Germany, Greece, Spain, France, Ireland, Italy, Luxembourg, the Netherlands, Austria, Portugal and Finland).

For three countries, much including the UK, in which both major parties were divided over the whole concept of the EC, this was a step too far. Eurosceptics, as the boo-birds became known, saw loss of control over their money as the final surrender of sovereignty to the larger body—which of course it is. What I find troubling about these events is that the pro-Europe adherents have never fessed up and won't simply fess up that they are indeed working towards one large federal state and, in spite of soft soap when asked awkward questions, always were. The reason they don't admit the obvious is that they know that without the fiction that the EC is really just a trading association with a few common rules, Britain might continue to stay outside the Euro and might even move to withdraw from the EC; and France, of all countries, might also kick up a big fuss.

By 2005, when the EC constitution, as drafted by former French president Giscard d'Estaing, was revealed, Great Britain could fairly say—as Eurosceptics were saying more and more—that they had been suckered into something quite different than they were led to believe would be the final deal. In order to get a more precise handle on this point I can do no better than refer you to *The Great Deception: The secret history of the European Union* by Christopher Booker and Richard North, two well-known British journalists and authors. To be fair, this book contradicts—and it seems was intended to contradict—the more popular history of this matter contained in Hugo Young's earlier book, *This Blessed Plot*, which is little short of sheer, unrestrained joy at the notion of Britain being in Europe all the way. Again in fairness, Booker and North are also regarded almost with contempt by Chris Patten, one-time European Commissioner for External Relations (and also the man who oversaw the handing back of Hong Kong to the Chinese), who, when defending Britain in his book *Cousins and Strangers*, quotes a 1960s speech made by Edward Heath in a Commons debate with Prime Minister Harold Wilson. At that time Heath said:

> Those who say that the British people must realize what is involved in this [the Common Market] are absolutely right. There is a pooling of sovereignty. Member countries . . . have deliberately undertaken this to attain their objectives and, because they believe that the objectives are worth that degree of surrender of sovereignty, they have done it quite deliberately. . . . When we surrender some sovereignty, we shall have a share in the sovereignty of the community as a whole, and of other members in it. It's not just, as sometimes thought, an abandonment of sovereignty to other countries, it is a sharing of other people's sovereignty as well as pooling of their own.

These words of Mr. Heath are not, in my research, much seen these days and in any event, while they may have satisfied Hugo Young, they certainly didn't so affect Messrs. Booker and North. And in my view they are nonsense. To illustrate my point using a Canadian example, if all Canada's provinces gave up some of their power to Ottawa, does anyone seriously suggest that BC would get a sufficient share of the new power structure in the federal government as well as a share of power from, say, Ontario to make up for its loss of sovereignty? The answer is clearly no because the exercise of that new power would be in the hands of two powerful provinces, Ontario and Quebec. The analogy to Europe is apt because Britain would trade its total sovereignty over, say, currency to a new body in which they could and probably always would be outvoted.

In *Cousins and Strangers* the estimable Chris Patten, a man long involved in the European Community, also deals with the expansion of the Union and the benefits this has brought both the union and the new members. But saying that is so and demonstrating its truth are two different things. Nearly twenty years after the wall crumbled, Germany is still dealing financially with the addition of East Germany. Larger members mutter under their breaths and through clenched teeth that new poor members, by refusing to raise taxes to the level of the more prosperous members, are in effect "tax dumping"—which they are. Patten concedes this but says without much conviction that all will come right in time. In the meantime, the Union plays out a sort of reverse "Ponzi" scheme, this being a scam where a promoter keeps his original investors quiet by feeding them some of the money he gets from new investors. The scheme collapses when the new money is not enough to supply old obligations. In the EC the newly acquired countries, instead of sending money back to the old players—though not enough to satisfy those to whom it's owed—in fact buy poverty, country by country, and send that back through the chain.

Patten does make one important point that must be addressed: the EU has kept peace and may in fact bring it to the Balkans. It's a seductive argument but a misleading one. The main wars, it's true, have always had Germany, France and Britain in the midst of them, but these countries are at peace because Germany and France made common economic cause. To extrapolate from this that Russia, reinvigorated, will never make claims again in the Baltic or that the presence of the EU will keep Balkans countries from each others' throats requires more than just saying that it's so. Still it is an argument made by EU fans and, in fairness, must be laid on the table.

Looking at the history of what Eurosceptics see as an ongoing exercise in deceit, Booker and North make the points that de Gaulle didn't blackball Britain in the first place out of spite—though God endowed him with lots of that—but because he saw Britain as a country that looked overseas to the Commonwealth and the United States and wasn't emotionally able to divest itself of those historical relationships. This to de Gaulle meant that the UK could never stomach the bargain France insisted upon, the Community Agriculture Policy (CAP), which was geared to subsidize French farmers, allowing them to stockpile and dump their products onto the world markets, thus keeping that sector—which traditionally has made or broken French political parties—happy.

When it became clear that the UK would go along with CAP, it was invited to join. But these authors go much further. They allege (and to my mind prove) that every inch of the way the UK was assured by its leaders and European Union leaders that the UK would never have to surrender any of its sovereignty. This brings in to play two terms—"intergovernmental" and "supranational." British politicians, including Edward Heath, Harold MacMillan, Harold Wilson, Margaret Thatcher (for whom the light went on too late) and Tony Blair, convinced themselves that the game was "intergovernmental" only and that it was little more than fine-tuning a "common market," the term first used for the association. All vigorously denied, each step of the way, that the game was really "supranationalism" where each country would be, in terms Americans and Canadians would understand, states or provinces of a country to be known as Europe.

Such a result may or may not be a good thing. My point, and that of Messrs. Booker and North, is that this is not what the British public was told, not when they approved of the European Union by referendum or in 1975 or since then. It is argued that, if what the European Union was really all about was put fairly to the British Public, they would have had no part of it. If current polls are correct and have legs, a referendum on the Euro, as proposed by Chancellor of the Exchequer Gordon Brown, would fail. If it did and a new EC constitution also failed in the UK, as is likely, it's difficult to see how Britain could remain in the union.

British taxes now subsidize French farmers who can outbid British farmers for the UK market. The substantial British fishery has now been utterly destroyed by French and Spanish fishermen — not damaged but destroyed. Once Britain was in the Union—with the rules being made from Brussels, not Westminster—all other members could fish British waters. Spanish fishermen could and did register their boats in Britain, fly the Red Ensign and take their British "share" then fish under the flag of Spain and take another "share" and there was nothing Britain could do about it.

Enormous numbers of business regulations, passed by bureaucrats in Brussels who have no responsibility to any politicians, have driven thousands of British businesses into failure. One example the authors give is of the butcher who, for years, got his meat from an abattoir across the street. In stepped Brussels saying you can't do that because the meat must be frozen in the abattoir and delivered that way to the butcher.

"But," said the butcher, "it's across the street!"

"Too bad. Best build a refrigerated tunnel."

There are several indicia of sovereignty, one of which is: do you or someone else make the laws by which you are bound? In the EC most significant laws are made in Brussels, not by the politicians but by bureaucrats, and every day more areas of jurisdiction are moving without so much as a parliamentary farewell from elected British MPs to the bureaucratic offices in Belgium.

Another sign of sovereignty is whether you control the issuance and supply of your own currency. Those who are now using the

Euro as currency have surrendered this critical power to the EC and, in the cases of smaller countries, don't even have a say through their membership in the Community. Plucky Denmark is outside the Euro, and so far, so is Britain.

The third aspect of sovereignty is whether as a nation, you govern yourself by reason of having your own constitution? The UK could have once answered, "Yes" (though the British Constitution is, by centuries of tradition, unwritten). Now, at best, the UK can only say, "Partly." If Great Britain approves of the Giscard d'Estaing Constitution it will have to say, "No. We have lost our one-thousand-year-old constitution and, to all intents and purposes, we must turn Parliament over to the tourism people, it having little else left to do." Holland voted against the Constitution, France has rejected it but can and will be bribed into submission because this entire exercise has been mainly about bribing the French, and France cannot risk losing what it has gained. The UK has postponed its vote on the reasonable assumption by Prime Minister Blair that under current circumstances it will fail badly.

The British public has been duped. I don't think it was so much deliberate in the sense of malicious as negligent. There was a dream out there that politicians could buy into because it was so far off. And how easy it was to think—No more war! Europe, the cause of two worldwide conflagrations will be at peace. Germany and France, two countries that in seventy years fought three crippling wars (with Germany winning all three had the British and Americans been taken out of the equation), will not only be at peace but will be partners in a wonderful new undertaking that will ensure both peace and prosperity.

What a dream for Britain to buy into! She had, after all, to deal with Louis XIV in the eighteenth century, Napoleon in the nineteenth, the Kaiser and Hitler in the twentieth. God, please, oh please, find us a way out of this cycle of war and don't bother us with tiresome details! In a sense it was a national attitude similar to that after Chamberlain's Munich deal with Hitler, but in this case the sense of relief has stretched out over decades.

All of this begs another critical question: what if this is all cobbled together into a nation called Europe and some country wants out? The break-up of most federations—Norway/Sweden and Czechoslovakia providing exceptions—is usually a nasty and often bloody affair. When you consider that we're dealing here with fifteen or more nations, must we not assume that there's a strong possibility, if not probability, of discontent leading to a demand for secession?

And are we not sure to see, as Booker and North foresee, cliques within the new European nation? Are not France and Germany in an echelon of their own, if only in their own minds? Won't Britain be in its own echelon and perhaps mentally go back to the 1700s and the years following where she constantly sought, with considerable success, to create alliances to balance off any combination of possible enemies? And has anyone thought of Russia? Russia, the nation that lost so much face—not to mention land and influence in 1990–91—and now seeks to restore her former pride? Does she simply sit by licking her wounds for the rest of time? In short, isn't the vision of peace for all time by means of uniting all traditional foes a bit blurred?

The selling of a dream is so much easier than the selling of a nightmare. Those who opposed the idea of a united Europe could be put down so easily as "little englanders," reactionaries, Colonel Blimps and so on. Either you were with change that would bring prosperity and peace or you weren't. And if you raised cruddy arguments about the pound, the Queen and the constitution, you just weren't with it in modern times. You were pre-Beatles, Carnaby Street, Kings Road and the "New Britain." You were back there, bathed in dreams of the "empah" of old, unable to see what was so clearly to be seen. As usual in such cases, ad hominem attacks and put-downs take the place of reasoned argument and put the final question in much starker terms than anyone would want.

How easy it's been for the Europhiles to sing the song of the future without worrying about how the song ends! What a cinch to shout down with personal insults any who dared question the dream. How easy it was to answer all questions with weasel words and comforting, all-knowing bleatings of blessings to come. For when it's done, there will be no point in looking back or assessing whatever faults show through. It will be over and done with.

The two players in this tragedy who only found out too late were Margaret Thatcher and John Major. It occurred to Mrs. Thatcher that the common currency and a constitution meant that Britain didn't just yield a *bit* of sovereignty—it gave it all to Brussels. But by the time she found out, it was past the time she could stop it, though to her credit she tried. Even the "Iron Maiden" had been duped into thinking that this was an exercise in "intergovernmental-ism" not "supernationalism." John Major, ironically, was brought down because he was victimized by the Exchange Rate Mechanism (ERM) he had agreed to, a device of the Europhiles that, when it failed, allowed them to kill Mr. Major. The only near hero of the piece was poor old Norman Lamont, the Chancellor of the Exchequer, who fought Europe and lost because Europe—that is to say the Europe of the Europhiles' dreams—had all but bankrupted the UK.

Now "New Labour" must face the question all its predecessors put off until a later day. Gordon Brown, the heir apparent to Mr. Blair, has placed conditions on Britain joining the Euro that on the one hand seem insurmountable and on the other hand are so vague as to not admit any interpretation. What seems obvious is that there will be a referendum on either the Euro or the Constitution or both. Britons are much better informed than they were in 1975 when they favoured entry into Europe in a referendum, and all three political parties know this. Would any British government dare take the next step without a clear mandate from the people? That would be a brave, foolhardy government indeed!

The trading partnership, banded together for commercial

purposes only—don't you dare use that word "supranationalism"—now has two capital cities, Brussels and Strasbourg, a parliament, a government, a flag, a national anthem, an executive, a common currency, a growing armed forces and a constitution. All that remains for Denmark, France and the UK to become states or provinces in this scheme is to buy into the Euro and the Constitution. And so it is that the mess Britain finds herself in today is precisely why Churchill saw Europe as the other side of the Channel. Not for the first or only time he saw the future with a clarity that has been thoroughly vindicated.

The EC and Racism

What is it about the Constitution of the European Community, soon to be simply Europe, that bothers the French public so much where it doesn't seem to bother the politicians? The answer is that the people have to live with the document in practice, not in theory or in esoteric constitutional challenges in the courts. And the bottom line is that the French don't like Muslims very much.

In *Foreign Affairs* Milton Viorst wrote an article called "The Muslims of France: Islam Abroad," a summary of which was as follows:

> Four or five million strong, France's Muslims, mainly from former North African colonies, have made Islam the country's second religion. Invited to immigrate in a decade of boom, Europe's Muslims are less welcome today and considered threats to jobs and security. In France, a faith uneasy with assimilation comes up against a government offering integration into society on its own determinedly secular terms. A battle over a head scarf reveals deep cultural rifts.

It must be noted that the number of French Muslims is a result of French colonial policy, which until 1962 held that Algeria was an "integral part of Metropolitan France." This meant that all residents were as French as if they had lived for centuries in the Loire Valley. (This "nationalizing" of peoples from colonies has also caused lots of heartburn for Britain, Spain, Holland and Portugal amongst others.) In France the numbers of Muslims have increased to the extent that National Front leader, Jean-Marie Le Pen, whose main ticket is racism, got into the run-off for president in 2004. Since then we've seen the terrible riots in the fall of 2005. And now the impending arrival of Turkey into the European Union has become the catalyst for the rejection of the Constitution by the French, though the arrival date is still uncertain and depends upon Turkey attaining certain goals. The worry in France is that this will mean an influx of Turks into France, adding to the Muslims already there. While EU officials say that Turkey in the EU will not necessarily mean right of passage for Turks to the other regions of the Union, the French are skeptical.

From my perspective the problem is pretty simple. The EU has simply gone too far afield. Protestant and Catholic Europe, spawned by the Treaty of Westphalia in 1648 that ended the Thirty Years War, verified the notion of the "nation" and created a commonality of Christian culture which kept the main branches of Christianity, Protestantism and Catholicism, from each others' throats. For many reasons, Christians and Muslims have not done this, as witness the troubles in the Balkans of recent times. Germans have been concerned about Turks who have come there to work—at German invitation it must be said—and, we are told, about the many Turks who would emigrate in a moment once they have that power through membership in the EU.

The EU has gone a country too far and its very existence depends on it working its way out of this pickle.

The Forgotten Player

When the people who know about these things calculate the power structure in the world to come, we hear a lot about the United States, and of course, China. For some reason no one mentions Russia, at one time the second most powerful nation in the world and the scariest. It lost its "powerful" designation by political implosion, thus transferring its leadership in the "scary" department to fundamentalist America. When the Iron Curtain fell in 1989 and the USSR disintegrated shortly thereafter, there was a collective sigh of relief in the western world. World peace at last! So, we said, why not create a "peace dividend" out of the money we no longer spend on armaments? After all, Russia gave up so much with scarcely a whimper. Much more surprisingly, there was also scarcely a murmur when the Ukraine, its buffer on the west seceded, and when the resources-rich East Asian republics stated their independence. Georgia, the home of Stalin, went too, taking the former foreign minister of the USSR, Eduard Shevardnadze as its first president. When Russia did little other than growl a bit after the Coalition was formed for the first Iraq war, it was clear that peace and democracy were overtaking Russia—or so we told ourselves. There was that niggling worry about all those aging nuclear weapons but, hell, let's not sweat the small stuff.

We have, of course, been sleepwalking. Churchill, no mean prophet himself, once said you can only see as far ahead as you can see the past. We would do well to look back at Russia, for perhaps four hundred years past, at least to the time of Peter the Great, to see what consistent ambitions she has had, ambitions that transcend whatever political power that has been in place at any given time.

Looking back, we see Russia as a very large empire constantly extending its boundaries. We see a country always very concerned about two things—security (internal and external) and a warm water port. The concern about external security is not hard to understand. Over the years Russia had been invaded by the Swedes, the Poles, the Lithuanians, the French and, in the twentieth century, once by Japan and twice by Germany. The USSR lost over twenty-two million people in World War II, so even after 1943 when the tide had turned in his favour, Stalin was still open to a deal with Hitler and engaged in backroom negotiations through Sweden. After World War II, much was made of the Soviet ambition to communize the world. The idiotic "we will bury you" remark by Nikita Khrushchev tended to confirm western fears of Soviet political and economic aggression, but clearly the USSR did not intend spreading communism by starting another world war, and any such ambition to spread their system was a sideshow to the real fear for security.

The overriding reason for the "Iron Curtain" was not some religious zeal to convert countries to communism but to secure Soviet defences. This was determined beyond doubt by George Kennan, the US State Department man in Moscow, whose famous memo made it clear that the answer was containment, and that since the USSR was just as frightened of a nuclear war as was the US, this was the policy to follow. (It's strange for me, who lived through both World War II and the Cold War, that hawks in the US were able to get so much mileage out of the notion that the Soviet Union would risk a nuclear conflagration in order to spread the gospel of communism. For an excellent account of US policy after World War II, I highly recommend *The House of War* by James Carroll.)

The concern by Russia for warm water ports is as much in evidence today as in days of yore. Arguments with the Ukraine over the Crimea and disputes with Turkey over the Dardanelles reflect this continuing concern. Indeed, the dispute with Turkey goes back into the mists of time. Which inspires this thought—just because an argument has waned or seems to have disappeared is no reason to think it has gone away. Like poison ivy, it will most likely reoccur and be all the more irritable for the passage of time.

When wars were fought by land, Russia always had two big defences: its sheer size and Old Man Winter. Napoleon made it to Moscow in 1812 but slunk home with his army in tatters, followed along the way by the bitter cold and the partisans who picked off their quarry using the weather and local knowledge. Hitler nearly made it to Moscow—there is a memorial in the outskirts marking the furthest point reached by the Nazi advance guard—but again winter came. But while it is true that the bitter weather helped to defeat Hitler's ill-clad troops, an even larger obstacle was the sheer size of the country, which literally kept the various German armies out of touch with each other and provided the perfect set-up for partisans who could and did hit and run with considerable effectiveness. But the problem with these two defences is that for all their success, the armies of both Napoleon and Hitler laid waste huge amounts of Russian land and inflicted enormous hardships and death on the Russian people. The Russians, then, though confident they cannot be beaten, know that a successful defence is hugely expensive, which is why in 1945 it seemed much better to Stalin to have other peoples' lands suffer—as buffers—before Mother Russia began to suffer, too. Thus, starting May 1, 1944, the Soviet Army stayed its fight for two months and watched as the Nazis utterly destroyed the last bits of Warsaw, which had seen the largest partisan uprising in history.

What was little noticed were the agreements at Yalta among

the Big Three of Churchill, the dying Roosevelt and Stalin over the new boundaries of Poland. In effect, Poland was moved to the left by being forced to give up much of its eastern land to Russia and taking in compensation all of Prussia and much of Germany's eastern provinces of Silesia and Pomerania. Millions of Germans were forcibly moved out of the new Poland into what was left of Germany. Then not only did Stalin impose a communist government in Poland, it reshaped the country to Germany's disadvantage.

The question is: Now that Poland has thrown off the Russian yoke, will it be able to keep its German booty? It's true that Germany recognized the new boundaries and accepted Poland as is, where is, but will that agreement pass the test of time? History is full of "permanent land settlements" with the issues remaining dormant for decades or even centuries, only to come to a head again amid enormous bloodshed.

Lest there be any doubt as to how long these sores fester, cast your mind back to old Yugoslavia and how the ancient enmities quickly swam to the surface after centuries of relatively peaceful cohabitation once an opportunity to settle old quarrels arose. For many years during the first half of the twentieth century Japan and Russia had a little reported but very hot war going on the China-Russia border. Then in April 1991 we saw the ancient Russia–Japan quarrel revive when then Soviet President Mikhail Gorbachev visited Japan, and Japan demanded the return of the Kurile Islands, taken from Russia by Japan in 1905 and given back to Russia along with the lower half of Sakhalin Island in 1945.

So now we're well into the twenty-first century and what do we see? Well, not a damned thing if we don't look inside the Kremlin where the latest Russia strongman, Vladimir Putin, is slowly but surely taking power away from Parliament. Russia's burst of unbridled capitalism has ended. Government corporations, sold off under Yeltsin, are slowly being taken back. The Republic of Ukraine, the oldest non-Russian part of ancient Russia, is being harassed because Putin doesn't care for the independent nature of its government. As well, the Muslim and resource-rich republics are feeling the heat from Moscow. And Russia remains a nuclear power second only to the United States, its nuclear program no doubt only in abeyance until the money pot is refilled.

Today the situation in Russia is not being seen as it should be. The hot border that extends in a great semi-circle starting in Finland and moving across the Middle East into Asia and north to the border with the United States in the Aleutians is holding back an ancient warrior nation that has been asleep for fifteen years. But now the giant is awakening, flexing its muscles and getting back in the game of pleading for advantages or demanding them or a combination or both. Long the biggest country in the world, Russia has always wanted security on its borders, warm water ports, and a prestigious and powerful place amongst nations. Mr. Putin is restoring his nation to the strongman politics it has always known.

It's time we noticed.

The Muddle East

Mair's Axiom No. 1 states that "You make a serious mistake assuming that people in charge know what they are doing." If proof is necessary, just look at the Middle East, the US and the UK. The problem is fundamental: everything changes. Everything. Today's allies become bitter enemies tomorrow. Enemies become friends. Neutrals become warlike and so it goes. To make matters worse, the changes can range from difficult to impossible to predict. As Churchill said, one must be able to predict with certainty then explain why it didn't happen. Who would have thought that Iran and Iraq who fought, less than twenty years ago, one of the bloodiest wars in modern history would now be pals? It's the old Arab adage: The enemy of my enemy is my friend. Thus, the common enemy has become the US and the UK.

Let us look at the Middle East—sans Palestine/Israel for the time being—as if through the eyes of US and UK "experts." On our left we have Egypt, which is a good friend. Then comes Saudi Arabia and, as pictures of President Bush and the Crown Prince holding hands will demonstrate, there's a pal loyal and true. Then we have Syria, which is nasty but without any serious ability to hurt us. Iraq, what's left of it, we have under our control. Iran is a bit of a stickler, but we know that between the Russians and ourselves we will keep the lid on there. We next come to Afghanistan, but we won the war there and on the border is good old loyal Pakistan under our great good friend, General Pervez Musharraf. That's how she sits, boys. Everything is under control. Or is it?

I don't want to make guesses as silly as those being made by Tony Blair and George W. Bush, but let's review those scenarios and see what might well happen. Pakistan is an assassin's bullet or a heart attack away from having a political upheaval of considerable proportions. Musharraf is seen by enough Pakistanis to be a traitor to his religion and to be toppled as soon as possible and replaced by? You guessed it, a Taliban-supporting, fundamentalist Islamic government.

Afghanistan teaches us every day why no one in its entire history, going back to and including Alexander the Great, has been able to control it. The US has "won" there the same way the Soviet Union "won"—it has won the right to have its troops murdered on a day-to-day basis, rather like the death from one thousand cuts. Afghanistan is now under a US puppet, just as it was once under a Soviet one. The one constant force is—are you ready for this?—the Taliban. In short, if the US leaves, the end of Musharraf will likely follow and Iran's eastern neighbours will be controlled by hard-liners.

It is hoped that Russia will help keep Iran under control as it has in the past. And it may well do so, but shouldn't one remember that President Putin has only one thing in mind: What's good for Russia? If Russia helps the US—or should I say to the extent that Russia helps the US—it will be because Russia is well served.

The threat from Syria much depends upon what happens in Iraq, which is now, in spite of what George W. Bush says, in the midst of a civil war—a three-sided one to boot. If—no, when—the US and the UK pull out, Iraq will likely be more than happy to help Syria make life difficult for Israel.

Saudi Arabia is a barrel of rotting fruit about to collapse. It is, experts say, also overestimating its oil reserves and is thus becoming of fast-shrinking economic importance to the US, with the result that its regime can't be shored up much longer. And the alternative to the Saudi royal family? The Wahhabi, the fundamentalist Islamic faction that spawned Osama bin Laden and nearly all of the "heroes" who took out the two World Trade Center buildings and the Pentagon plus another jumbo jet full of innocent people.

Now let's look at that great good pal of the UK and the US, Hosni Mubarak. He is seventy-eight years old and clumsily trying to put his son into the presidential palace. His government is totalitarian and corrupt, a very bad combination. Tourism, one of Egypt's main sources of hard currency, is in a free fall after several deaths including a massacre of tourists in front of the Cairo Museum. Even his country's middle class, long the unwilling supporter of the dictatorship, is rapidly losing interest. The opposition grows stronger by the day. And who will take over? While the main opposition party is the liberal Ghad [Tomorrow] Party, fundamentalist Islam is not far behind.

I have deliberately left the Israel–Palestine conflict out of the equation because here, surely, in itself is proof that nothing stays the same. For every minute of hope seems to be followed by ninety seconds of hopelessness. But let us for a moment take the sunny view and assume that Israel and a new State of Palestine do reach an agreement of *modus vivendi*, most unlikely at this writing. Will that be the end of the matter so that the US and the UK can go home and let the region look after itself, knowing that there will be peace and amity throughout? Does anyone really believe this is likely or even possible? It must be remembered that bin Laden didn't attack the US because of Israel but because of the US presence in Saudi Arabia.

It has not been my plan in this essay to make any predictions about the Middle East but to demonstrate that the hopefulness of the US/UK allies about the good guys and the bad guys coming to terms rests on quicksand. Moreover, since the US and UK went into

Iraq in order to get rid of weapons of mass destruction that weren't there, they have created a dandy mess from which there is no safe exit. Indeed, they are proof positive that you do make a very serious mistake assuming that people in charge know what the hell they are doing.

Terrorism: What Is It?

The overwhelming issue of our times is terrorism and, of course, nowadays we think of terrorism as a Muslim plot to subvert our society. And it is. But that's not all it is. It's a form of warfare that has been practised by earthlings since time immemorial. That doesn't make it right, of course. That the charge of terrorism might presently be specifically directed at fundamentalist Islam countries and groups because of their involvement in the Middle East may be fair, but it is axiomatic by any moral standard that it is wrong to deliberately kill innocent civilians.

What we need first is a working definition of terror. How does this suit? Terrorism is the use of deadly violence to cow civilians so as to demoralize them and encourage them to urge their government to change policy.

When we in the West deplore terrorism, we are on very weak ground indeed if only because the Allies used mass terrorism in World War II (as did the Nazis, of course). It wasn't just the famous raid on Dresden we must look at. Before that, Churchill expressed horror at what was happening to Hamburg, which was, for some days, the "Target for Tonight" as the wartime movie was called.

There were, of course, declared military targets for all these bombings, but they also created firestorms that killed enormous numbers
of civilians. The strategy of terrorizing civilians was even more
amply demonstrated in Japan where the US bombings, especially
of Tokyo, were even more brutal than in Europe.

You can argue that since we weren't there, immersed in the
mood of the moment, we shouldn't presume to judge. It must also
be said that any decisions in wartime will usually be based on short-
term practical considerations without any longer term perspective.
Of course, it's pretty easy to ignore moral issues when you are trying
to end the biggest war in history, but that doesn't excuse us from
examining what was done from the perspective of a little time. I
don't have to be convinced that if the Allies had been forced to
invade Japan itself there would have ensued a horrible bloodbath.
All the signs pointed to that. The largely American island-hopping
exercises that led the Allies so close to the Japanese mainland had
been made at incredible human loss. Japanese soldiers fought with
a fanaticism that was guaranteed to make the taking of any territory they held, but especially their homeland, hugely expensive in
human terms.

During the spring and summer of 1945, the issue of how to
defeat Japan was front and centre. Hitler had been defeated and
Japan remained to be dealt with. How to do that? The accepted
wisdom was to use the same methods as had been used in
Normandy—land troops, establish a beachhead, and fight until surrender came. It was on that basis that the question of whether to use
the new atomic weapons was settled. If the loss of Allied lives could
be greatly reduced, who wouldn't go down the atomic bomb road?
Whether or not civilians should be terrorized was weighed against
the saving the lives of perhaps hundreds of thousands of, mostly,
American boys. My research of the times shows very little, if any,
concern about saving Japanese lives. On those terms of reference,
the atom bombing of Hiroshima and Nagasaki makes military sense,
but isn't there a moral question here?

Hiroshima, the first to be bombed, over sixty years ago on August 6, 1945, had no military significance. The target was clearly the civilian population. The bomb was dropped to coincide with the morning rush hour so that the maximum casualties would be caused. If terrorism is intimidating civilians in order to achieve a political or military goal, Hiroshima and Nagasaki were clear and egregious acts of terrorism. The bombing of Tokyo was an even clearer case of terror against civilians because Tokyo had long ago lost any military significance, yet on March 9–10, 1945, it was fire-bombed by low-level B-29s at a cost of an estimated one hundred thousand lives in that one night. General Curtis LeMay, with the blessing of Franklin Roosevelt and later Harry Truman, com-manded those B-29 operations against Tokyo as well as the massive incendiary attacks on another sixty Japanese cities. Though precise figures are not available, the firebombing and nuclear bombing campaign against Japan, directed by LeMay between March 1945 and the Japanese surrender in August 1945, may have killed more than one million Japanese civilians.

LeMay had a career revival in the sixties when he became chief of staff of the US Air Force. He was not a success. He was a bel-ligerent, totally committed anti-communist and he clashed repeat-edly with more flexible minds, notably those of Robert McNamara, Eugene Zuckert and General Maxwell Taylor. LeMay lost a number of significant appropriation battles (for Skybolt ALBM, the F-111, and the B-52 replacement, the XB-70) as well as losing his campaign for a much more vigorous engagement in the Vietnam War. The quote that "we should bomb Vietnam back into the Stone Age" is often attributed to him. His passion for promoting strategic air campaigns over tactical strike and ground support operations did come to be reflected in the Air Force, which became disproportion-ately strong in favour of strategic bombing operations during his ten-ure. Area bombardment of Vietnam, Laos and Cambodia led to the deaths and maiming of hundreds of thousands of innocent civilians during the wars in those countries. (In the Peter Sellers movie, *Dr.*

Strangelove, George C. Scott played General "Buck" Turgidson, a strategic bombing enthusiast who was a thinly disguised take-off of General Curtis LeMay.)

This brings Southeast Asia in general and Vietnam in particular into focus. The bombing of North Vietnam was, for the most part, hardly a military exercise. Though docks and airfields were the stated targets, the North Vietnamese weren't into building planes and tanks but relied on soldiers who could live on bugger-all a day and get by on bicycles. Therefore, that bombing can, for the most part, only be described as terrorism, an effort to make civilians turn on their government. Was it then justifiable terrorism because the American cause was clearly right? If so, millions of Americans, especially those of draft age, didn't agree. In fact, one of the architects of the American military effort, Robert McNamara, changed his mind and became much opposed to the war he had done so much to encourage while in office. Was the war a just one until McNamara changed his mind and an evil one thereafter? Of course not. It was an unjustifiable war from the beginning.

What, then, about the American attack on Baghdad, the so-called "shock and awe." Here's what one of the authors of the strategy, Harlan Ullman, wrote in the *Economic Times* about this massive attack on Baghdad on March 21, 2003:

> We want them to quit. We want them not to fight . . . so that you have this simultaneous effect, rather like the nuclear weapons at Hiroshima, not taking days or weeks but in minutes. . . .

Ullman went on to say that it would work as well in 2003 as it did in 1945:

> Super tools and weapons — information-age equivalents of the atomic bomb — have to be invented. As the atomic bombs dropped on Hiroshima and Nagasaki finally convinced the

Japanese Emperor and High Command that even suicidal resistance was futile, these tools must be directed towards a similar outcome.

Clearly, then, "shock and awe" was terrorism with the only question being: Was it justified? The only answer that makes any sense is that terrorism cannot be justified on the basis of right or wrong motives, that it is terrorism whether practised by Osama bin Laden or Harry Truman or Curtis Lemay or George W. Bush.

A question of semantics enters the discourse here. Is terrorism against civilian populations an evil thing in itself or is it something that can be good or evil depending upon the motives? We use it in the present context as being something inherently evil, and if *that* is our all-time definition, then Hiroshima and Nagasaki were, however successful, evil. On the other hand, the argument used by Allied leaders, especially President Truman, was that this was a war against evil, and such wars must be fought with no sentimental concerns about the enemy whether military or civilian. In fact, the case was nowhere as simple as posited by Mr. Truman because there's even a nagging doubt upon the *strategic* necessity of using the atomic bombs. Less than a week after Nagasaki, Russia was scheduled by the Yalta Agreement to enter the war against Japan—and it did. In any case, by the summer of 1945 Japan was finished because it had no natural resources and had been depending upon imports to keep going. Water supplies and lines of supply for food had been deliberately destroyed by the USAAF, and by this time the Allied blockade was complete. Japan could not have held out much longer.

So, given our record, can we claim that terrorism is evil and uncivilized? For answer, I simply say that when George Bush and Tony Blair rail against terrorism as evil, they ought to know that much of the Muslim world sees this as the epitome of hypocrisy.

Some years ago I watched an Egyptian woman being interviewed about Muslim terrorism, which at that time took the form of hijacking, kidnapping and deaths in the 1972 massacres at the

Munich Olympics and aboard the *Achille Lauro*. She was asked how under these circumstances she could condone terrorism. She almost spat out her answer. "How can you," she asked, "speak to me about terrorism? You who sent a generation of young men out of their trenches into certain death by murderous machine gun fire? You who deliberately killed civilians by the hundreds of thousands in Germany . . . you who killed 250,000 with two atomic bombs! How dare you talk of terrorism?"

Of course, one can and should consider the terrorism that the West has employed, but luckily for us, we won and never had to face the question seriously. Quite apart from their own manifold sins and wickedness, if the Japanese and Germans had won, would they have been entitled to assume that the West was terrorist? This point becomes particularly apt when you consider that virtually all the terrorism we face today comes from Muslims.

I did not start out as a tolerant person. I was born in intolerant times where racial slurs were common, when words like nigger, kike, wop and chink were common and were said without the slightest embarrassment. But World War II, the central theme of my pre-adult period, brought changes to my generation to the surprise and sometimes annoyance of our seniors who didn't really take seriously the notion that it was a war to end racial and other prejudices. While I knew that Catholics went to a different church, it never occurred to me to think anything special about them or their church.

My parents' generation was quite different, as illustrated by the fuss that arose in the early fifties when one of my cousins married a Roman Catholic. In my parents' time, marrying a Jew was almost unthinkable; marrying someone "of colour" *was* indeed unthinkable. This attitude wasn't confined to "WASPS"; Catholics insisted that any children of a mixed marriage be raised as Catholics, while many ethnic groups in Canada—the Greeks come quickly to mind—made it all but impossible for someone outside the community to marry into it. But my generation was the one that spawned the hippies of the sixties. We were the ones who cheered Jackie

Robinson on as he fought his way into organized baseball in 1946, and we actually believed in the Atlantic Charter that Roosevelt and Churchill agreed upon in 1941.

However, with the horrors of 9/11 came an understandable knee-jerk reaction against Muslims, especially those who came from the area known as the Middle East, that "middle" now evidently stretching from Pakistan to Morocco. Much of the pre-conditioning for a strong prejudice against Muslims from that region arose from the hijackings, kidnappings and especially suicide bombings. For "liberals" like me, this was a very difficult period because we were as shocked and revolted as anyone else by Muslim terrorism, but we avoided blaming Islam, the religion. It was just a few mad mullahs, we said.

But as we reached the middle of 2004 it became very difficult for me, at any rate, to maintain my limp-wristed liberalism towards Islam. While like most "liberals" I had since 9/11 repeated the mantra that Islam is really a religion of peace and only a few wackos were misreading the revealed word in order to justify Osama bin Laden and al Qaeda, I began to have the uneasy feeling that I was wrong. I had this nagging sense that while much of what I'd said and thought was undoubtedly true, there is a capacity for madness in Islam that was being successfully exploited by some pretty bad people. However, in order to keep my limp-wristed liberal button, I dutifully noted that there is also much capacity for madness in Christianity as well and that it has manifested itself countless times over the centuries. But I knew that true as this statement was, I was using it as an excuse not to deal with the reality of Islam.

My epiphany came in early August 2005 when I saw an interview on BBC *Hard Talk* with Muslim cleric Omar Bakri Muhammad, who openly supported Osama bin Laden, constantly praised the nineteen "heroes" who did 9/11, and refused to criticize the London bombings. He said that, if Europe failed to heed bin Laden's offer to end terrorism in exchange for all foreign troops being withdrawn from Iraq within three months, terrorism would continue and increase. Indeed, he said that, without that truce agreement, Muslims would no longer be restrained from attacking the western countries that play host to them. "All Muslims of the West will be obliged," he said, to "become his [bin Laden's] sword" in a new battle. Europeans take heed, he added. "It is foolish to fight people who want death—that is what they are looking for." Bakri is scarcely alone among the Muslim clerics in London and elsewhere.

I asked myself what would happen if an Anglican priest, a Catholic priest, a United Church minister or a rabbi, were to utter these words? They would surely be disciplined and probably defrocked. But that's because these religions are hierarchical, which Islam, leaving aside the Ismaili and their Aga Khan, is not. Islam has no equivalent of the archbishop of Canterbury, or the pope, or the moderator of the United Church or the chief rabbi. This means that Bakri and his ilk have no superiors to discipline them. To make matters worse, senior mullahs largely agree with him or, at least, certainly don't openly oppose him.

Then the obvious next horrible conclusion hit: If this is so, there must be a great number of Muslim clerics, unrestrained by any discipline, who are no doubt preaching the most terrible things in places like London to large congregations that include a great many young people. These clerics are not at Speakers' Corner with the other wackos—where encouragement of violence is not permitted—but in mosques where they can't be censured. While there's no shortage of outrageous quotes in the Bible that Christian preachers could use to inflame their congregations, they're under the discipline of a higher-up, and while kooky offshoots like the Branch Davidians do horrible things, the major churches would not countenance much less condone violence.

It became clear (though deep down I had always known it) that there is a reason for Muslim terrorism that we all have trouble understanding. Muslim fanatics don't have tanks, jets and rockets, at least not in quantities necessary to fight a conventional war. And

I'm glad they don't. But they do have the armed forces and weapons that rest in the minds of mad mullahs and the breasts of young people prepared to kill themselves. The issue for a long time, of course, has been Israel, which much of the Muslim world sees as a major ongoing American intrusion. Moreover, they regard the presence of "infidel" troops in the Middle East, especially in Saudi Arabia where the holy cities of Mecca and Medina are located, as blasphemy. But these fundamentalists have watched the Arab world lose every war it has had with Israel, and they realize that a conventional war is simply not on. What then to do?

The clear answer is terrorism. Terrorism with huge impacts, terrorism with lesser horrors. From their point of view, 9/11 in the United States and 7/7 in London are but two successful examples. Terrorism has the advantage of being cheap with enormous worldwide impact. The object is not necessarily to kill people in revenge for American, British and Australian involvement in Iraq—though this no doubt is part of it—but to make people so scared that they will pressure their governments to pull out of Iraq and Afghanistan. It is a tactic that forced the Spanish government to yank its troops from Iraq. Added to this poisonous mix is that Iran is clearly embarking on a program of nuclear weapons and, among its government leaders at any rate, is bent on destroying Israel.

There are many in the West who say that the Islamic cause against the US, Britain and Australia is a just cause. They also say that, given our record of terrorism when it suits us, we are fine ones to talk about terrifying civilians in pursuit of political aims. But two wrongs don't make a right, and the killing of innocent people whenever and wherever it happens is abhorrent in a civilized society. This is all the more scary because the US, Britain and Australia are not going to let their actions be swayed by Islamic terror no matter what form that terror takes. They say that no nation can permit itself to be cowed by terrorism.

Or can it? The United States succumbed to North Vietnam when the number of body bags became politically intolerable. Spain got out of Iraq as a result of fear aggravated by an enormous terrorist attack, which is perhaps why Germany and France didn't go into Iraq in the first place. I believe it would be a mistake to assume that terrorism will get the US out of the Middle East, but the Muslim terrorists clearly believe that Vietnam shows how the Americans can be beaten. This means that we in Canada—who are at least pencilled on the list because of our presence in Afghanistan—and the Americans, British and Australians will have to fight a defensive war against ongoing attacks. There will be many who will say get out of Iraq and Afghanistan and avoid the horrors to come. This may or may not be a legitimate argument, but what is clear is that none of the governments involved will go down that road.

We will all, I'm afraid, have to view Islam, wherever it is practised, as a continuing potential danger. That doesn't mean that we should treat Muslims badly but it does mean that Islam must be carefully watched as a special group. This is hard for me to say but I just can no longer pump out the mantra that Islam is a peaceful religion when, as it is practised to an alarming degree, it harbours and encourages terrorists who put my community and family at risk.

Do We Have to Be Stupid
When We Deal With Terrorism?

The English have an extraordinary ability for flying into a great calm.

—ALEXANDER WOOLCOTT

The maxim of the British people is "Business as usual."

—WINSTON CHURCHILL

The terrible bombings in London in July of 2005 horrified us all. Terrorism had reached the London Underground, and had Wendy and I been there, as we often are at that time of year, we could easily have been victims.

However, Vancouver isn't exempt—nor is any other city, for that matter—for while it certainly isn't a major target area, to terrorists it just might seem sensible to show the infidels that small centres can be hit too. So there are lessons to be learned, and I think we will have a good opportunity to advance our thinking in the days to come when we realize how well the British authorities handled their crisis.

First—and many will perhaps hate me for this—we must fairly evaluate these events. In World War II one V-1 or V-2 rocket hitting London could have caused as much damage and loss of life, while the destruction of a 9/11 attack would hardly have counted as a decent air raid. If you were to ask survivors of the Blitz, or more importantly those who lived through the Allied bombings of Germany and Japan, they would certainly express deep sorrow but shake their heads at the media reaction. With perspective of five years, 9/11, horrifying though it was, would have been, taking deaths and injuries, about the same as a middling Allied air raid in World War II.

Why do I say these things? Not to hurt anyone. I wept as I watched the coverage of these tragedies, and I thought about the hundreds of times Wendy and I have been on the Circle and Piccadilly lines, both of which go through our local Tube station at South Kensington. I was shattered by what I saw.

But our problem is that we don't understand that we're in a war and that it is a type of war that is damned near impossible to fight. The enemy sees us but we don't see them except in the aggressive war images set by Messrs. Bush and Blair. We're like the big heavyweight trying, with blinders on, to beat a featherweight who can hit as much as he wants against a helpless foe.

So 9/11 and 7/7 have brought us a lot of silliness, and one can only assume that this is because governments want to make us feel as if they are being helpful. I mean truly, does anyone seriously think you check terrorism or catch terrorists with the sorts of idiotic questions we're asked at the airline counter?

"Did you pack the bag yourself, sir?"

"No, it was done by Abdullah, my butler, who has, you know, a brother in al Qaeda."

"Has anyone asked you to carry anything in this luggage?"

"Come to think of it, yes. Abdullah asked me to take a package to his brother. I noticed it was ticking but Abdullah assured me it was just an alarm clock."

I suppose, given past events, we must take our shoes off to show we have not secreted bombs in the heels, but in my case this only exposes the holes in the toes of my socks because I'm a negligent toenail cutter. Then it's hand luggage time and after a thorough check they locate those nail clippers I should use more often and note there is a tiny little nail file attached. Without a by-your-leave it is snapped off and consigned to the rubbish. Can't you just imagine terrorists streaking down the aisle in first class waving little half-inch nail files like this one, shouting, "Death to the infidels!" On a recent trip, I had a small tube of Krazy Glue seized—I had bought it in order to attach a tip on my walking stick. What was it I might do with Krazy Glue? Cement the pilot's hands behind his back after he has been subdued by my nail clippers?

I say all this not to make light of security measures. Decent, intelligent measures make sense. But we know that since 9/11 several newspaper reporters, to prove a point, have boarded airplanes with hunting knives and God-only-knows what else. You can't get nail clippers on board but big knives are easy.

So what should we learn from what happened in London? Be prepared. A pre-war prime minister, Stanley Baldwin, once opined that "The bomber will always get through." It was in another context of course, but he was right. To stop the sort of bombing London got is all but impossible. What the Brits showed us, however, was how to prepare for these things, execute your preparations, and, as citizens, be calm.

Am I playing down the need for security?

Not at all. I hope that the authorities are now doing the work that ought to have been done before 9/11. Because, you see, 9/11 was no more difficult to pull off, using just nineteen men, than was the London tragedy. We tend to forget this and, because we don't want to look stupid, to accept the rantings of President Bush that it was planned and executed in a massive and complicated undertaking.

But it wasn't that at all. Had not Bush lashed out so desperately and in such climacteric manner, it would have been clearly seen that he and President Clinton bore responsibility for a security system that had passengers being asked silly questions while men who scarcely looked like first-class types went into first class with one-way tickets and large clumsy weapons. In truth—and horror—9/11 was blindingly simple as long as airlines would let men with first-class one-way tickets carrying box cutters onto a plane.

In this war, we cannot prevent attacks on us. If we could, Israel would have done so decades ago and the IRA would have been as dangerous as a Boy Scout troop. All we can do is minimize them with good, on-the-ground police work because these bombings are not being planned in the foothills of the Himalayas but within a short distance of where the outrage will be perpetrated. In a *Time* article right after the London disaster, there was an interview with a young Muslim who was on the waiting list to kill himself while blowing innocent people to smithereens! A waiting list, for God's sake! And in London! So this is on-the-ground, tough, undercover police work we need here. And we must be as alert as London was.

One final note: Wendy and I went to London a month after the bombing and again in November and yet again over New Year's. Moreover, we used the usual Underground stations—especially the Circle and Piccadilly lines—as always. We wore t-shirts with a Canadian flag and the Union Jack bordering the words "If you're not scared, neither are we." Was that because we're brave? No. It's because we know that the odds are very long indeed that we'll have trouble and there's nowhere in the world that is safe anyway. And we're not about to let the terrorists accomplish their purpose.

The London tragedy taught us all—at least ought to have taught us all—that terrorism can hit everywhere, that we must live with it, and that it can be minimized, but only by sound, solid police work, not silly questions at the airline counter.

PART FOUR

The Free Press and Other Myths

The Rear-View Mirror

I wanted to call my 2004 book, *Rafe: A Memoir* and subtitle it, *Is that a swan I hear singing?* but my publisher thought it a poor idea since I had much more to do before I was finished with writing. Since that was three books ago, I suppose he was right.

The last comment I made about my career and the people I had met along the way was in *Rafe: A Memoir,* and was really inspired by my receiving the Bruce Hutchison Award for Lifetime Achievement at the Jack Webster Awards in October 2003. That award came as a great surprise to me and it couldn't have happened at a better time. I had been fired by CKNW, where I had been working for nearly nineteen years, only a few months after they had signed me to a three-year contract making me the highest paid broadcaster in the province—at least so I was assured. Ten days before I was canned, my ratings were fantastic, and I have kept the letter of flowing praise sent me on that occasion by the program director, Tom Plasteras, which read in part, "Rafe Mair dominates the 8:30–11 A.M. slot with a 17.8 share, up from 17.0 last fall. *Rafe has an amazing average quarter hour audience of 99,900!!* [Emphasis his] The next closest station is QM-FM with a 12.1 then QM with an 11.6 share . . ."

I was in one way happy to get out of NW because the last few months there were sheer torment for Wendy and me as it became clear they wanted to force me to quit so they wouldn't have to pay me a year's salary. Under the release I was eventually compelled to sign to get my money, I'm not permitted to give any of the details leading up to the firing but I think I can say this: It was bullshit.

A couple of weeks after I was fired I received a phone call from Jack Webster Jr. who informed me that I had been unanimously selected for the Hutchison Award. I honestly thought he was kidding. Then, for some strange reason I can't explain, I didn't really care. I think I was feeling sorry for myself and all of a sudden I hated the industry. As so often happens, Wendy put it pretty clearly. "Honey," she said, "this is your industry, your colleagues telling you they think a hell of a lot of you and don't think much of the way CKNW treated you." Then she reminded me of how, after I was fired, Shiral Tobin had risked her job at the CBC by going very public and telling the world what she thought of me and how I was treated, and how all my past producers, all of them women, had offered to do the same thing. As the weeks passed leading up to the Webster dinner, I became overwhelmed with pride, but more than that, deep gratitude for what my colleagues had done for me and my morale—and Wendy and the rest of my family—and for what they were saying about me.

Now I'm also in the Canadian Association of Broadcasters Hall of Fame, and as with the Hutchison Award I'm in damned fine company.

I don't kid myself about these awards. When my then station, 600AM, found out about the Hall of Fame, their great newsman—and I mean *great*—Cam McCubbin did a piece, a collage on me on very short notice, and it was marvellous for me to hear his words. When I thanked him he laughed and said, "If I go on for another fifty years, maybe I'll get there, too." He meant it as a joke but I suddenly felt badly. He was right, of course. He is a great veteran and has been in the business a lifetime, whereas I elbowed in at the top with no previous experience and was the Hutchison winner before I'd been in the game twenty-three years and the Hall of Fame before I'd reached twenty-five. Life just isn't fair.

I have reminisced before about things I have done, places I have been and people I have interviewed, and in all it hasn't been all that remarkable. I am proud of some work I've done, especially in environmental matters and constitutional affairs. I think I've been a pretty decent prod in the ass to governments, especially in the area of mental health. I've also taken a few bumps along the way and am glad I was able, much through good luck, to pick myself up and start all over again, as the old song goes.

But there is one thing I am very proud of. When I went into talk radio in early 1981, I said that before I was through I wanted to change the face of talk radio by dealing with major issues, not just tiddly little things like hookers on the street or a politician with his hand in the jam jar. The pattern of talk shows had become pretty standard. Three hours and three guests, each guest a fifteen-minute interview, then calls from the public. My colleague Gary Bannerman used to do a rambling editorial off the top (we all tend to ramble!) and in the old days Jack Webster did *City Mike*, which you would properly infer dealt mostly with civic issues. But I wanted to make waves. Like a dog with a bone, I badly wanted to get onto issues. I didn't want to just do so for the sake of doing it, but I genuinely felt that we all needed a good shake. Things were happening that the public wasn't paying attention to. Canadians were so shy, so accepting of government abuse.

I had three areas where I felt I could do some good at shaking things up a bit. I had been in politics and knew where the bodies were buried. I knew that the BC legislature—and the House of Commons for that matter—was a sham like the old Iron Curtain parliaments where government legislation was rubber-stamped. I also knew about how the "spin doctors" worked, having employed many myself.

I knew something about constitutional law, not just from law school but from having been in the thick of it during the run-up to the patriating of the Constitution in 1982. I knew the double-talk that had British Columbians anaesthetized against reality. I knew well that constitutional matters were going to heat up and I wanted the public to understand the issues. I think I succeeded when the Meech Lake Accord came along, followed by the Charlottetown Accord. At about year two of Meech Lake (the provinces and parliament had three years in which to support it) Doug Rutherford, CKNW's program director, who to his great credit never interfered with what I did, asked me if I thought the public cared about all these esoteric arguments I was making day after day about Meech Lake. I replied, "Doug, they will care and when they do the story will be ours." And so it proved to be.

I am also an environmentalist and had been environment minister when the BC government confirmed the deal I'd made with Seattle Light and Power so that in exchange for giving the Americans power from our grid system to make up for the power they would lose if they didn't raise the Ross Lake Dam (as they were entitled to), we could save British Columbia's part of the Skagit River from becoming a lake instead of a beautiful trout stream. The kudos for that go to the Run Out Skagit Spoilers (ROSS) Committee, which never quit even when it seemed the cause was lost. That I was able to negotiate the saving of that wonderful stream is one of the high points of my life. Later in radio I was also involved in several major environmental issues, including the Kemano Completion Project (for which I won the Michener Award), the Pitt River gravel conflict and, of course, the Atlantic salmon fish farm issue.

I leave it all with this. I wanted to change talk radio and I think I did. Whether it was really just a case of *post hoc ergo propter hoc*, which, loosely translated, means "Just because the rooster crows when the sun comes up doesn't mean that the sun came up because the rooster crowed" or whether it had something to do with me is for others to judge. Rather than actually making a difference, it's just possible I came along at the right time. That it happened, however, cannot be denied.

The Journalist's Duty

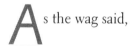s the wag said,

> *You cannot hope to bribe or twist*
> *Thank God the British journalist.*
> *Considering what the man will do*
> *Unbribed, there's no occasion to.*

The best defence the journalist has, of course, is the same safety net that protects the negligent surgeon: Who is going to report the biased journalist and who will print that report? I think the best place to start this discussion is with the proposition that no one is free from bias but, unfortunately, that truism has been used to excuse bias blatant or subtle instead of identifying it and dealing with it.

The problem with wanting objective journalism, which I assume all of us think a good idea, is that the unfairness starts with the editorial decision whether to report on a subject or not or, if it is to be covered, how much space will be given to it. A good and amusing example is from many years ago when King George VI and Queen Elizabeth visited South Africa. The English-language papers gushed with patriotic pride while the main Dutch paper had an item on the social page announcing that "Mr. and Mrs. George Windsor" were in town! Married to the problem of whether to report on the subject and how much space to give it is the editorial decision as to how much prominence to give a story.

Owners habitually hire editors who do their bidding—or else— so is it any surprise, then, that editors don't have to tell newsmen and women to remember their kindly old publisher when submitting work? Though it is tough to prove a negative, I suspect that editors usually don't have to censor because writers have mortgages to pay and kids to bring up. As a result, I would say that almost all of what you read or see has passed either formal censorship or self-censorship, meaning that all allegations in print, on air or on screen must be taken with large doses of salt.

I think, too, that it is important to note that criticism of the publisher's favourite political party is permitted—it would be impossible to run a paper or a station unless it was—but it sure as hell isn't encouraged. This is what makes objective criticism of the media so difficult. Whether, for example, the CanWest approach to past Liberal governments has been tough enough is a matter of judgment, and CanWest can always point to tape or newspaper inches to show coverage and claim that those who complain are probably biased Conservatives or NDPers. It is for this reason that one must ask the question, "Is there bias in the media?" and then take care with the answer. Whether there is bias in the article you are reading is difficult to determine, but if it passed muster by not displeasing the editor and publisher, that should give you pause for concern. What it is easier to do—though this requires patience and diligence—is to examine what is reported and see if it contains editorial comment mingled in with the reporting. The test is a simple one: that which is not clearly factual contains opinion, and the whole piece must be seen in that light.

What this means is that there must be good editorial content, and this is not as easy as it sounds. Those who write editorials anonymously for a paper are not the people I am concerned with here; those shadowy figures clearly do what they are told. I am talking about columnists. And I'm sad to report that there are more than a few columnists these days who have jobs either because their pens are seen to be in a safe pair of hands or because it is difficult to take a high moral tone when you have a mortgage and a number of mouths to feed. I have to say that I am in no position to criticize these hard-working columnists because I have been fortunate in that I have never, save for two instances I'll talk about in a minute, ever had the slightest pressure to do or not do anything. I've been damned lucky that for most of my media career I've been free from interference and, indeed, during my days at CKNW before Corus took over, management told advertisers that the reason they could advertise to such a large audience is because they left their broadcasters alone.

The two instances? One I've related elsewhere and involved some unfriendly remarks I had made about Brian Burke, then with the Vancouver Canucks, a team owned by the Griffiths family who also owned CKNW. In spite of that, the Canucks could sell their broadcast rights to anyone and that rightly frightened the CKNW management. Burke, who has the thinnest skin of any public figure I've ever seen, complained about words I had used to describe him; I believe that "asshole" was amongst them. Program director Doug Rutherford pled with me to apologize. He ran the full gamut from threatening to suspend me, which he had no right to do, and tearful pleading. I told him to go fuck himself and the next day on air I told the story. The matter was never raised again.

The second happened more recently when I was at 600AM. After we had received unpleasant news about a recent ratings "book," manager Gerry Siemens told me, "Rafe, some of my golfing buddies complain that you do too much on fish farms." I was frankly astonished and simply replied, "Gerry, perhaps you should go fishing once in a while." I have no doubt that his comment was a symptom of advertiser pressure and that it led a few months later to me being fired. Otherwise, it was a move that made no sense. I was told in October 2005 that he wanted a better bottom line for 2006. Well, since my contract ended on August 31, 2006, and he had to pay me until that date, he didn't save all that much by firing me before then. And when you consider the severance the two producers he also fired were entitled to, it would not have been much of a financial burden to bear had Siemens continued my show until my contract ended.

So I say that I *think* I was forced out because of advertiser pressure because there is no other sensible explanation. I must say that I have no bitterness toward 600AM, Siemens or Jimmy Pattison, who owns the station. I have always felt that owners could hire and fire as long as they lived up to their side of the deal, which 600AM did. What I do say, however, is that there is no one left across Canada, as far as I can determine, who will consistently stand against the Establishment, ask the questions the people want asked, and press for the answers. There is no one left who, seeing an injustice, will fight to see it rectified. That saddens me.

The tough journalists are gone from the mainstream media. The late Jack Webster, the Stevie Camerons, the Claire Hoys, the Andrew MacIntoshes and, yes, the Rafe Mairs are gone, not to be replaced. There is no eternally vigilant media to nip things like the federal Liberals' sponsorship scandal in the bud and, if there are journalists who would play that role, there is no money for that exercise.

The Modern Media
and What to Do About It

Freedom of the press is guaranteed only to those who own one.

—A.J. LIEBLING

Free speech, which is to say the right to say or write anything subject to reasonable libel laws and prohibitions from inciting wrongdoing, no longer exists in Canada nor, from what I can determine, anywhere else. There are two ways this has happened: 1) the government has taken away the right to say and publish certain things and plans more restrictions, and 2) there is simply no way to get words published or broadcast if owners don't want that to happen.

The government acts this way. In the Criminal Code of Canada, publication of hate literature or inciting hate or violence is a crime. This facet of the law is rarely used and I leave debate of matters like the Ernst Zundel case for another time. What I'm more concerned about is that under the very broad language of the Criminal Code, the CRTC can effectively censor what can be said and done on radio and TV but not, one must observe, in newspapers or on the internet. In an article called "Wrong Wavelength" published on page 15 of *The National Post* on June 24, 2004, Pierre Lemieux says this:

> Under the legal verbiage of regulatory offences, the CRTC blames CHOI for violating "Canadian values." Criticizing some comments made on-air, the CRTC ruled on July 13 that "their broadcast on public airwaves does not constitute programming that reflects Canadian values." The CRTC's decision adds: "The regulation prohibiting abusive comment that tends or is likely to expose a person or a group to hatred or contempt is necessary not only to avoid harm to the persons targeted, but also to ensure that Canadian values are respected for all Canadians. . . . This harm undermines the cultural, political and social fabric of Canada."

We have to ask who determines what Canadian values are? The prime minister? The moderator of the United Church? Perhaps, for impartiality, we could invite Jerry Falwell and Pat Robertson to do the job. And upon what authority does the CRTC make this ruling? Lemieux has this to say:

> The CRTC justifies its censorship by the fact that the airwaves "are public property," that using them is a "privilege," and that broadcasting is "a public service essential to the maintenance and enhancement of national identity and cultural sovereignty." Disregarding the last point, which is an open plea for state censorship, there is no economic foundation to the claim that the electromagnetic spectrum is a public good that needs to be public property. *There is no more reason for a state bureau to allocate frequencies*

*on the electromagnetic spectrum than to distribute forest
acreage to those who need wood to make newsprint to publish
newspapers.* [Emphasis added]

This view was supported by the *Globe and Mail* on September
7, 2005, when in an editorial it said:

> What can regulators realistically do to control content in
> this new world of specialty broadcasters and choice-hungry
> consumers with hundreds of channels at their fingertips?
> Sooner or later Ottawa is going to have to accept that its
> rationale for regulating broadcast content—control of the
> public airwaves—is as archaic as the vinyl record.

The station that got into trouble with the CRTC on this ground
of violating "Canadian values" was CHOI in Quebec City. Some
background, again from Lemieux:

> CHOI is the most popular radio station in the capital of
> Quebec. It is a rock station, but with politically incorrect and
> controversial (and anti-nationalist) talk shows and hosts. Its
> broadcasts attract up to 46,000 listeners, according to Cossette
> Média data. The CRTC received 9,417 "interventions" in
> favour of the renewal of CHOI's licence, and 38 against. On
> July 22, between 35,000 and 50,000 people demonstrated
> in the streets of Quebec City streets against the CRTC's
> diktat. By yesterday, the station claims, 209,016 individuals
> had signed its petition asking Parliament to overrule the
> CRTC.

Lemieux concludes:

> Contrary to CHOI, few radio and TV stations dare to violate
> the CRTC's "Canadian values," precisely because they don't

want to put their licences at risk. So, in practice, the CRTC exerts its censorship on the contents of broadcasting from the new licence applications to their periodic renewals, and to the forced auto-censorship in between.

I couldn't agree more. An old friend, Terry Moore of CFAX in Victoria, got into heavy doo-doo for allowing a Muslim author to say what were perfectly awful things about Jews in general and what should happen to them. On reading a transcript of what was said, I think the words may indeed be actionable under the Criminal Code of Canada and I can say, though I suppose it is irrelevant, that on my program this guest would not have got away with what he said on this show. Terry should have stopped him and should have done a better job of answering his guest's outrages. But this same interview could have been published in Q&A form in any newspaper in the country without any government interference save, perhaps, from the RCMP laying charges under the Criminal Code in which one has (still) the presumption of innocence going for them in a court of law. This basic civil liberty doesn't exist in the rarefied air occupied by the CRTC pointy-heads who use their power to license and de-license to impose standards they can't begin to define.

As Pierre Lemieux says, it is nonsense to make exceptions for what is broadcast because it is the "use of public airways," an argument that makes as much sense as censoring newspapers on the grounds that they are made from trees that came from publicly owned timber. No, the problem is that Canadians are too damned stupid to see that government enforcing manners, as they define them, is a denial of free speech, plain and simple.

The CRTC also censored in advance when it approved the adding of al-Jazeera, the Arab equivalent of CNN, to the Canadian cable package, but on exceptional terms. As Lemieux observes:

> The agency also took an unprecedented step in allowing cable companies to alter or delete "abusive comments" from

al-Jazeera programs. Currently, it is illegal for distributors to delete programming, but in this case, the commission made an exception.

At the same time, the CRTC has refused permission to add the Fox News channel to the cable package. It might well be argued that Fox is little more than a mouthpiece for the Republican Party, but surely this is, if true, beside the point. Canadian citizens, not regulators, ought to deal with that question.

Canadians, at least far too many of them, are concerned that without government censorship through the CRTC, "naughty" things—at least what is naughty to their ears and eyes—will be said and shown. Canadian Jews, for example, object to what they see as al-Jazeera's stereotyping of Jews in general, which is the Canadian Jewish Congress' ill-disguised code for "It gives the Arab point of view." Undoubtedly, many Jewish people would take great offence at what al-Jazeera has to say, but since when has free speech been defined as that which doesn't offend? If the "offensive language" violates Defamation Laws or the Criminal Code of Canada, there is a process for dealing with it. If not, it is—or should be—part of the rough and tumble of debate in a free society. Indeed, it is this right to be rude that separates freedom from tyranny.

Let's look at a book I guarantee very few Canadians have ever heard of. I follow the book reviews religiously and I've never seen it mentioned, but it is a well-written blockbuster. The author, Susan Nathan, is a Jew born in Britain who didn't migrate to Israel until she was fifty. She regarded herself as a Zionist, was given instant citizenship in Israel under their "Right of Return" policy, and moved to Tel Aviv. (It's surely fair to point out that displaced Palestinians don't have a "Right to Return.") In her book, *The Other Side of Israel: My journey across the Jewish-Arab divide*, Ms. Nathan tells a compelling story of her move to Tamra, an Israeli Palestinian town of about 25,000 where she is the only Jew. Now remember, this book is not about Palestinians *beyond* Israel's borders but

Palestinians who are in fact living within Israel *as citizens*. In the following several paragraphs I will summarize just a few of the facts contained in her book.

Israeli Palestinians are considered and treated as second-class citizens at best. They make up 20 percent of the population of Israel and, though they can vote and do send members to the Knesset, and although Israel's government is always formed from broad coalitions, not one Palestinian has served in the government since the nation's inception in 1948.

Nearly all arable land taken by Israel in wars has been confiscated by the state then parcelled out to Jewish Israelis; so seldom is that land reallocated to Palestinians that one might as well say never. The Israeli government regularly confiscates land held by Israeli Palestinians who have never left it and hold title deeds to it; as soon as they evict the proper owners, the government bulldozes down all buildings. Lands taken from Arabs who fled the advancing Israeli army in 1948 were all confiscated without compensation and have been given to Jews. Israeli Palestinians wanting to visit families across the border and Palestinians who wish to go to Israel are consistently harassed, beaten and too often killed by Israeli troops just as an exercise of power.

The original "right of return" for Jews stated that anyone anywhere in the world who had a Jewish grandparent could claim Israeli citizenship upon arrival in Israel. This was broadened in 1970 to extend the right to immigrate to non-Jews who are either children or grandchildren of a Jew, to the spouse of a Jew or to the spouse of a child or grandchild of a Jew. However, no Palestinian who resided on land conquered by Israel, even though his family resided there for centuries, can return and claim his property, much less citizenship.

Israeli Palestinian communities receive virtually no financial help from the government and are constantly refused the right to expand. Because Israeli Palestinians are not permitted to join the army, while Jews *must* serve, young Palestinians don't get any of the help with mortgages and land acquisition that the government gives to young Jews. Per capita, Israeli Palestinian children get less than one quarter the money spent on them than do Jewish kids.

Many thoughtful Jews both inside and outside Israel see Israeli treatment of their Palestinian co-citizens in much the same way Nazi Germany treated Jews (with the obvious exception of the Holocaust).

The chilling part of this story is that the state of Israel doesn't deny any of the basic statements in Ms. Nathan's book. So the question we must ask ourselves is this: Why don't these atrocities and this unfair discrimination get reported? Why haven't we seen "specials" in newspapers and on TV about this? Why haven't we been told that far more Arabs than Jews have been violently killed? Why haven't we debated how we can support Israel when it denies basic human rights to one million of its citizens? Why, in short, have we for the most part seen the issues through the eyes of Israeli Jews, the government of Israel and Jewish organizations abroad, and learned nothing about the way they are seen by the Palestinian citizens of Israel?

If you live in Vancouver, the answer is pretty easy. All the main newspapers plus a hell of a lot of community papers here are owned by CanWest, which also owns the largest TV station, Global/BCTV. And CanWest's stated policy is that news from the Middle East must reflect well on Israel. This raises the touchy issue that CanWest is owned by the Asper family, who are Jewish, but the issue is far too broad to go down that road. Rupert Murdoch isn't a Jew and he is the biggest media power in the world, and you will not see much of the concerns of Israeli Palestinians in his newspapers either. The truth is that even the mighty "broadsheets" unfailingly spout the line of the publisher, so the concentration of media ownership has drastically limited the number of points of view expressed. James Winter, in an article published in the May/June 2002 edition of *Fair*, explains how CanWest imposed its publisher's line on its newspapers:

CanWest set off the media furor in December [2001] with its decision to require all of its daily newspapers to run corporate editorials produced in its Winnipeg head office. Initially, the company sent out one editorial weekly, but said this would increase to three times a week. The company also said locally written material should not contradict the party line handed down in corporate editorials.

Winter said that the dispute that ensued put the topic of "media concentration on the political agenda as seldom before." He went on to say:

In January [2002], organizations representing journalists across Canada called for a parliamentary inquiry into media concentration, especially at CanWest Global Communications. The Canadian Association of Journalists (CAJ) and the Quebec Federation of Professional Journalists (QFPJ) denounced actions of the media giant as "a disturbing pattern of censorship and repression of dissenting views."

He quoted the vice-president of the Canadian Association of Journalists, Paul Schneidereit, as saying that the federal government needed to examine the issue of media ownership concentration. And he stated, "We feel it's time for the elected officials of this country to be looking at what the repercussions [of media concentration] are for the general public." The Newspaper Guild of Canada, the largest journalists' union in North America, demanded that CanWest "immediately cease its attack on divergent opinions" and called for the Winnipeg-based media conglomerate "to adopt principles that would respect the editorial autonomy of each paper and its columnists, and allow editors, rather than corporate headquarters to make news judgments."

How did CanWest gain such control? In 2000 the company bought up the Hollinger and Southam newspaper holdings from media mogul Conrad Black. A year later it acquired majority control of Black's *National Post*, the Toronto-based Canada-wide daily. In addition, CanWest now owns 14 large city dailies, 120 smaller dailies and weeklies, and Canada's second-largest private broadcaster, the Global TV network, which includes Global/BCTV, the largest in BC.

The rest of the media picture in Canada is just as grim. In fact, Canadian media ownership is, as kids say, as tight as a gnat's ass. The telephone company Bell Canada owns the *Globe and Mail* as well as CTV, the largest private television network; it also controls Sympatico, a web portal and high-speed internet link. Montreal-based Quebecor owns the *Sun* newspaper chain, magazines, cable TV, the Canoe internet portal, music and video stores and the private TVA network in Quebec. Torstar Corporation, publisher of Harlequin romance novels, also owns the *Toronto Star*, Canada's highest-circulated daily, as well as four other dailies and sixty-nine weeklies. Rogers Communications has interests in cable, radio, television, magazines, video stores and wireless telephone. Mr. Winter concludes, "You can fit everyone who controls significant Canadian media in my office."

In discussing managerial interference with free speech in the Canadian media, Vince Carlin, chair of the School of Journalism at Ryerson University in Toronto, told the *Washington Post* on January 27, 2002, that it was "not a healthy situation." He continued:

> Who has been affected by this? That's not an easy question to answer since those given the pink slip are, not unnaturally, hoping to find a new source of mortgage payments. We do know that author and Southam columnist Lawrence Martin's contract was not renewed in 2001 because of his criticism of Liberal Prime Minister Jean Chrétien—a friend of Izzy Asper, who once led the Manitoba Liberal Party.

Toronto Sun columnist Peter Worthington was also critical of the Aspers and had his column pulled from the *Windsor Star*, a

Southam paper, as a result. Doug Cuthand, a First Nations columnist for the *Regina Leader-Post*, wrote an essay in early January 2001 sympathetic to the plight of Palestinians in the West Bank, comparing them to Canada's indigenous peoples. The Aspers, who are, according to the *Toronto Star* (January 12, 2002), "well known for their unstinting support of Israel," had the column killed. Stephen Kimber, a columnist for fifteen years with the *Halifax Daily News*, quit in January 2002 after one of his columns was killed by corporate headquarters. It was eventually published in the *Globe and Mail* (January 7, 2002). Stephanie Domet, another freelance columnist for the *Halifax Sunday Daily News*, resigned a few days later after writing a column in support of Kimber for *The Coast*, a Halifax weekly. Her column was later posted on the CBC's website (January 7, 2002).

Carlin's comments in the *Washington Post* conclude with these words:

> CanWest's owners, Winnipeg's Asper family, which made its fortune in the television business, appear to consider their newspapers not only as profit centres and promotional vehicles for their television network but also as private, personal pulpits from which to express their views. The Aspers support the federal Liberal Party. They're pro-Israel. They think rich people like themselves deserve tax breaks. They support privatizing health care delivery. And they believe their newspapers . . . should agree with them.

But the repercussions of CanWest's managerial interference did not end in January. A number of reporters at CanWest's *Regina Leader-Post* were suspended for five days in early March for talking to outside media, and another six were given letters of reprimand after they withdrew their bylines in protest after management censored a story by reporter Michelle Lang about a speech critical of CanWest.

Of perhaps more concern is the self-censorship issue I touched upon in the last chapter. Writers want desperately to do a good job and speak frankly about issues but, having mortgages and families, they recognize realities and pull punches. I know of several in British Columbia and in other parts of Canada who clearly write with considerably more tact and circumspection than they once did. This fact must be combined with what I call censorship by omission. What articles are not written because journalists fear to write them? And if they did write them, who knows whether they would be accepted by the editor? And what about the specials that editors never commission? You can't quantify any of this, but I have no doubt that the reason there is little hard-hitting journalism on environmental issues is simply because editors know that publishers—and their advertisers—don't want it, and writers take the hint.

The Aspers have never been anything but frank about their mission. In 1991, after acquiring a 20 percent stake in New Zealand's TV3, the late Izzy Asper gathered two hundred employees of the station in the cafeteria and astounded them by asking a journalist, "You, what business do you think you're in?"

The journalist replied that "The business we're in is to make sure our audience gets the most carefully researched news and information possible." Asper asked the same questions of the drama and entertainment departments and got similar answers.

"You're all wrong," he said. "You're in the business of selling soap." It was his way of telling all who wrote for him that their first duty was to the advertiser. That being so, it is our duty as consumers to bear it in mind when we're consuming!

What can be done?

First, we must note that this is scarcely a new problem. In 1970 at the time of the Davey Report, media concentration was considerably less than it is today; the three biggest chains controlled a mere 45 percent of the daily circulation. Just a decade later when Kent Commission reported on the media, those three chains controlled 57 percent. Today the concentration of newspaper ownership is far worse than either Keith Davey or Tom Kent could have imagined. According to the Campaign for Press and Broadcast Freedom, the three biggest chains now control more than 74 percent of daily circulation. One company alone — CanWest Global — owns or controls more than 40 percent of English language circulation. Particularly troubling is the fact that there exists a complete monopoly of the daily press in Saskatchewan, New Brunswick, Prince Edward Island and Newfoundland.

An editorial comment by the Campaign for Press and Broadcast Freedom (www.presscampaign.org) states:

> Faced with this possibility [of legislation] in the past, media owners have argued such measures infringe upon their individual rights and transgress freedom of the press. While we are sensitive to this argument, the truth is the case for imposing limits on media ownership is based solely on democratic, social and journalistic concerns. The media have a social responsibility that makes them unlike other commercial activities. As such, freedom of the press is not just the proprietary right of owners to do as they see fit. It is a right of the Canadian people.
>
> For this right to be respected, therefore, we need to actively encourage diversity and openness in our media. That means enacting policies to promote wider participation in the media industries and reverse the concentration of media power in fewer and fewer hands. Other countries and jurisdictions have recognized this basic principle and have developed measures to confront the threat of media ownership concentration. Others are taking action now:
>
> The European Commission is proposing legislation to restrict the reach of big media corporations and control the spread of cross-media ownership.
>
> In Britain, television broadcasters are limited to 15 percent of the national audience. In the case of newspaper

mergers, the British Monopolies and Mergers Commission, unlike Canada's Competition Bureau, is required to assess the impact on "the accurate presentation of news and free expression of opinion" when deciding whether to approve a merger.

Sweden has a long-standing press subsidy scheme whereby a diversity of newspapers, not always supported by private corporate advertisers, are provided public financing.

The Italian Broadcasting Act of 1990 sets concrete limits on media concentration. Under the law, no one person or company may own or control more than 20 percent of all the media.

In Germany, whenever a merger enables a company to control a specific press market or strengthen its already controlling position, the federal cartel office is required to intervene to prevent the merger. The regulations have been used several times and with some notable success. Most recently, the cartel office prevented Springer from acquiring monopoly control of the Munich newspaper market.

The French government restricts any group or individual from owning more than 30 percent of the daily press. However, if a company or individual has substantial interests in the broadcast media, it may only control up to 10 percent of the daily press.

Clearly, Canada is lagging behind most of the developed world when it comes to regulating media ownership.

It's nigh on impossible to deny the foregoing but what should be done? What can be done? These are the recommendations proposed by the Campaign for Press and Broadcast Freedom:

1. The total number of daily newspapers, radio stations, or

television stations owned by one company or individual in any market should not exceed 50 percent.

2. No one company or individual should directly or indirectly control more than 25 percent of the circulation of daily newspapers in Canada.

3. To limit cross-media ownership concentration, we propose that no one person or company may own or control more than 20 percent of all the media.

4. The current Competition Act should be amended so that it contains the following clause: "The Director of Research and Investigation shall report whether or not a merger involving media interests may be expected to operate against the public interest, taking into account all matters which appear in the particular circumstances to be relevant and having regard to the need for accurate presentation of news and free expression of diverse opinion.

I'm afraid that I don't have much confidence in the foregoing recommendations although passing them can hardly make matters worse and may bring some reforms. And I must confess that I don't see any other reforms that would improve things. However, I believe that the solutions rest elsewhere, for example, with the question of government regulation of the electronic media. The fact is there is no longer a need for any regulation whatsoever. Moreover, in the case of satellite radio, the government cannot regulate anyway, except in a roundabout way, such as where the satellite radio is owned in whole or in part by a company (let's say Telus) that requires a friendly CRTC when it asks for rate increases for telephone use. The electronic media can — and more and more do — provide competition for the newspapers, and the more competition the better. The government should not concern itself with the sensibilities of Canadians, but let the defamation laws and the Criminal Code act as protective devices. I go further: the American case of Sullivan v. the *New York Times* should be made the law in Canada so that for a public official to maintain a defamation case it must be demonstrated that not only is the statement untrue but malicious. Since the mainstream media do as their advertisers wish, how can this help? It helps modestly in the sense that, where a publisher has no personal reason for the remarks not to be published but fears a lawsuit, journalists will be encouraged to boldly put politicians' feet to the fire, not hesitatingly as now.

After all this gloom, there is a very big ray of light ahead: the internet and satellite radio. When electronic outlets no longer need "frequencies" or "channels," government regulators will be put out of business, except in cases like the Telus one cited above. This will bring some problems with it to be sure, but censorship by owners or government will not be one of them. I suppose this last comment must be modified to accept the fact that governments can still pass laws about content, but the reality is that they will find enforcing those laws one hell of a problem. Technology through the internet provides the hope for knowledge dissemination much as the Irish cloisters protected and perpetuated knowledge in the Dark Ages. It is here that thought and opinion can flourish. Of course, there are nations that are looking for ways to control this new limitless availability of information. Whether they can do so or not remains to be seen. What we do know from history is that every time a government censors, people find their way around their laws.

I write for *www.thetyee.ca*, a marvellous online outlet for opinion in my neck of the woods. If you read it, you will see many familiar names, and unless I miss my guess, you will sense a freedom of thought and expression that has become rare in the mainstream. In short, good writers are even better when they are not under the nose of the censor. The internet, of course, suffers from excess of choice, and web newspapers must rely on links and word of mouth for expansion. Moreover there is so much stuff on the internet one is always tempted to abandon a "surfing" exercise that is getting tiresome. On the other hand, people are getting more and more aggressive as the mainstream media gets more and more censored. At least that's the hope.

But how long will it be before government extends its big blue pencil online? It already is considering action against kiddie porn outlets, and though there is no argument that can be made in favour of them, is this the thin edge of the wedge? Will governments extend their interpretation of what they believe is evil to portray and watch? They can take two tacks: they can view a site then prosecute for what they see as lawbreaking or they can physically shut down the site. But whether or not they can do anything more than nip at the edges, bearing in mind that censored websites will no doubt open up again, remains much to be seen. However, China is finding ways to stifle internet opinion; who says it won't happen here?

Unquestionably the problem is a very difficult one, and it is confounding nations throughout the so-called free world. At present we do not have free speech in our media, and the mainstream media that so readily espouses the cause of freedom of the press denies this fact every moment of every day. This is very bad news for a society that wishes to live in freedom.

PART FIVE

Some Thoughts on Religions

The Christian Right

The conversion of the Republican Party to right-wing Christianity is interesting. It comes at a time, I'm sure you will have noticed, when three of the world's major religions are at the forefront of world affairs, and each in its own way is scrambling for world supremacy.

The Jews—and I admit that's too broad a term—have their own state, one specifically declared to be for them. But while there are five million Jews in Israel, there are also one million Palestinians, and the Israeli Palestinians are not even second-class citizens. Quite apart from the astonishing fact that this is a "democracy" that actively favours one segment, there's not much question that Israel's discrimination against its Palestinian citizens is intended to encourage them to leave and to discourage the Palestinians who are demanding the right to return to lands confiscated from them during the 1948 war and after. Strictly speaking, this struggle is not between Muslims and Jews, but in reality religion has a huge influence on it. For the Israeli establishment the worry is that, given the birth rate of Palestinians as opposed to Jews, Israel could in the foreseeable future lose its Jewish majority. This fact is like death: you can go for a time without thinking about it but not for very long.

Islam claims to be a peaceful religion, but it clearly is nothing of the sort if you read the Koran. The Muslim duty to convert the infidel has always had a big presence in this religion as does the use of force. Where Muslim countries are indeed theocracies—and most of them are—the military threat they pose is very real. It is also true that Muslims can fight Muslims, as happened between Iran and Iraq, just as Christian countries have demonstrated that they too will replace the cross with a gun at the drop of a hat.

It's fair to say, I think, that while there are other underlying causes, the main factor in the Middle East is the Jews in Israel pushing their Arab brethren out of their lands. Of course, one might argue, as many do, that they are entitled to do so, but surely all must agree that this is not the way displaced Palestinians view the matter. In fact, it is fair to ask supporters of Israel how the Jews would have behaved had they been in residence for two thousand years when scattered Arabs came back and took their land. It is this usurpation of land, I think, more than any other factor that makes true peace in that region all but impossible.

Most people, until Jimmy Carter came along, thought that the United States was sort of an Episcopalian place that could accept a Roman Catholic president, though only after 184 years. Jimmy Carter, a born-again Christian, gave cause for alarm at first but only in theory, for Carter made it clear by his actions and words that he stood for separation of church and state. What no one seemed to notice is that the tectonic shift in American politics really started with Richard Nixon. Before Nixon, the general rule was that the North was Republican territory because the GOP, according to the South, tended to be more than just a bit too pushy on civil rights. Besides, the South had never forgiven that damned Republican president (the first, actually) Abe Lincoln. Thus, the Democrats could count on the South.

The change started with the case that integrated the schools—*Brown v. Board of Education*. But while Eisenhower, under whose watch this happened, did send troops to integrate Central High in

Little Rock, Arkansas, he was not big on civil rights. John Kennedy, under whose presidency the real civil rights war (and it *was* war) developed, was much more concerned than Eisenhower about civil rights. And it was Kennedy, much influenced by his brother Robert, his attorney-general, who sent the troops into the University of Mississippi and federalized the Mississippi National Guard in order to register James Meredith, a black. However, it was the Texan Lyndon Johnson whose civil rights legislation really began to irritate Southern whites because he supported civil rights with the zeal of a convert, which he was. And suddenly, in the eyes of Americans in the South, the Democrats had abandoned their right to be supported. It was the Republican Nixon, a Quaker in name only, who saw the possibilities of invading the South politically, and while the worm didn't turn immediately, gradually the South became a Republican stronghold, leaving the highly populated places in the North to the Democrats. This is admittedly an oversimplification, but I think this point is clear: regional loyalties had changed dramatically.

With the Southern voter came something quite new for the Republican Party—fundamentalist Christianity. The party of Nixon and before had been Christian—when it was religious at all—but always in the image of Billy Graham, a man who liked to be friends and play golf with Republican leaders. While Graham had started his career as an Elmer Gantry sort of preacher, he mellowed considerably and was seen as the kindly old pastor who could be relied upon to say a prayer at the Republican national convention and not much more. Now there were two men on the scene who would change the makeup of the two main parties dramatically and, for our purposes, permanently. The not-so-slow and relatively sure way the Christian Right, also called the Christian Coalition, founded by former presidential candidate Pat Robertson and joined by the Moral Majority movement of Jerry Falwell in 1989, is taking over the Republican Party has made the Conservative Party of Canada sit up and take notice. The fears of many old-line Conservatives that a merger with the Canadian Alliance, née the Reform Party, would bring radical right wingers into the new party seems to have been well-founded.

I am not a conservative, large or small "c"—except in environmental terms—and though I consider myself a Christian, I doubt that Roberta Combs, leader of the Christian Coalition, would consider me one. I follow the view of Queen Elizabeth I, who said, "There is only one Lord Jesus Christ and the rest is a dispute over trifles." And I accept Jesus' commandments that "Thou shall love the Lord thy God with all thy heart and all thy soul and all thy might," and "Thou shalt love thy neighbour as thyself." Many overlook his next line, which says, "Upon these two commandments hang all the law and the prophets." And that's it. No more doctrinal mysteries to absorb and proclaim. I do not consider the Bible to be holy writ nor can I believe that anyone else who has their wits about them can either. Having said that, let me say clearly that this is not an attack upon Christians or Christianity but an assertion that no book, though seen as holy by some, can be permitted to govern our society be it the Bible, the Talmud, the Koran or whatever. When that happens, you have a theocracy, not a democracy. We are a secular state and must stay one if all people of all religions or no religion at all are to have equal shares in making the laws.

When I speak of the Christian Right, I am not talking about Christians who may consider themselves fundamentalists yet respect the principle of the separation of church and state. I am not speaking of "born again" Christians per se. I am talking about people who, despite the many mental hoops they must go through, believe that each and every word in the Bible is the word of God and must be obeyed not just by Christians *but by everyone else*. What I am talking about are those who interpret the Bible literally and believe that I must be compelled, through legislation and policy, to obey their interpretations of what that book says. What I'm talking about are those who believe that every law, bylaw, utterance and policy of those who govern us must first pass the Christian Right's biblical test—their interpretation of what the Bible says. What I'm talking about are those who deny the principle of the separation of the church and state. Here is what Pat Robertson has to say on this subject: "There is no such thing as separation of church and state in the Constitution. It is a lie of the left and we are not going to take it anymore." *And, further,* "We're going to bring back God and the Bible and drive the gods of secular humanism right out of the public schools of America."

If there is one thing for sure about the Christian Coalition, it is that they believe in a theocracy, with themselves as the theocrats. Here's more of what Robertson had to say:

> The mission of the Christian Coalition is simple . . . to mobilize Christians—one precinct at a time, one community at a time—until once again we are the head and not the tail, and at the top rather than the bottom of our political system. . . . We have enough votes to run this country. . . and when the people say, "We've had enough," we're going to take over!

Robertson also said this:

> When I said during my presidential bid that I would only bring Christians and Jews into the government, I lit a firestorm. "What do you mean?" the media challenged me. "You're not going to bring atheists into the government? How dare you maintain that those who believe in the Judeo-Christian values are better qualified to govern America than Hindus and Muslims?" My simple answer is, "Yes, they are."

The Christian Right deals in moral certainties and, having determined what they are, wishes to enforce them not from the pulpit but from Congress, the White House and the Supreme

Court Chamber—and now, perhaps, from the House of Commons. One only has to look at the question of gay rights and gay marriages to see how the Christian Right works. In order to build a biblical case against homosexuality, they had to do a lot of research and make many questionable interpretations, but after consulting Deuteronomy, St. Paul and other sources—I've had them all submitted to me in great detail by those seeking my soul to save—the Christian Right would deny gays the secular entitlements others possess. (It is ironic that the Christian Coalition shouts from the rooftops that there is a "gay agenda" to take over "straight America" while having a very powerfully backed agenda of their own which has as its goal nothing less than the takeover of the American government including the Supreme Court.) However, during this entire and often ugly debate, I've heard no one suggest for a second that churches be forced to marry gays or to do anything for that matter. No legislator would for a moment make such a suggestion. Nor is anyone offering gay people any special privileges.

Women should also take heed because, unless you believe a woman's place is in the kitchen, the nursery or in bed, you ought to know Pat Robertson's view on feminism. He says:

> The feminist agenda is not about equal rights for women. It is about a socialist, anti-family political movement that encourages women to leave their husbands, kill their children, practice witchcraft, destroy capitalism, and become lesbians. . . . I know this is painful for the ladies to hear, but if you get married, you have accepted the headship of a man, your husband. Christ is the head of the household and the husband is the head of the wife, and that's the way it is, period.

One has to ponder this: If the religious right were to take over Canadian government, presumably they would try to annul gay marriages and other privileges even though the Ten Commandments don't mention homosexuality, even by inference. Yet, the Ten

Commandments expressly forbid adultery. How can you enforce biblical law against homosexuality (which doesn't make it onto the Ten Commandments list) and not against those who commit adultery or, Heaven forfend, have sex before marriage? Will we return to the days when adultery, fornication and homosexuality were crimes? Atheists must beware, too, for here is what George W. Bush says: "I don't know that atheists should be considered citizens nor should they be considered patriots. This is one nation under God." He might have added, *my* God.

Drawing civil laws from biblical injunctions utterly denies that fundamental rule of freedom that says that, as long as you're not hurting someone else, live and let live. I don't deny anyone the right to push for whatever legislation they wish, even bringing back the Sunday Blue Laws or making legal injunctions against fornication. But my right and your right is to find out whether or not a person running for office will, if elected, legislate in keeping with Christian Coalition leader Roberta Combs' notion of what the Bible says or in accordance with the wishes of the majority of voters. Here is the most sinister part—the Republican Party is split because the Christian Coalition knows how a minority can easily take over organizations.

Meanwhile, Canadian Conservatives tell me that the Christian right already has a disproportionate influence within the party and that this influence is growing. This places the Conservative Party in a pickle for, unlike the Republicans, they don't get elected to positions of power very often. The argument could be made that since Lincoln, the Republicans have been the natural governing party in America, but no one would make that claim for the Conservative Party of Canada. When the Tories do gain power, they rely on a very broad coalition of differing backgrounds, including many Canadians whom the religious right would consider sinners beyond redemption. Canadians for the most part are not attracted to radical anything, be it radical Christianity or the radical right or left wing.

The essential question now becomes: To whom are our elected

officials accountable—we the people or someone's interpretation of the Bible? I suggest that most Canadians would say, "Let us by all means have decent, moral people in government who bring high standards to their job, but let them be answerable to God in private when their time comes. In their public deeds they must be answerable to the public."

The Catholic Church

My complaint with the Catholic Church is not about the religion itself or the millions of individuals who practise that faith around the world. In fact, as an Anglican I have, at various times in my life, thought of converting to Catholicism. (I have no such thoughts now because I'm having trouble enough with my own church's catechism much less that of Roman Catholicism.) My argument is that Catholicism and the doctrines it compels the faithful to follow have cost untold millions of deaths around the world—and here I am only talking about recent days—and the toll increases at an alarming pace.

Churches in general have an insatiable hunger for power, not necessarily by exercising it directly but by strong control over those who run things. Sadly, imperialist countries (I mean that in the traditional sense not the communist definition) have propped up so many evil dictators and advised so many people not to revolt, it is beyond the counting. When Catholics in Nicaragua tried to modernize the church's teaching and embrace things like land reform—which today is still a central issue of basic justice in such countries where 99 percent of both land and wealth are controlled by less than 1 percent of the people—it was vigorously opposed by John Paul II with the backing of the United States. The Pope seemed completely unable to grasp the difference between the peasant's struggle for basic human dignity and a soviet state even when his own archbishops, such as Archbishop Oscar Romero of El Salvador, travelled to Rome to talk about it. Instead, Pope John Paul II told Romero (who was later assassinated by the very people with whom John Paul urged him to cooperate) to shut up and stop stirring up the people. And when the Pope travelled to Nicaragua in 1986, he told the crowd to shut up and give up "unacceptable ideological commitments."

We have an example close to home. Quebec, until the Quiet Revolution begun by Premier Jean Lesage in 1960, was in the iron grip of the Roman Catholic Church, made possible by careful understandings with men like Maurice Duplessis. Today it has little impact in political matters. But it is not just evil countries that Catholicism turns a blind eye to; it is not out of the ordinary today to see Mafia thugs buried with the full ceremony and the very long funeral service of the Roman Catholic Church.

The fight against AIDs in Africa—there are five million HIV and AIDs sufferers in South Africa alone—is being badly compromised by the Catholic Church's ban on the use of condoms. "Using condoms as a means of preventing AIDs can only lead to sexual promiscuity," says Archbishop Dominique Bulamatari of the Democratic Republic of Congo, his words accurately summing up the opposition of the Catholic Church to the most effective weapon against AIDs apart from abstinence. And Ugandan President Yoweri Museveni has accused the West of promoting condom use in Africa "for selfish economic gain." If the Devil has a catechism, it could scarcely be more harmful to humanity than this disregard for human welfare and suffering.

But the ban on the use of condoms does more than condemn millions of Africans to a horrible and premature death. That ban has contributed to huge families amongst the poor in all parts of the world, though especially in the Horn of Africa and the sub-Sahara region in general. Of course, the immense birth rate in these areas is scarcely all the fault of the Catholic Church. Where poverty is grinding and apparently permanent, couples need children to look after them when they get older. And because child mortality is so high, they deem it necessary to have, say, a dozen children in order that two or three survive to adulthood. This problem is multi-faceted and must be handled that way, but having said that, the Catholic Church's position on condoms and birth control in general is scarcely helpful.

While the Catholic Church promotes an AIDs program that bans condoms, it continues to preach adherence to the church's policy on homosexuality (don't do it) and continence. This so-called policy has even cost several hundred lives of gay Catholic priests but the Vatican remains unmoved. The *Kansas City Star* reports as follows:

> The Roman Catholic Church has no national policy on dealing with priests who have HIV or AIDs. Nor does the church have specific guidelines on educating priests about sexuality. Priests and seminarians are expected to rely on church doctrine on homosexuality and celibacy and to follow their bishop's or superior's lead in ministering to colleagues afflicted with AIDs.

This attitude may be consistent with Catholic dogma but it's horribly inconsistent with Jesus' command to "love thy neighbour as thyself." In fact, Catholics—as well as most Protestant churches—must split an invisible hair to find homosexuality a sin.

I was astonished that at the death of John Paul II he was seen by the world's press, and I daresay by many people generally, as a great man. That he showed immense personal courage during World War II and the communist regime in Poland and when he was shot is beyond argument, but his record as the leader of a world-wide religion was appalling. This was a Pope who took prominent stands against abortion, birth control, the use of condoms to prevent AIDs, homosexuality, divorce, the ordination of women and the right of priests to marry. But it is in the area of child molestation that John Paul is seen in the worst light. He treated the sexual predations of Catholic priests and brothers on young children as about as sinful as failing to pay a parking ticket. The *Boston Globe* said this:

> In the case of almost every predator priest, church officials had reports of abusive behaviour but allowed the priests to remain in ministry, documents show. In many cases, accused priests were sent for brief periods of psychological evaluation then returned to parishes — where they abused again.

Whether or not the Catholic Church permits the ordination of women priests is, I suppose, an internal matter except it tells the world that the largest of Christian churches sees women as inferior to men.

There is no hope in sight because to right itself the Catholic Church must have new, young, modern leadership throughout the church, and how on earth can that come about when the College of Cardinals who appoint new popes are usually all appointed by the ultimate reactionary pope just past and are conservatives from another era? An all-male, aging if not aged group, appointed by a man who demanded the strictest adherence to his version of Catholic doctrine, is expected to replace that pope, on his death, with a modern reformer? It is not going to happen. In any event, one has difficulty seeing the College of Cardinals, however and when-ever appointed, as a body with an open mind and liberal leanings.

It is said, of course, that there are so many devout Catholics in the world and the church is so rich it will always survive. But that is what they always say about empires until they lose their moral compass and pass into the hands of bad leaders — and come to an inglorious end. The fall of the Roman Catholic Church will be like the death of a great elephant — it will, in fact, be dead long before it actually collapses and hits the ground.

A Thought on Sin

To paraphrase Will Rogers, I belong to no organized religion, I'm an Anglican. My church, like most Christian churches, is having gut-wrenching trouble dealing with homosexuality, and I wonder why?

To build a case against homosexuals one must trawl through the Bible, especially Leviticus, which—while it condemns sodomy—also seems overly fond of slavery, war and the oppression of women, yet doesn't deal with lesbianism or oral sex between partners of the same sex. So what I wonder about is why, instead of spending so much effort on finding ways to keep gays from becoming priests or getting hitched, churches don't look at the Ten Commandments for things to keep them busy. Indeed, one should note that homosexuality is *not* one of the sins included in the Ten Commandments given to Moses and that, during a time when homosexuality was widely practised, Jesus uttered not one word on the subject.

However, while there's nothing on Moses' stone tablets about homosexuality, there is, clear as a bell, a prohibition on adultery: *Thou shall not commit adultery.* Thus, where biblical evidence is at best vague on whether homosexuality is sinful, especially when it's not male-to-male sodomy, there is no doubt at all about adultery. Nor is there any doubt about sins like coveting things like your neighbour's wife (husbands seem to be okay) or taking in a ballgame on Sunday. But it seems to me that it would make as much sense to stone adulterers in the marketplace as it does to pillory homosexuals, though at least there can be no doubt that the Bible does regard adultery as a sin. The problem is, I suppose, that if the Ten Commandments were enforced, there would be few priests left and even fewer candidates for the priesthood.

PART SIX

Idle and Not-So-Idle
Thoughts

Small Can Be Beautiful

I love small things. I suppose being hung like a squirrel all my life, liking little things is, in part, making a virtue of necessity. I prefer small cars, for example, even though I now drive a Chrysler Sebring convertible. I have an excuse: after driving a sports car for years, I got tired of being backed into in parking lots and then, for my pains, being asked, "Where the hell did you come from?" The defining moment came when a bus driver, demonstrating that the law says he can do whatever he damn well pleases, nearly killed me because he couldn't see me beside him as he was changing lanes.

But I am at my best, or worst if you prefer, when it comes to small stores.

When I had just been called to the bar in May 1961, I badly needed a new suit. On $125 a week, with a wife and three—soon to be four—kids, this was a big, very big challenge. I went to the Hudson's Bay Company, looked at suits, and found one I fancied at $90 off the rack. (Bear in mind that in those days a small glass of beer cost 10 cents and the best Scotch went for about $8.) I needed credit so was sent to the credit department and, while I wasn't turned down, I wasn't accepted either. I was told by an abrupt young prick, who probably got his cruddy suit at a big discount, that it would take a few weeks.

It being the time of day one thinks of as "cool beer time," I sauntered over toward the favourite watering hole of the young white collar set and UBC types, the Georgia Hotel beer parlour, but on the way I did a bit of window shopping and, looking into the window of Warren-McCuish Men's Wear, there was my suit! Exactly the same as the one in HBC. Tremulously I entered the store and was greeted by a short, stout and very jovial man named Jerry Lapointe. I asked him how much "my" suit was and he said $90.

"Jerry," I said, "I have just been called to the bar and am barely making fuck-all a week. What kind of credit can you give me?"

"What can you afford?"

"How about $20 now, and the rest when you catch me?"

"Done," said Jerry, starting a relationship that lasted about fifteen years. I bought all my clothes from Jerry thereafter, and as I got a bit more prosperous, Jerry's investment in me and my character paid off for both of us.

But I never really did get over my slow burn at department stores. I had been brought up to detest Eaton's because they were a Toronto company that was almost vicious in its parsimony and hardheartedness toward its employees. The worst of it was that these eastern bastards, these snotty-nosed excretions from Upper Canada College, had bought out our very own David Spencer's Limited, wiping it off the map.

It was my Nova Scotia gram who put me up to my loathing of Eaton's. As a Cape Breton Islander she regarded Toronto as the source of all Canada's evil and none of its virtues. I must say that any time I shopped in Eaton's (which I occasionally did after my gram had died), I had a lousy experience. Then I would look heavenwards (for where else would Gram be?) and say, "Gram, you were right, dammit, right as rain!"

Mostly, I disliked Eaton's for being what they were—large and, until a few years ago, very successful on the backs of overworked and underpaid employees; indeed, any employee who even whispered the notion of a union was fired. They, along with the Hudson's Bay Company, put a lot of small businesses in the downtown area out of business. I know that's free enterprise and all that, but dammit I loved stores like James Inglis Reid ("we hae meat that ye can eat"), Purdy's Chocolates and Harkley & Haywood, the fishing tackle experts where you could learn to tie flies by watching the neat Scots lady do it in the store. (She once told me she never fished a day in her life!) It will no doubt be argued that the Hudson's Bay Company was standing exactly where it is now in Vancouver when the small businesses I mentioned were all doing well. That's partly true, but what happened is that the chains opened up branches in malls and that killed the small merchants downtown. And the Hudson's Bay Company and Eaton's were amongst those chain stores who, by going to the burbs, piled on the little guys.

I made one exception to my boycott of department stores: when our own BC chain, Woodward's, was still around I went there without hesitation. Charles "Chunky" Woodward was a good man to his customers and mostly loved by his employees. When he died, his successors sold all the property Woodward's owned, thus making the stores pay rent for the first time. It was then only a matter of time.

I must, before moving on, also admit to visiting Harrods in London whenever Wendy and I are there, but that is just to visit a shrine to conspicuous wealth, not to buy. It is truly a spectacular emporium and boasts that it can get you anything in the world. One lunchtime, it is said, a gentleman entered their most expensive restaurant and ordered an elephant sandwich. "Certainly, right away, sir," said the waiter in tails and white tie. About five minutes later the waiter returned, looking as down in the mouth as a bloodhound with a bad cold. "I'm very embarrassed and sorry, sir," he said, "but it seems we have run out of bread."

As for bookstores, I must confess that I do go into Chapters-Indigo sometimes, but to my credit, I hope, when I find a book I want, I write down the particulars and take it to my friend Mary Trentadue who runs 32 Books in Edgemont Village in North Vancouver. If Mary hasn't got it—and more often than not she has—she will order it for me and I get it three or four days later. My small sacrifice gives an independent bookseller a sale while taking it away from a mean-spirited corporate bookseller. ("Why '32' Books?" I once asked Mary. "Because," she told me, "my name, Trentadue, is Italian for 32, so why not?")

I must also confess to going into the big Waterstone's store on Piccadilly (in the old Simpson's Department Store building) and Foyles and Blackwell's, both on Charing Cross Road, but I rarely buy there. Instead, I see what I want, price it, then go to the wonderful independent store around the corner from our Tube station, Bookthrift, which invariably has what I want with at least 10 percent off, or I check it out with the British Book and Stationery Store on Oxford Street near Selfridges. But if it appears that the book I just *must have* can be obtained in Canada, it goes on Wendy's list for Mary and 32 Books.

I spend more than I should—and more than I can afford—on clothes and books and am happy, nay proud, to say that most of the money goes to David, not Goliath. I like the feel of small entrepreneurial stores. They usually have found that fine line between being helpful and being a pushy nuisance. They have personality and atmosphere, including an odour—a nice odour—of caring. (I must add, by way of postscript, that I also love used bookstores, especially small, one-owner shops.)

I like smaller communities. My home is a small townhouse in the village of Lions Bay, about thirty-five kilometres north of Vancouver on the road to Whistler, and it is just how I want to live. I can be as snuggly and neighbourly as I want, which in my case is not much. I know more dogs' names than people's. It's better that way, I think. We have a nice general store and a tiny shopping area that includes a small café that serves very good food, and there is an artist there, complete with gallery. There is an hourly bus service to Caulfield Shopping Centre and return. We have famous people living in Lions Bay, and most of us don't know who they are—nor do we want to know, though Paul Hogan lives there in the summertime and I think it would be neat to walk a dog with him. We don't have a neighbourhood pub because no one wants one in or near his backyard; we respect that decision and no one pushes. Our townhouse is a short walk to a beach I call Chauncey's Cove, and this is where he goes for a swim every day of the year and has done since he was ten weeks old. Usually one or more seals drop by to check us out, there is a family of otters who swim past, and often we see an eagle in one of the trees. One day Wendy counted nineteen seals, one otter and a bald-headed eagle.

As the hippy-dippy crowd in the sixties used to say, "Small is beautiful." They were right.

Things I Can Do Without

I can do without people patting me on the tummy and asking "When is it due?" or some such droll utterance. My answer is invariably, "When we get a bit older, we do one of two things—we put on weight or lose our fucking manners." If I'm in one of my periodic weight loss modes, and someone says, "You're on a diet, I see," I say, "No, I have stomach cancer."

I wear knee braces and walk with a stick because playing bad squash resulted in bad arthritis. I'm always astonished at how many people consider it quite appropriate to discuss my arthritic knees ad nauseam as if they were public property, punctuating their helpful suggestions by references to an uncle or brother or someone else who had *just* the same problem as I, but who, after two operations, now spends his spare time climbing the Matterhorn. An astonishing number of people ask me, "What's that you have in your hand, eh?" I answer, "It's called a walking stick, though it's more commonly known as a cane. I'm surprised you didn't know that before!"

And because, with my arthritic knees, I must walk with the aid of a stick, it is especially annoying to me when I am walking down a busy street and a group of five abreast, holding hands and oblivious to their surroundings, bear down upon me. They force me to lose my gait and hit the gutter to find some way around them.

I hate some foods with a passion. A partial list includes pork, turnips, parsnips, vegetable marrow, squash (especially zucchini of which there is obviously a worldwide oversupply), asparagus, liver, kidneys no matter how they are presented, all fish except a freshly cooked trout for breakfast (but always excepting shellfish which I like a lot), eggplant, pickles and on it goes. What mildly amuses me—and pisses me off—is the person who says, "What, you don't like liver? There's nothing better than liver and onions the way Mom used to cook it." In fact, to me there is little good in liver no matter who cooks it, and I growl, "Different strokes," under my breath.

I hate cigar smokers. Yes, I once smoked. A lot. But I quit forty years ago, which, I submit, puts me outside the category of a "reformed" smoker. I also hate a law that, while it clears smokers out of indoor eating places, allows them to smoke outside in the summertime, meaning that non-smokers must stay inside when the weather is fine. And I hate it when people all too successfully turn an argument around by an irrelevant shift, such as, "Before we ban smoking in public places, we should deal with the carcinogens caused by cars and other things." It is an outrageous irrelevancy but it works far too often.

I hate queues. I won't queue for dinner. Even more, I hate queue jumpers, especially those in cars who, when two lanes are melding into one, either won't let you have your turn or who start to cut in ten cars too soon, buggering up the entire otherwise orderly scheme of things. I hate lineups to pay for something; a customer should never have to wait to pay his bill.

While recognizing their usefulness in a car when an emergency arises, I hate cellphones. I cannot imagine who all these people are talking to and about what. I have a cellphone in my car but no one—not even I—knows the number. And besides, it's never on, anyway. But I think cellphones are more than just a nuisance. When they go off at the symphony or in the middle of a play, they are a sign of abominable manners and make one think—only briefly, of course—that maybe we should bring back the lash. Moreover, they are destroying the last vestiges of our right to privacy. The pager was bad enough but at least it gave you time to figure out what the hell excuse you should give your wife for still being at the bar. Now, you are expected to be available—and accountable—to everyone who has your cell number and uses it at whatever time suits him.

I get really pissed off at authors who give a quote in a foreign language and don't add the translation. There are, I suppose, some foreign phrases that are well known to all, but an author I recently read went way over the line with nearly five sentences in Greek! It's ostentatious, pedantic bullshit, and editors who permit this stuff past their blue pencils should be put on the ducking stool.

I get annoyed at newspapers—all of them—who unburden themselves of editorials without identifying who wrote them. There is a sort of "royal we" about this, a pretence that they, hiding their faces like the Delphic oracle, possess superior wisdom. In fact, editors are lucky that, because today's paper is on the bottom of the birdcage the next day, no one remembers the rot they peddle. What is more galling is that these editors are quick to hold columnists like me to account for our unwelcome views while hiding behind their own anonymity and denying the reader a response.

I get annoyed as hell when, while dining out, just as I am unburdening myself of the punchline to a wonderful story I heard that afternoon, a server, without a by-your-leave, sticks his/her head into the midst of the group and says, "Good evening, folks! My name is Jonathan/Sarah, and I'm your server. Here are the specials for this evening!"

I hate it when people, at what is supposed to be a casual, friendly social occasion, begin to spin racist crap, leaving you in the position of either getting into an argument or, by your silence, being seen to agree with them.

I hate it when people who ought to know better, such as the

Canadian media, don't admit that Parliament and the provincial legislatures are mere charades of democracy but persist in pumping out the garbage that we have "responsible" government where the prime minister/premier and cabinet are only in power on the sufferance of the MPs/MMPs/MNAs. God only knows how much this kind of media crap has stifled decent debate and long overdue reform in this country. Even worse, we teach this to our kids. Is it any wonder that the average citizen hasn't the faintest idea what really happens in government? The system needs reforming in a big way. That can't begin to happen until the people know the system and see it for what it is: political make-believe.

I hate playing any game against someone who is such a "good sport" that they don't care a bit if they lose. Where's the fun in kicking the crap out of people like that? I used to try like hell to beat my kids at their Christmas games!

Now that I fly "economy" again, I hate people in the seat in front who shove their seat-backs into your knees, spilling your beer all over your lap.

I hate compact disc covers. It's damned near impossible to get the cellophane off them, the cases crack, and if you carry more than three at a time your room will soon be full of flying missiles.

Help for Stats Canada

At the time of the census before the current one, I was doing an open-line program in Vancouver and did the story of several women who had refused to fill in the long census form and maintained their position until, as I had suspected would happen, all the threats to prosecute them just went away. With the latest census, I gave my own actions a lot of thought, and I now wish to repent as I realize that it is very good for our government to know every last detail about me. That lot at the CIA with their Patriot Act know everything, so why shouldn't my own government? After all, if I've nothing to hide—well, you know how the argument goes. And if you can't trust your own government, who can you trust? So herewith I offer my own list of questions to better able the census folks to troll through the lives of Canadians:

A. How many squares of toilet paper do you use, on average, after a bowel movement?

    (1) 1 to 10

    (2) 11 to 50

    (3) I still have a backlog of old Eaton's calendars

B. How much alcohol do you consume every day?

    (1) 0 to 10 ounces

    (2) 11 to 20 ounces

    (3) I'm far too pissed to answer

C. Have you ever had sex with more than one partner at the same time?

    (1) 0 to 5 times

    (2) many times

    (3) I live in Bountiful, BC

D. If you have had sex with more than one at a time, were the other partners the same sex as you are?

    (1) yes

    (2) no

    (3) I haven't the faintest idea

E. If you believe that the notion of marriage should be expanded, what should it include?

    (1) a ménage a trois

    (2) anything goes when the whistle blows

    (3) shepherds and their sheep but only opposite sexes for we can't let this go too far and seem kinky

F. This question is for males only. If you use a condom, who puts it on?

    (1) me

    (2) my partner

    (3) my butler

G. Should the government ban recreational drugs? If so, what should they be?

    (1) marijuana

    (2) cocaine and its derivatives

(3) only the most serious and dangerous ones like alcohol and tobacco

H. If from outside the Lower Mainland of British Columbia, what's stopping you from moving to Vancouver where the action is?
    (1) it rains a lot there
    (2) it rains a hell of a lot there
    (3) I love shovelling snow and freezing my balls off

I. Are you in favour of Canada having a governor general and if so, what ought the criteria be?
    (1) chinless British aristocrats who wear uniforms with a couple of dozen medals they haven't earned
    (2) a politician whom the prime minister wants to reward or get out of his hair
    (3) a cutesie-pooh female of colour, a CBC-type who is an immigrant and will enhance the prime minister's chance of getting elected

J. If you are a well-read person, where do you get the information you need to stay on top of things and make your mind up whom to vote for?
    (1) the print media
    (2) the electronic media
    (3) my barber or taxi driver depending on which I last listened to

K. How do you think medicare can be most improved?
    (1) get rid of the politicians
    (2) make all doctors take a year off
    (3) both of the above

L. What should Canada do in a military way to do its bit in this turbulent world?

(1) whatever George W. Bush wants us to do

(2) whatever George W. Bush doesn't want us to do

(3) crawl under the sheets, cover our ears and hope for the best

M. If you believe in an afterlife, what do you think will happen?

(1) I'll be mobbed by forty virgins and I'll have forgotten what it is one does next

(2) I'll be reunited with the turkey I divorced

(3) I'll be spending an eternity asking them to turn the heat down

N. If you go to church, why?

(1) I am secretly in love with one of the choirboys

(2) I just love mumbo-jumbo from people wearing extravagant cloaks and vestments

(3) I'm too hungover on Sunday mornings to do much else

O. Do you secretly hope Kim Campbell will make a comeback because

(1) both she and her term of office were short

(2) I agree with her that elections are a lousy time to discuss issues

(3) everything else we've had since has made her look very good indeed

P. When a cell phone starts playing "Hi-ho, hi-ho, it's off to work we go," what do you think your rights ought to be?

(1) to sing along

(2) to seize the phone and smash it to bits

(3) to kill the owner of the phone

Q. For your safety Transport Canada makes clerks at the airport ask you if you packed the bag yourself and has it every been out of your sight, etc. Which of the following additional questions should be added?

    (1) Are you related to Osama bin Laden?

    (2) Is that ticking sound a bomb?

    (3) Do you think that George W. Bush is cute?

R. How do you heat your swimming pool?

    (1) from my furnace

    (2) with a special heater

    (3) warm piss from neighbourhood kids

These questions don't, of course, exhaust the possibilities—not by a long shot. Excellent work is being done, we're told, at little known Muskeg U. in northern Saskatchewan, which is entirely funded by senior Ottawa mandarins out of their own pockets just for the sheer joy of seeing that their work is carried on from generation to generation.

The Longest Year

In 1999, even though I had years to prepare for the event, I nearly lost it. I was, you see, born on December 31, and every New Year's Eve in a year ending with 9 I have had a fight with someone—often everyone—as I tried to explain to the ninnies that the next day was not the start of a new decade but the last year in the current one. I remember my birthdays in 1959, '69, '79 and '89 very well, but it all came together in 1999 when I went to a "Millennium Party" at the Vancouver Club and spent the night mumbling, "But it's the wrong day! It's next New Year's Eve!"

I know that readers are all ready now to shout back at the page, "You're wrong! Can't you count?" The answer is, yes, I can count very well. For January 1, 2000, to be the first year of the new millennium, the first year of the first millennium A.D. would have started on January 1, 0. In fact, to be consistent, it would have had to start on January 0, year 0. Or, come to think of it, month 0, year 0. During the year 1999 I heard every imaginable argument including when Jesus was born and so on. But you cannot quantify anything with zero because zero denies any quantity whatsoever.

Let's run over this using a book as an example. If it contained

2,000 pages, where would you start? On page 1, of course! Right, and where does the book end? At the end of page 1999 and the start of page 2000? Of course not! You still have page 2000 left to read. Do the test yourself. Or make it easier by agreeing that the principle is the same with a 100-page book. (It's the same for a 10-page book if you really want to save yourself some counting.) Begin at page 1 and start counting. Page 1 is the first page—well done!—page 2 is the second page. . . . Now you have the hang of it.

Fast forward to the end. Page 98 is the 98th page, page 99 (like the year 1999) is the 99th page, and the very first word on the next page *starts* the 100th page and when you have read *all* of page 100, you will have *finished* 100 pages (2,000 years). It's important to remember that you will not have read 100 pages until you have read that whole page, just as you haven't completed 2,000 years until the last second of the year 2000. The next page will be the 101st page, and the very first word will therefore start the next hundred pages (the twenty-first century). Put simply—you can't finish the 2,000-page book until the very last word has been read and you're just turning over to page 2001—and it's the same for centuries.

We often talk about zero degrees Celsius or, for that matter, Fahrenheit. But there is no zero degree. Don't take my word for it. Look at your thermometer, your neighbour's thermometer or any thermometer in the world. There is no zero degree. There is one degree below a line designated zero and one degree above it designated plus but no zero degree. That's because zero denotes the invisible line between minus-1 and plus-1 and is not a degree itself.

There likewise was no year 0. During 1999 I offered a thousand dollars to anyone who could tell me of anything that happened in the year 0. My money was and remains safe. It went (using the old terminology) 1 BC followed by 1 AD. Since there was no year 0, for 2,000 years to pass we had to wait until the year 2000 was *finished* at the precise moment that December 31, 2000, turned to January 1,

2001. It's no more complicated than this: we count 1, 2, 3, 4, not 0, 1, 2, 3, 4, whether it is apples or years.

The problem with the millennium year was twofold. First, three zeroes are fun and to get to 2000 seemed to be the logical target. Second, there was a lot of money and hype on the millennium, and no one was going to let a little matter like accuracy get in the way of making a bundle. (It's rather like the way baseball has made Abner Doubleday the father of the game and Cooperstown the place where it was first played. He wasn't and Cooperstown wasn't, but what the hell does that have to do with anything when there's a buck to be made off it?) The worst of it all was that when I wanted to celebrate the proper year on December 31, 2000, heading into 2001, no one cared!

I could only console myself with this thought: I can count and a hell of a lot of people on this planet cannot!

Dogs and a Couple of Cats I've Known

Just this side of heaven is a place called Rainbow Bridge.

When an animal dies that has been especially close to someone here, that pet goes to Rainbow Bridge.

There are meadows and hills for all of our special friends so they can run and play together.

There is plenty of food, water and sunshine, and our friends are warm and comfortable.

All the animals who had been ill and old are restored to health and vigour; those who were hurt or maimed are made whole and strong again, just as we remember them in our dreams of days and times gone by.

The animals are happy and content, except for one small thing; they each miss someone very special to them, who had to be left behind.

*They all run and play together, but the day comes
when one suddenly stops and looks into the distance.
His bright eyes are intent; his eager body quivers.
Suddenly he begins to run from the group, flying over
the green grass, his legs carrying him faster and faster.*

*You have been spotted, and when you and your
special friend finally meet, you cling together in
joyous reunion, never to be parted again. The happy
kisses rain upon your face; your hands again caress
the beloved head, and you look once more into the
trusting eyes of your pet, so long gone from your life
but never absent from your heart.*

Then you cross Rainbow Bridge together. . . .

—AUTHOR UNKNOWN

My first memory of a dog was when I was about three. He was an English sheepdog named Skipper, and I must confess that I may confuse memory with snapshots of me in a playpen and Skipper just outside, but I *think* I remember him. My mom told me that Skipper was so protective of me that only she and my dad could touch me when I was in that playpen. I don't remember Skipper dying, but I do credit this first involvement with a dog as at least partly the reason I've had a lifelong love of that wonderful creature. My next real memory of a dog was Mandy, a black cocker/springer cross who became Tonto to my Lone Ranger. No matter where I went, Mandy was sure to go. My friend Denis Hargrave, who had an Airedale called Jake, and I would take bicycle trips and the two dogs would run along with us. This was no mean trick for Mandy because she had contracted distemper as a pup and it had left her lame though still very game.

Both our dogs were with us the day Denis and I went to Wreck Beach at the mouth of the Fraser. (It is now renowned as a nudist beach, but Denis and I claim to have been the first nude swimmers.) In those days there really was a wreck out there, and for reasons I have never been able to fathom, we swam out and stole the anchor. It was a whacking big thing—I should know my anchors better but it was like the one Popeye had tattooed on his arm. Somehow, an eleven-year-old and a twelve-year-old dragged that damned thing ashore without drowning and up the steep cliff path, balanced it between our bikes and took it back to my place—which would have been a least two miles, much of it uphill. We dumped it on my front lawn just as my dad arrived home from work.

"What the hell are you going to do with that?" he asked, not unreasonably.

This was something that Denis and I had not considered. Indeed, what the hell *were* we going to do with this monstrous mass of rusting iron?

There was but one thing we could do. Dump the damned thing on the vacant lot next to our house, a lot that is probably now 6391 McCleery Street. I have often wondered what happened when the people clearing the lot came across that anchor. Were archaeologists called in? Were there musings that this anchor was perhaps from Drake's flagship, the *Golden Hind*? (We now know from Sam Bawlf's wonderful book, *The Secret Voyage Of Sir Francis Drake*, that the old sea dog did get this far north and perhaps even farther, a piece of information that annoys San Franciscans who believe he went that far and no farther.) Even if our anchor was just thrown away, it must have got some tongues wagging.

Not all the dogs I knew in my youth were especially nice. The Earl Adams family (he was a long-time Vancouver alderman) lived on the corner of Marine and McCleery and they had a pretty daughter named Barbara and a nasty Doberman pinscher named Pete. Whenever I took my bike past their house, I had to walk it a bit, otherwise Pete would come charging out of the Adams yard and get hold of my pant leg. I, of course, would fall to the ground. The late Denis Wotherspoon, who became one of the great characters in Vancouver, was sweet on Barbara at the time, and when he came visiting on his bike, he got the same treatment from Pete as I did. Perhaps that's the reason Denny and Barbara didn't last.

Across the street from us lived the Steuart Erskine family with their kids, Patsy and Johnny (has the ring of a song title, doesn't it?), and a wretched little Scotch terrier named Pointy. Besides pooping on our lawn (much to the annoyance of my dad who tried to train Mandy to crap on the Erskines' lawn), Pointy was a little bastard who was utterly devoid of any affection—unless biting people counts. For those who wonder how Pete and Pointy, with their nasty biting habits, survived the gas chamber, I must explain that things were different in those days. We were much more tolerant of neighbourhood annoyances and there were no "higher purpose persons" (in Denny Boyd's wonderful phrase) charging around with pencils and petitions.

I don't recall when Mandy died, but the next dogs I got to know were the foundation for my love of Labrador retrievers. My uncle and aunt, Dr. Bill Hatfield and my dad's twin sister Lois, owned the island just off the shore at Woodlands on the North Arm of Burrard Inlet. Uncle Bill sort of raised Labradors. I say "sort of" because I don't remember any litters. But he was a good friend of the late millionaire Austin Taylor Sr. who did breed Labs and perhaps that's where Uncle Bill sent his dogs. There were two of his black Labs I especially remember (no one owned chocolate Labs in those days). One was a shorter-legged, very broad-shouldered male named Dike. He looked like—and perhaps was—an English bred Lab. He was the gentlest of dogs. If you asked him to take you to Aunty Lo, he would grab your hand ever so gently but nevertheless firmly and walk you to wherever she was.

His pal, and I believe sometime partner, was a beautiful, sleek bitch by the name of Darky. Can you imagine the fuss today if someone named a black dog Darky? But those were different days, and racist words were thoughtlessly part of most vocabularies. (Our black cocker/springer cross, Mandy, had been given her name because in those days it was patronizingly considered to indicate a black woman.) Darky was a patient dog. She would sit on the dock at water's edge and wait for shiners to come too close to the surface, whereupon she would snap them up and toss them onto the wharf behind her. It was not uncommon to go down to the dock and see a dozen shiners, one or two still in the throes of death, piled up behind this canine fisherman!

During this time our family had a dachshund named Gussie. "Daxies" are great little dogs—a dog and a half long and half a dog high—and Gussie was no exception. As daxies are bred to hunt badgers, digging and going underground were second nature to this beautiful little creature. At night she would get under the covers and snuggle down to sleep at my feet. How she could breathe is beyond me.

Her main claim to fame came each Christmastime. Staying with us was a remarkable Austrian, a year or two my senior, named Peter Bishop. (His original last name was Ippen, but he had changed it to the name of the sponsor who got him from Austria to the University of Pennsylvania.) I met Peter when he moved into the Zeta Psi House at UBC after he came to Canada when his US visa ran out. He was a brilliant man whose specialty was international studies and political science. He worked his way through university as a draftsman for a large engineering firm and eventually got his doctorate in political science and became a professor at the University of Toronto with his own show on CBC. Though Peter had come safely through the war, he was always tortured by inner fears. Today he would clearly be diagnosed as bipolar, but doctors didn't know much about that stuff back then. Sadly, around 1960, he killed himself.

But back to Gussie, Peter, and Christmas. Peter used to send an enormous number of cards at Christmas, and after he had written his messages on the cards, they had to be, of course, put in envelopes, stamped and mailed. And that's where Gussie came in. Peter would sit at the kitchen table, and after each card was duly autographed, he would hold the envelope down to Gussie, who would delightedly lick the flap so it could be closed and then would lick the stamp. It was a small assembly line, to be sure, but a very efficient one.

At that time, circa 1952, I was attending UBC and still living at home, which was on the very lovely Minto Crescent in Shaughnessy. In the front we had a very large rhododendron bush right where the driveway crossed the sidewalk. We also had an enormous Persian cat named Tiger, who was well named, as you will see. Tiger had a habit of lying under this rhodo waiting for dogs to come by, at which point she would fly from the bush onto the poor bastard's back and hang on, all claws imbedded, riding him as a rodeo performer might ride a bull. It got so dogs with some experience would, when they came to our property line, quickly cross the street, always keeping a sharp eye on the rhododendron bush.

As a young husband and father, living in Richmond in a very tacky little house, I acquired, over the mild protests of my wife Eve, a very large black Lab. I don't recall the circumstances, but I know I got him at a farm and the farmer assured me that I needn't be concerned that Beauregard, as he came to be known, would grow too big just because he had paws the size of large pancakes. This dog came, I was assured, from a line of Labs that were rather small. In fact, he became roughly as big as a medium-sized Shetland Pony. Beau (he was named Beauregard after the dog in the comic strip *Pogo*) became a wonderful dog for the three young children we then had. My late daughter Shawn, when a crawling infant, had a habit of inching over and grabbing Beau by the balls. Beau would simply push her away with not a suggestion of bad temper.

My son Ken, then about five, used to play with his friend Hughie from across the street. Often they would wrestle on our lawn, and if one or the other would seem to have an unfair advantage, Beauregard would saunter over, gently grab the one on top by his belt and pull him off. When he finally became just too big for the house and the neighbourhood, we had to give him away to some people in the country.

A year or two later, we acquired a border collie named

Macgregor. He was a super dog but he had one failing—he hated bicycles and motorbikes. When one passed, Macgregor would grab the trousers of the rider, hang on like a burr, and bring rider and machine to the ground. The local kids kind of got used to this and, because they rather liked Macgregor, they would dismount their bikes when he was around. Unfortunately, one day a delivery boy on a motorbike came by, and at the end of the resulting unpleasantness the bike and rider went through a neighbour's basement window. The rider was not amused and neither was our neighbour. Macgregor had had his last chance.

In the mid-1960s the kids pestered us for another dog so Eve and I, answering an ad, found a litter of little black dogs of utterly undeterminable origin. Because there were two left and it was Christmas Eve, we took them both for twenty bucks and named them Taki and Tar to go with the Siamese cat named Tiki we had somehow acquired along the way. The first thing the pups learned was to give Tiki a very wide berth indeed for she was not impressed with these two little intruders in her domain. Unfortunately, Tar was killed by a car but Taki soldiered on—always giving Tiki the widest possible berth—into old age.

Taki hated the mailman, an emotion returned in spades. This meant we had to keep her indoors at mail delivery time. It also meant that we had better be close by the mail slot because she would sit patiently for her nemesis to appear, then snatch at the mail as it came through the slot and rip it up.

One day in 1969 after we had moved to Kamloops, my heart melted at the sight of a small black pup in a pet store window. I bought him, a Lab whom we named Wallace after the race-baiting governor of Alabama, George Wallace. We thought it appropriate that a man so intolerant should have a black dog named after him—though, of course, he never found out. I have two abiding memories of Wally, as he became known. The neighbours across the street had a short and stocky black Lab named Duke, who was, so to speak, cock of the walk, and no one messed with him. Wally was scared shitless of Duke as, from time to time, Duke went after him when he crossed the line into Duke's territory. But, like everything else in this world, dogs get older. We lived on the Thompson River and one crisp March day Wally and Duke met on the beach in the mode of the shootout down at the OK Corral. Duke's owner and I tried to break them up but to do that would be to court serious injury—to us, not the dogs. They were in a fight for all that mattered, and Wally, the younger and fitter, kicked the crap out of Duke. From that point on *he* was the cock of the walk and his territory included Duke's old private domain. It was Wallace who now did all the policing.

My other abiding memory of Wally concerns the times I would take him fishing. If, as was often the case, one or more of my kids were along, Wallace would sit up on the bow of our small boat as we motored to where we were going to anchor and cast our flies. As we chugged along, perhaps due to the hum of the engine, Wally would often doze off, and the next thing we would know he had fallen into the lake. Any who have tried to get a very wet Labrador retriever from the water into a small rowboat will know that this is no mean trick! Sadly, Wally was killed by a car right in front of my youngest daughter Karen, who was Wally's best pal and vice versa. She was inconsolable.

About that time we moved from Ridgeway Terrace in Brocklehurst to a bit of property on Bank Road in Westsyde along the North Thompson River. By this time I had become involved with a group who had bought the Cherry Creek Ranch between Savona and Kamloops on the Trans-Canada Highway. (To any city slickers who have seen the silvery barn on that property with its "Polled Herefords" sign, it just means de-horned!) My new partners gave my family a "cow dog" that we named Amigo. (We were spending Christmas in Mexico in those days.) Amigo was mostly border collie and was truly a fun dog. He had one very bad habit, however. We had a couple of horses and Amigo loved to get in behind one of them, jump up, grab the tail and go for a ride. Now if he'd done this with cows, he would have been okay, but horses, as we all know, can throw their hind legs behind them and kick. Which one of them did, leaving poor Amigo with broken ribs and other assorted injuries for which we paid an enormous veterinarian bill. But Amigo had no sooner recovered and come home than he did it again—same horse, same result. Back to the vets and a new big bill. This time he learned his lesson.

In 1975 we built a new house above the Cherry Creek Ranch with a magnificent view of Kamloops Lake below us. And a short time before moving there we got another Lab, Kona, a beautiful black bitch, small and sleek, with a delicious sense of humour. She and Amigo roamed together in the wonderful sagebrush hills, but the very first time they were out, they came back with a gillion cactus spikes in each paw. These had to be removed, of course, in what has to be as difficult an operation as exists in this world. What was remarkable was that this was the last time either dog got a cactus spike! Even Amigo had learned!

Not long after we moved to Cherry Creek our lovely daughter Shawn was killed in a car crash. I've told the story before but suffice it to say our marriage split (it was my fault) and I no longer lived at Cherry Creek. In the midst of this ongoing tragedy neither of us thought to have Kona spayed, and lo and behold, she had a litter. In fact, it was actually two litters. Until that time I didn't know that a dog could be impregnated twice, but they can, and Kona had a litter of "cow dog" crosses (Amigo strongly suspected as the father) and a litter of purebred Labs by a yellow Lab from the neighbour-ing property. I came for a visit some weeks after the litters were born and all that was left was a yellow pup that Eve didn't know what to do with. Three guesses where he went! He became our Casey, the only Lab I've ever heard of who was afraid of the water! According to Eve, every time Kona would lead her pups around to the front of the house, they passed the swimming pool. Casey, the runt of the litter, was always the one bringing up the rear and he habitually fell into the pool! He thereafter looked at water with a passionate dislike.

Casey was a lovely dog whose only bad habit was escaping, an act that required a mass neighbourhood search. When my new wife Patti and I moved to North Vancouver, we puzzled as to how we could keep him confined during the day while we both worked. First we tried the garage but on Day No. 1 Casey had all but chewed his way through the door by the time we got home. So we got a spacious wire kennel for the back yard. On the first day Casey lifted the latch and escaped. We got a lock, though I told Patti he would probably learn the combination and be out faster than you could say Harry Houdini! In fact, we came home to see that, just as the Allied prisoners did during the war, he had all but tunnelled his way out. With the help of a neighbour, we secured the back yard. Actually, he did the work and I brought the beer because anyone who sees me trying to be a handyman knows that the best plan is to keep me amused doing something else. This manoeuvre contained Casey all right, but he sat in the back yard and howled to the point that the helpful neighbour suggested that we take down the fence and let him run away to his heart's desire.

Then we decided that what he needed was a companion—and we were right. We bought an adorable American golden cocker named Pujah and, as we had the sense to have her spayed, we thereby provided Casey with a bosom buddy for the rest of his life.

Casey wasn't through roaming, though. If a door to the outside opened, he could sense it and he was out of there like a shot. This happened every month or so, and just as firemen react to the bell, our neighbours, hearing the shout that Casey had escaped, would all take up their battle stations and the search would be on. As often as not Pujah had escaped with him, but on the occasions she was left behind, as soon as we brought Casey back into the house, she would run up and bite him on the nose. In this case the "alpha male" was actually the small spayed female.

As Casey got older his escapes were no fewer but since he could only go downhill now, he was easier to find. He died of old age in 1989 and Patti and I resolved not to get another dog. Two days later we were at a breeder's in Aldergrove looking at a huge litter of chocolate Labs. Which to pick? One of the pups came up to me and lay on my foot. Thus Clancy, Duke of Deveron, came into our lives. I have written in past books about Clancy and his successor, Chauncey, so I'll be brief here.

Like all chocolates, Clancy had a touch of madness. He loved swimming and since we had a pool that was no problem. He had a rubber "kong" that we would throw into the pool for him, though this could get pretty tiresome as it was a game without a time clock. Wendy came into our lives when Clancy was four and the bonding was immediate and lasting. We moved to Lions Bay in 2000 and, while Clancy lost his pool, he gained an ocean in which he swam every day. He had a number of unique habits but none so embedded as when Wendy and I would have a bedtime nightcap. Clancy would plant himself at Wendy's feet and sit there in unblinking concentration until she gave him the ice cubes from her recent glass of Scotch. It was like he had died and gone to heaven if Wendy had a second.

After Clancy died, Wendy and I decided that we would not get another. After all, we live in a condo that is so small that if you bring a box of beer in, you must take a case of empties out! But one night about a week after Clancy died, I picked up a book of poetry, opened it randomly and saw this poem, which, choking with tears, I read out loud to Wendy:

> *Father in thy starry tent,*
> *I kneel a humble suppliant.*
> *A dog has died today on earth,*
> *Of little worth*
> *Yet very dear.*
> *Gather him in Thine arms,*
> *If only*
> *For a while*
> *I fear he will be lonely,*
> *Shield him with thy smile.*

The next day we began the search that led to Big Valley's Chauncey of Deveron, who brought with him all the idiosyncrasies of Labrador pups including that tinge of madness I spoke of that seems to be part of the chocolate variety. Though now nearly five, he is still a puppy, in superb condition from daily swimming and running and is loved by all who know him.

Ambrose Bierce defined a dog as "a kind of additional or subsidiary deity designed to catch the overflow and surplus of the world's worship." Mark Twain said, "If you pick up a starving dog and make him prosperous, he will not bite you. This is the principal difference between a dog and a man." Robert Benchley said, "A dog teaches a boy fidelity, perseverance, and to turn around three times before lying down." Finally, Dan Bennett said, "Nothing in the world is friendlier than a wet dog." If your pooch is, like Chauncey, an incurable swimmer in any and all available waters, you know the truth of that.

I've long pondered why Wendy and I are such dog lovers and, more specifically, devoted to Labradors, though I suspect that we would be fans of whatever dog we had. You notice I did not say "own." We "own" Chauncey as far as the Village of Lions Bay records are concerned when they license him, but in our family he's one of us. If I were to say our equal, it would probably downgrade his actual position.

I suppose one of the reasons we love him so much is that he's so much fun to be with. He has an endless variety of games involving his rubber kong, his pal and lover Octopus (a large six-legged floppy moppy), his rag doll or a tennis ball. After thirty seconds with Chauncey it becomes pretty clear why Labradors are called retrievers. (I digress to tell you that Octopus with its multi-coloured legs has been Chauncey's sex object from the outset, so when we took him to Agneta and Willy's place in Enderby to be bred to the lovely Asha, I told Agneta she had better paint Asha's hind legs in splashing colours or else Chauncey wouldn't be able to find his way!)

One of the great joys in life comes when after breakfast we take

Chauncey to the beach and use a catapult to throw a tennis ball for his minimum of eight long swims followed by a trip to the cul-de-sac for at least thirty long throws up the hill. He does this every day of the year, regardless of weather. Of course for Chauncey, the harder it's raining, the better. Needless to say he is the picture of health and good condition. (Maybe I should do the swimming and chasing!) One day in December when I was sending Chauncey in for his swim, a lady came down and asked crossly if I was going to "make" that poor dog swim in that icy water? "Madam," I replied, "the problem is precisely the opposite."

Chauncey is important to us not just for the love he gives us, and the opportunity he gives Wendy and me to love him. It's more important than that because he acts as a conduit through which passes the great love between Wendy and me. Differences of opinion don't last long when Chauncey, sensing the tension, brings us a tennis ball to be thrown—right now! Thus ends the quarrel.

But the love he gives is not just for us. Jack, the man who looks after our hot tub, comes every Wednesday, and every Wednesday morning Chauncey sits up on the windowsill in Wendy's office to watch for him. When Jack arrives, it's hell bent for election to his toy box for a boing boing for Jack to throw for him. And he gets positively sappy with little kids. They adore him and he they.

But I think, if I'm honest, one of the main reasons for my affection for Chauncey is that in many ways he reflects what I wish I were. Not that he doesn't have moods. Just watch him when Wendy is packing a suitcase or for some reason Jack doesn't come. But he snaps out of them. He is loyal to a fault, has an enormous sense of fun, is clean and takes care of himself, and he loves Wendy and me no matter what we do. Mostly, I suppose he is, in our vet Moe Milstein's words, a happy dog—and that's catching. When we've been away, I'm as excited as a kid at Christmas to get home and see my dog. . . . No, Rafe, not your dog, but the family member you have badly missed.

To people who don't care for dogs none of this makes sense,

I'm sure. But it makes a lot of sense to Wendy and me, and when "our boy" comes back home from Enderby to fill the void left by his absence, it's as exciting as it gets. But I daresay it makes some sense to lots of you, too.

Tiger's the Best, Period

Is Tiger Woods the greatest golfer of all time?

He has some claims. No one has won so many routine tournaments and so many major tournaments so fast. Tiger, by everyone's agreement, set a new bar for golf from the time he teed up for his first PGA tournament. After he had been on the tour a few years—especially after his US Open win at Pebble Beach in 2000 by fifteen strokes—he dominated the game. By common consent, he had the rest of the pro golfing world scared of him. He had them spooked. Some very good players literally lost their games; David Duval, the previous #1, Davis Love III and Colin Montgomerie come to mind. Tiger's so-called slump, when he didn't win a major in eleven tries, resulted not in another dominant player emerging but eleven different winners. If any two players emerged out of that, they were Vijay Singh and Ernie Els—now joined by Phil Mickelson—but while the rest of the pack had respect for these fine players, it was always felt that they could be beaten.

The claim for best golfer of all time is made for Bobby Jones, Ben Hogan, Jack Nicklaus and, of course, Tiger. Back in a much different era, Jones won with hickory-shafted clubs and golf balls

that were uneven in quality to say the least. The courses were short-
er, and it's hard to gauge the competition because the Professional
Golf Association (PGA) tour was, at best, little more than the same
small group of professional golfers playing perhaps a dozen tournaments that one could consider first class. But out of that, Jones and
Walter Hagen certainly fathered the modern golf swing and thus
modern golf.

Ben Hogan has, in my opinion, a better claim because, not only
did he win most of his majors after a devastating car accident, he
established a golf swing that is still taught today. He was the first to
properly analyze the swing, and his book, *Five Lessons: the Modern
Fundamentals of Golf*, which first appeared as serialized articles in
Sports Illustrated, is a classic. (Butch Harmon, a Hogan disciple,
was once Tiger Woods' coach.)

Perhaps the one with the best claim to being the all-time best
is Jack Nicklaus. Very unpopular at the start because he thrashed
TV idol Arnold Palmer, he went on to win eighteen majors, each of
them at least three times. What is harder to gauge is the quality of
the opposition he faced. Palmer was a good player past his prime.
Gary Player was certainly a high quality golfer as was Lee Trevino,
though Trevino simply couldn't adapt his game to Augusta and had
a pitiful record in the Masters. Tom Watson was also a great player
whose record is often overlooked. What was lacking in the Nicklaus
era was the enormous competition from Europe and to a lesser
extent from Asia that there is now. It is to the credit of Jack Nicklaus,
Arnold Palmer and Tom Watson that they made the British Open
the competition it is today, thus, in a sense, making the European
Tour a major league in prestige if not yet money. (The money was
to come, not coincidentally, after Tiger arrived on the scene.) These
men had a feel for the game of golf and its history and vowed to get
the Open its deserved prestige back and they did. Incidentally, a former US Open champion, Tommy Bolt, was asked who he thought
was better, Nicklaus or Hogan. He replied, "I've seen Nicklaus go

out to the practice fairway to watch Hogan hit golf shots but I've never seen Ben go out to watch Nicklaus."

All the men I've mentioned, very much including Tiger plus many others like Ben Crenshaw, Bernhard Langer, Seve Ballesteros to name just a few, have done yeoman work in making modern golf the way it is but, more importantly, keeping the history and spirit of the game alive. In a sense, Vijay Singh epitomizes what I'm talking about: golf is a game where the only policeman is the player, and Singh was caught cheating on the Asian tour many years ago and since then has never really been accepted. Nor should he be.

The acid test for the best comes down to this: the only thing anyone can hope to be is the best of his time as Bobby Jones, Ben Hogan, Jack Nicklaus and Tiger Woods clearly were and are. To my way of thinking, when it comes to dominance over their colleagues, a superiority that bred fear, all four men had it. However, I think Tiger Woods has that quality in greater abundance than his predecessors. While he was in his majors slump for three years, it was like when the cat's away, the mice will play. And play they did but now the cat is back big time, and the mice are acting like mice again. His victory in the 2006 British Open where he had the patience and will to play short off the tee and avoid fairways bunkers wasn't rocket science, but the overarching fact is that Tiger and Tiger alone had the long iron skills to pull it off.

What outstanding individuals the four of them were: all super players, all credits to the game, all with an indelible place in history. They played in different eras with different equipment on different golf courses. Tiger has a long way to go to match Nicklaus' record in the majors, but comparisons by scores simply cannot be made. And while I note that Tiger has said that Nicklaus was the greatest, based on the superiority over colleagues and hating to contradict Mr. Woods, I break the deadlock to say I think Tiger is the all-time best.

On Writing and Language

I am no good at writing but, as Robert Benchley put it, "by the time I realized that, I was too famous to quit." Admittedly my own fame is both fleeting and narrowly confined, but this is book number seven, and I couldn't begin to tell you how many newspaper columns I have written. I started with political columns for the Kamloops papers when I was an MLA, then not long after I left politics in 1981 I began writing for the *Financial Post* and, with some gaps in between, wrote for them until CanWest took over. I don't know whether I was fired, retired or just what. All of a sudden I had my regular column returned with a terse note saying that my services were no longer required. A nice touch and just what I would have expected from that lot.

I wrote for the old *Equity* magazine and a good mag it was. My editor was Mike Campbell, who for years has done a finance show on radio, and he let me write whatever I wanted and gave me the enormous advantage of having Dan Murphy do my cartoons and Charlie Smith, now editor of the *Georgia Straight*, as a colleague. I have many of Dan's originals hanging around the place. The one of Grace McCarthy as "Wonder Woman" is one of the best caricatures

I've ever seen. About the time *Equity* sadly folded, I started writing for the *Georgia Straight*. The memory fades but I think I was there for a couple of years under the editorship of Charles Campbell and a very good one he was. Somewhere along the way I got hooked up with the *Courier* (it was the *Kerrisdale Courier* when I was a tad) under the editorship of Mick Maloney who was another good 'un who left his writers alone. During this period I also was syndicated to the NOW newspapers, a prosperous period.

I was seduced away from the *Courier* by Mike Cooke of the *Province*, which, considering my rocky (to say the least!) relationship with the Southam-cum-Asper press, took considerable courage. Mike wanted me to write on general topics, not just timely political ones, but when he left, my new editor Joey Thompson saw things differently and things deteriorated. I was reduced from a weekly column to once every two weeks, and both Joey and I became uncomfortable with the arrangement. In summer of 2002 Russell Mills, long-time journalist and editor with the Southam papers, was fired by Leonard Asper because of criticism made in a speech about incestuous relationships in the media. Shortly after that, my friend Gordon Gibson was fired by the *National Post* for a column they didn't like. So I resigned my column in the *Province* on-air and suggested that people who were tired of these bullies ought to cancel their subscriptions to the *Sun* and the *Province* and thousands did just that.

The thing blew over, as these things always do but the relationship between those papers and me remains rocky at best. Shortly thereafter I had lunch with Rick O'Connor of the David Black newspapers, and I've been writing for them ever since though I went from weekly to monthly early in 2005. I now write a weekly column for *thetyee.ca*, a wonderful online newspaper. As well, over the years I have written numerous freelance articles for various newspapers and magazines. The point of all this being, I suppose, that for a non-writer I seem to have done a lot of writing! So it's time to tell you of my prejudices and areas of utter bafflement at the uses of the English language.

Whenever I have a new editor, I tell him/her that I have a serious "which/that" problem for which I ask blanket forgiveness for all time. It is invariably granted. When I get manuscripts back from the editor, they are replete with stroked out "whichs" and "that" written above or vice versa.

Unlike Andy Rooney, I like apostrophes and probably learned to use them when I wrote for Mick Maloney who, without exception, contracted phrases such as "I am" into "I'm" unless emphasis was required. He was right, too. I also learned that it made two words into one and this little trick, when you're fighting a word limit, can be very useful. Of course, if you're being paid by the word, that is quite another matter!

I generally dislike semi-colons except when I'm making a list and a comma just won't do. I like the dash—such as that. I also like a series of dots (ellipses) . . . but my editor says I use them incorrectly and generally removes them. (I'm told that I write like I talk, which probably accounts for my idiosyncrasies.) I often start a sentence with a conjunction. But I sometimes get the editor's blue pencil for doing what I just did.

I don't use words I don't understand, words like "paradigm" and "didactic," and some words I don't use because they seem to have a multitude of meanings that are, I think, contrary to one another. Such a word is "sanguine." I often use short sentences that have no verb or object. I split the hell out of infinitives and end sentences with prepositions.

Then there are clichés—as the man said, "All clichés are suspect including this one." But let me dwell for a moment on a few I like. Some years ago I heard "at the end of the day" and I kind of liked it. I still don't find "end of the day" as bad as many seem to, though "in the fullness of time" reminds me of Sir Humphrey in the *Yes, Prime Minister* series. I hate the term "stakeholders," mostly because it is used not to describe someone who is holding the stakes to be delivered to the owner of the winning horse, but rather anyone who thinks they ought to have a piece of the action in a public handout.

Come to think of it, "piece of the action" isn't a great cliché but it's not all that bad either.

"Back to the drawing board" offends many people but not me. I remember a marvellous *New Yorker* cartoon back in World War II that shows a plane crash, ambulances and fire trucks racing to the scene, and a couple of men descending in parachutes, while walking towards the reader with a wry grin on his face is, obviously, the designer of the tested and failed plane. The caption reads, "Well, back to the old drawing board!" It's okay if not overused. "Bottom line" was bad enough before the bean counters took over everything but now it has caught on to the point it's hard to find a synonymous phrase.

The list of clichés is endless—to use a cliché—but I think the problem with them is that they often very neatly sum up a thought and convey it to someone else who will understand because it's his lingo, too. In fact, if you listen to people who fight to avoid clichés, they sound stilted. I think the rule ought to be: Don't use a cliché if you can avoid it without making matters worse.

And we all have lapses in grammar. I have a terrible time, as I said, with "which" versus "that." I can never remember the rule. I'm also prone to say "between the three of us" instead of saying "among." Sometimes I hear myself making other mistakes of which I am now about to complain, but in my defence I must tell you that I know when I do them and if possible correct myself.

Prepositions, such as "with," "to" and so forth take the accusative (objective) case yet it is common to hear people say "with you and I" or "to you and I." The test is a simple one: if the use of "I" standing alone is absurd—such as in "to I" or "with I," the word you seek is "me." This is an error much on the increase and I'm shocked at how common it has become in England.

Not all rules about prepositions are sacred, however. Where we were once taught we should never end a sentence with a preposition, that rule is honoured much more in the breach than in the observance ever since Churchill mocked it by saying "That is something up with which I will not put." Similarly, it is no longer considered bad form to occasionally split an infinitive or to use sentences without predicates (verbs). Moreover, as writing takes on a more conversational tone, starting sentences with a conjunction such as "but" or "and" is done in the best of writing circles.

Like prepositions, transitive verbs take the accusative, yet you'll hear people say, "The noise scared my wife and I," and similar clangers. "To be" is a copula (linking or connecting) verb and as a result takes a complement in the nominative or subjective case, for example, "It is I you must blame for that." But this rule is losing its force as we see from the title of Patricia T. O'Conner's highly amusing little grammar book entitled *Woe Is I.* Indeed, it would be hard to sing, "It's only *I* from over the sea, it's Barnacle Bill the sailor!" I suppose, even as an aging curmudgeon, I might concede on the verb "to be" but on prepositions *never!*

I can't believe how many people don't know how to use simple words properly. Many, including experienced broadcasters, simply do not know the difference between "flout" and "flaunt." One flouts the law, while a chesty lady might be said to flaunt her substantial mammary glands. It's difficult to understand how anyone who talks for a living can mix these two words up!

A former premier and one-time education minister adds the letter "i" to the word "mischievous" so it comes out "mis-chee-vee-ous." Many others do the same, of course, but it's no more correct for that. A regular on my radio show always said "rout" when he meant "route," as in Nat King Cole's "Route 66." But perhaps he can be forgiven his lapse because he is an American by birth.

The younger set—some of them not so young any more—have devastated linguistic intercourse. They use the word "like" to start each thought: "Like Charlie like picked me up and we like went for like a drink and like I had too many beers." Even worse, this group uses the word "go" instead of the verb "say": "I go hey Jack what's up and he goes not much and I go. . . ." You know the rest. Most often the "go" and "like" words are used together: "I go like hi John and he goes like hi Jane and I go like do you feel like. . . sexy? and he goes like what did you have in mind and I go. . . ." You get the drift. (Imagine if one used the "f-word" instead of "like"!)

I concede that languages change and, in the case of English, though it is the language of Shakespeare and Churchill, that additions from other languages permit a golden sack of synonyms that (which?) have made it the world's language of commerce. (Indeed, it has been to the considerable detriment of the French language that L'Academie Francaise censors and prevents foreign words, especially English ones, from creeping into it.) English should always be in a state of flux, moving slowly but inexorably through the ages, adapting new words and abandoning old ones as circumstances warrant. But while it can take abuse, it must not be mangled by the wrongful and nauseatingly irritating use of words such as "like" and "goes." In fact, given the way the tongue is being treated these days, I do wonder if English teachers teach English anymore.

PART SEVEN

Collecting

Whither Books
and Other Good Things?

The computer has taken over so much of our lives it's hard to remember what it was like back when. I'm writing this on my computer, of course, listening to King FM out of Seattle—on my computer. That, of course, is nothing these days, but it makes me think. Where will it all end? Will everything the computer *can* control *be* controlled by it? Will the human element disappear? I argue that the answer is no—but I wouldn't want to bet on it.

When I was a lad in school, I recall the teacher informing us that one day no paper would be delivered to our doors because we would have a device on our dining room tables through which our papers would come, rather like the old stockbrokers' tape. This would mean, of course, the end of newspapers. It is certainly feasible and in a way has happened through online papers, but we still have newspapers—plenty of them—and so sure are the publishers that you will buy them that they also make their papers available, often free, on the internet. Indeed, these new freebies are available daily. There have been changes in newspaper production, of course—the print media has fallen into fewer hands—but still the papers flourish.

I think one of the reasons is that real newspapers are easier to read than the internet variety. You don't have to scroll or interpret a table of contents to see what to press to get where you want; moreover, it's nice to sit at the table and split the paper with your partner, she with the comics, you with the sports section. What has happened, in fact, is that the street handout or the paper in the bin at the bus stop has taken another bite out of the circulation of the traditional newspaper. As mainstream papers try to please all regions of the country, community papers have become much more popular. Sadly, most of them are now owned by the big publishers. At the same time we still buy from the big kids, maybe because we just like the heft and feel of the big newspapers.

I suppose the day will come when we will all get our news from a hand-held device that doubles as phone, camera, TV set and music provider—as you can now if you wish—but there is a hell of a lot of money out there that's betting that the *Daily Blat* will be with us for some time. I make this prediction with some trepidation because time and circumstances have dramatically changed the way we do things. Until the mid-1980s there was just ordinary mail and Telex. When the fax, short for facsimile, came into our lives, it was hailed as a great breakthrough in communications. But it wasn't. For forty years or more before that, news outlets had been sending "wire-photos," and if you could send photos you could send words. The fax's time just hadn't yet arrived. Now the fax has gone the way of the carrier pigeon because everyone is online.

About twenty years ago I interviewed a man, a "modernist" if you will, who predicted that grocery stores would simply become big warehouses and you would order your requirements through your computer and they would be delivered to your back door. Not only has this been possible for a long time, technologically it is child's play. It didn't happen because people, young and old, wanted a marketplace. Shopping alongside your neighbours is fun and a necessary part of life. Now, mercifully, shopping centres are going out of fashion and the shopping "village" is in. The more things change . . . .

But what of books? The technology is there and it's cheap to have all the books you want sent to your hand-held device. Why take a heavy book to bed when you can use a computer and soon, if not now, read whatever you want for a small fee?

Some years ago, when the new Vancouver Public Library was being built, the well-known futurist Frank Ogden called it a colossal waste of money because books would be passé very shortly. Well, the library is still there, is very busy, and has books like you wouldn't believe. It also has, interestingly enough, banks of computers for public use! Huge booksellers—Chapters in Canada, Borders and Barnes and Noble in the States, Waterstone's and Foyles in Britain—have stores several storeys high. Large book clubs, such as the Book of the Month Club, still thrive as do online sellers of books such as Amazon for new books and Abebooks for used ones. These giants make it tough for the small neighbourhood bookstore, but the locals can survive if they build a community base of regular clients. I think, or perhaps I should say I hope, that serious readers are turning away from the big book depots with their mandatory Starbucks and are going to community shops that look and feel like real bookstores and have a pot of coffee brewing.

But the question remains, why aren't we all beating on publishers' doors and insisting that they put all—or at least most—of their books online? Maybe a personal story will give part of the answer. At Christmas 2004 Wendy gave me a volume of all the cartoons ever put out by the *New Yorker* magazine. A few hundred of these are in the book and the rest—well over sixty thousand of them—are on disc. I quite often pick the book up off the coffee table and browse, yet, apart from seeing that they work, I have never used the CD-ROMs. I love the *New Yorker* cartoons and often cite very old ones in articles I write and speeches I give, but I don't throw the CD-ROMs into my computer. Why not? Partly it's laziness, but more than that the cartoons just don't look right on the screen. I can scroll (I hate that word) up and down, but it's not the same as leafing through a book.

I like the feel and the smell of books. I like being able to easily browse. If it's non-fiction, I like to riffle through and check out the photographs. Yes, you can accomplish the same with a computer but it's so damned impersonal. And mechanical! I also like to look at my library. I enjoy pulling out a volume and leafing through it. I like to reminisce about when and where I bought the book. I simply like to own books.

I'm a CD-aholic as well—I have over one thousand CDs—but I don't care to look at them. They are, frankly, a pain in the ass to store. If I could get my entire collection onto a computer—and technically I could—I would do it in a minute, but it would take weeks to track down all the stuff I have. Moreover, I doubt that all of it is available.

Will things change with the younger generation coming along? As yet I see no evidence that the younger people are eliminating books and newspapers from their lives, but probably there will be changes, though not nearly as dramatically or to the extent predicted by my futurist friends. Books have been with us too long to disappear without a huge struggle. I just can't imagine browsing through Waterstone's or Hatchards on Piccadilly, looking at CD-ROMs, pulling them from their slots and reading the labels. I suppose that when that point is reached, Waterstone's will be a one-room, back alley joint containing books on its computers that you can, for a price, download onto your computer.

Much about modern communications I like. It's nice to know that if I am in trouble I have a cell phone beside me. I can't imagine writing as much as I do each day using a typewriter. And though we've lost the fine art of letter writing, email is a wondrous thing, in spite of the many abuses it leads to. But while I like to be "with it" and even predict future societal habits, I must admit to being an old fogey on this one. I like books, period.

So, dammit, leave my books alone.

On Parting with Old Friends

I know we're told that soon we'll be reading all our books on the internet so there will be no more need for libraries, public or private, but I still think that next to death, the passing of a book is the saddest thing in the world. Am I just old-fashioned, clinging to my books? Perhaps, but if so, there are sure a lot of very young old-fashioned people in the bookstores I frequent—and that's a lot. Books are more than just words. They are a great comfort just to have around you.

However, recently I reached the point of no return. We live in a small condo and my office is wall-to-wall bookshelves, as is Wendy's office. We also have one bookcase against the wall as you walk upstairs, several portable ones and a special one for some of my Churchill stuff. I could not walk into my office for the books piled up and waiting for me there—most of them new and most unread. I needed space and so had to make often gut-wrenching decisions about what should go and what should stay.

I am not fishing anymore so it had to be the fishing books, which I reckon at about 150 volumes. I promised them to the Georgia Strait Alliance so they could raise some money. There would be exceptions, of course. No Haig-Brown could be touched. And there were all those fly-fishing classics I had paid a small fortune for—they would stay. Then there was a lovely book on British rivers that former Commons Speaker and old friend John Fraser had signed and given me. And Robert Travers' stuff—all that would stay. There was the late Jack Shaw's marvellous book on lake fishing that he signed for me. Can't let that go. And Arthur Gingrich's *The Joys of Trout* and the stuff by Arthur Ransome and Ray Berg's masterful *Trout* that a listener gave me. Then there were those great books on Scottish lochs by Bruce Sandison, the dean of British fishing writers, which had afforded me so much undiluted pleasure. Then there were Al McClane and John Gierach. Dave Hughes' masterpiece on fly-tying called simply *Trout Flies*. And, of course, all the marvellous tabletops gathered over the years. By the time I had sorted things out, the books to go were down to seventy-five. These books will be auctioned off in a few months.

As I write this, I'm looking at the pile of books to be boxed and sent to God-knows-who. If I live to one hundred I would never have reread these books, but for all that, they've been great friends, often comforting me with their silent presence. There is, however, a tiny sliver of silver in the lining—only people who love fly-fishing will bid on these books. Thus they will go to comfortable bookshelves and give pride of possession to an unknown brother of the angle (I may not fish anymore but I've certainly not left the brotherhood!) because they are all so beautifully written they will also take my unidentified friend away from his troubles and into a wonderful dreamland.

Farewell dear friends. You have work ahead of you giving countless pleasures anew.

Rattling Records with Rafe

As readers of past books will know, I'm a bookaholic, but I must confess that I am also a serial offender, big time, with compact discs.

I have always liked music and had pretty catholic tastes, which would have been more satisfactorily classical had I paid more attention to my mom. I didn't because one of her friends, a Mrs. MacKay, who seemed forever to be in our house, always bugged me about listening to Glenn Miller, Tommy Dorsey and that terrible boogie-woogie. Being about age twelve and having always had a strong anti-authoritarian streak, I did everything I could to annoy Mrs. MacKay. (I remember her visually because she didn't shave her legs, which were accordingly covered with jet-black hair. I was drawn to looking at those legs as one is drawn to looking at buckteeth or big boobs. Not a creditable habit but, I fear, an inevitable one.)

My bedroom was in the basement right under the living room so when the dear lady came to tea, I would put on some great boogie-woogie—perhaps Harry James' incredible "Boo Woo" with the equally great "Woo Woo" on the flip side—and let 'er rip, volume up as far as it would go. This would really piss off Mrs. MacKay, and

Mom would descend into my lair and get me to desist. It happened that I also loved Strauss (pere et fils) waltzes and had an album (six 10-inch records) and would play them as loudly as I could, knowing that Mrs. M thought that Strauss was for barbarians and would be seething because my mom—who also liked giving her friend the "mickey" on occasion—would say "Constance, see, Rafe does like classical music, too."

In high school I wrote a music column for *The Three Feathers*, our newspaper (so named because I went to Prince of Wales and his crest has three feathers on it), calling it "Rattling Records with Rafe." Part of my duties was to find out what was new and that would take me to Thompson & Page, the phonograph and records store on South Granville. Helen, the beautiful Helen, would let me play records all day and even let me have one once in a while (the only graft I ever took in a career that had lots of politics in it), knowing it would get covered in our school paper.

I remember when they came out with "unbreakable" records and I brought one up to my Hatfield cousins' place at 41st and Marguerite where there was always a crowd of guys, given my cousins' great beauty and my aunt's great hospitality. I came into the "rec room," tossed the new record onto the floor to show off its unbreakable qualities—and it broke into bits! Helen replaced it.

But I was only a modest collector of records because even with the long plays (LPs) the value wasn't there. It was not just the limited number of sides, but once they were scratched, which happened frequently at the kind of parties I went to, they were effectively finished. Oh, I had lots of records as most kids did, but a collection in any real sense they were not. I didn't really start any sort of a collection until the seventies when I got my first car with an eight-track tape deck. Now we were talking! The tapes didn't break—at least not too often—or scratch and the quality was infinitely better than records. Then came the cassettes where the quality was even better, the case was much, much smaller, and they had fifteen or more songs on each tape. That was the good news. The bad news was that if they got twisted, you were left with a hell of a mess of tape that couldn't be reassembled. When the compact disc arrived in the mid-eighties, it was heaven. The sound was much better than the tape and, when handled carefully, they lasted forever. Moreover, you got up to twenty-five songs per CD. It was at this point that my love of music became an addiction that has cost me dearly, though it has given me immense satisfaction as well.

In a way it's a bit like saving stamps — it takes time to be able to say you have a "collection" and are now in the process of adding to it. I suppose I really became a collector when Wendy and I got together, and we each brought about 100 CDs to the partnership. Her modern music was more up-to-date than mine, and she had some classical music that brought back memories of Mrs. MacKay but got me hooked nonetheless.

During the sixties, seventies and eighties I had listened to Pat Boone, Boney M, The Manhattan Transfer, Simon and Garfunkel, ABBA and many others in order to retain some sanity as my eardrums were being attacked by the stuff played first by my own kids then torturously extended by stepchildren. Happily for my collecting habit, digital remastering came in and we learned about AAD, ADD and DDD. By the nineties much of the stuff I had liked in those earlier years had been remastered and reissued on CDs. Then, as the twenty-first century approached, remastering was extended to more and more of the really great stuff from before the war, during the war and from the decade or so after the war but before rock and roll came in. By this time Wendy and I had an excellent base and could truly be called collectors. Not big-time collectors, mind, but collectors in the sense that we bought a lot of CDs and almost always had our collection in mind as we did so. I would think, after just rearranging all mine, that between us we have at least 1,500 discs. Maybe more.

From the outset, Wendy and I travelled a lot, up to five times a year with much of that time in Britain and at least once a year to New Zealand. In London we spent a lot of time in the HMV store on Oxford Street—not the one near Selfridges but the one to the east near Tottenham Court Road. Every year it has newly remastered stuff from innumerable European countries and for some reason from Australia.

When I was young, I was a big fan of Frankie Laine, but the only way I could get some of his good stuff was to pester the incomparable Jack Cullen, long-time deejay at CKNW, who would get me some taped stuff. Rock and Roll Hall of Famer Red Robinson was also a good and kind source in those days. So every time Wendy and I went to HMV in London I would come to the Ls and pray for some Laine other than "High Noon" or the crappy "Wild Goose" sort of rubbish. (Incidentally, when my father first heard "The Wild Goose," he sang out, "Bend right over and touch your toes, and I'll show you where the wild goose goes!") Then one day at HMV it happened. There was a CD with most of Laine's Atlas label stuff like "Someday Sweetheart," "S'Posin," "Coquette" and many others. There was just that one disc, but it was like I had died and gone to heaven. It was a start. Then, be damned if I wasn't in the Jazz section and there was Buck Clayton and his All-Stars with all but one song by Frankie Laine. And it was the remastered update of an LP I had borrowed from a friend then wore out I played it so much!

New Zealand is also a terrific place to get low-priced CDs and, again for reasons I don't fathom, the small town of Taupo is one of the best places. It has one outdoor stand that's half a block long. Auckland and especially Wellington are also very good places for bargains.

Closer to home, on the second floor of the Lonsdale Quay there is a great little spot for what must be called "different" CDs in that, while you will often know the artist, you will likely be unaware of that disc. I'm not sure where the proprietor gets his stuff but he has particularly good boxed sets of classics, and I have also picked up some neat jazz stuff.

I'm always surprised where I come across some of this stuff. For example, I had a tape of the Mamas & the Papas that I just couldn't find on CD. One day Wendy and I were in Alnwick in northern England visiting the factory and shop of the famous fishing equipment manufacturer, Hardy's, and I popped into a convenience store to get a soft drink. The shop had a tray of perhaps fifty CDs, and among them was the Mamas & the Papas I had been looking for! When I go into any store nowadays, I must look like a ferret as my eyes search for the telltale signs of a tray of CDs!

Now, of course, you can even get the old transcriptions on CD but finding the Buck Clayton CD and the early Mamas & the Papas show that you should always look everywhere, no matter how strange it may seem. For instance, not long ago Wendy and I visited Ostia, Italy, a nice seaside town that had been the seaport for ancient Rome. Out for a stroll one day, we came across a street market with a stall selling CDs—all sorts of CDs with no clear signs of distinction between types of music. My eye caught four Glenn Millers and two Duke Ellingtons I had never seen before. I couldn't tell by looking at them whether they had been remastered and, not wanting to take a chance, I bought one of each, took them back to the hotel, tore off the cellophane and looked inside the jackets. They were all DDD! Now I had to get the rest of them, but for five days we searched in vain for our wandering CD salesman. On our last day I spotted him and to my delight I found the remaining discs I wanted. It turned out that he actually has a large store in Rome and is only occasionally given a licence to sell on the streets of Ostia. I had got lucky. For the princely sum of forty-eight Euros I had six discs that are really collector's items.

Until a year or so ago, there was a classical music store near our London Hotel. Sadly, it went bust. For me this was a great store for I could get classical music—of which I was becoming more and more fond and was starting to learn about—especially on the Naxos label, at a reasonable price. One day I was browsing there and Wendy sidled up and said, "Hon, you're not going to believe this," and presented me with a package of eight Sinatra CDs—all of his pre-1950 stuff for the grand total of twenty pounds! (When Sinatra got into that Rat Pack crap and the Ol' Blue Eyes shit I couldn't stand the man. Before that, he was terrific.) In any event, these songs Sinatra made with Harry James, Tommy Dorsey and Alex Stordahl were terrific quality and I got them in a classical music store! And all remastered! A year later in the same "classical music" store Wendy found a twenty-CD box of Benny Goodman for twenty quid. They turned out to be fantastic quality for one pound per CD. As I've always said, you never know when the good things in life are going to happen!

Sometimes it isn't just your eyes you must keep open. A few years ago Wendy and I had popped into Covent Garden after Sunday Matins at St. Paul's and stopped by a funky little shop called Banana where occasionally you can find a bin of decent remainder books. As we were poking around, I stopped dead in my tracks. "Honey! Am I hearing things? Isn't that background music the Benny Goodman Quartet and isn't that Lionel Hampton I hear?" I shot up to the desk clerk and was told that yes, the two-CD set was on sale downstairs. Sure that they would all be gone, I pushed old ladies aside as I flew down the viciously narrow staircase and yes! There was a copy left. A two-CD set for $2.99 and, unbelievably, next to it a boxed set of Lionel Hampton at the same price! I took them—firmly clasped, I can tell you—back to the cash desk.

"Is the Lionel Hampton one remastered?" I asked.

"I haven't a clue," the young lady said, no doubt thinking just what I was telling myself: What the hell, Mair! For $2.99, take a chance! I did and it was wonderful.

In the winter of 2001 Wendy and I were in Prague, and swept up in this marvellous, indeed magic, city of the Czechs, I went into a CD store in the "New Square" (which is "new" only if you consider the fourteenth century recent). I had known of the great Czech composer Dvorak, of course, but had never "met" Smetana, but here it seemed that everywhere I looked both Smetana's and Dvorak's names appeared. I decided to take a chance—I'm a high roller, as you have seen. I would buy some Smetana as long as

Dvorak was involved so that I would at least have something I liked on the disc. As a result, I wound up a great fan of Dvorak and, as I climbed my long learning curve, of Smetana as well.

Are there any rules to buying cheap CDs? Not really. It helps if it says on the label that it has been 22-bit or 32-bit remastered (whatever the hell a "bit" is) or has AAD (good), ADD (better), or best of all DDD on the package somewhere. But you can get fooled. Sometimes the surprise is a happy one, sometimes not so happy. When I'm not sure, I'll ask. Often the cheap CD is not, for anti-theft reasons, in the display case so the clerk will let you have a listen. If you can do that, be sure you check several tracks. I bought a Lester Young CD with Oscar Peterson on the piano and listened to the first track but it was scratchy as hell. I was about to give it back but decided to try a few more tracks. The rest of the sound was terrific, making a CD with one lousy track and fifteen good ones a great buy at five bucks. But I'll tell you who will piss you off. Verve. They have great stuff, especially great jazz, but they never tell you the quality, evidently because they believe that their name is sufficient. The galling thing is that they're usually right!

I must tell you that those who have always had classical music as part of their lives will know just how gauche my working my way into the classics is. I was unlucky enough to have been a silly little boy who enjoyed pissing off Mrs. MacKay, but I wound up having, late in life, the adventure of exploring that which the more cultured have always taken for granted. I suppose I took some of it in by osmosis—pieces such as Beethoven's "Appassionata," which my mom played a lot and I had to admit I liked. Then there were popular songs like "Tonight We Love," which Freddy Martin stole from Tchaikovsky. He and his pianist Jack Fina also stole "Bumble Boogie," a huge hit in 1945, from Rimsky-Korsakov's "Flight of the Bumble Bee." Contributions to popular song also came from Chopin's "Marching Polonaise," Rachmaninoff and others. So the base was always there, and not even memories of Constance MacKay and childhood stubbornness could keep me from giving classical stuff a good listen every once in a while. I even started going to concerts, though after three stifling nights of opera, I gave up opera for nice recordings of the overtures. I have the attention span of a gnat and anything that lasts longer than two hours has me begging the clock to go faster so I can get the hell out of there.

One advantage of not having been steeped in the classics from birth is that Wendy and I can go to a classical concert in the Royal Albert Hall in November and be entranced by the actual cannons fired in Tchaikovsky's "1812 Overture." Or go to the symphony with, in my case anyway, the zeal of a convert. I'm too old to be embarrassed by my ignorance and will ask all sorts of what I think are stupid questions. Of course, after broadcasting for twenty-five years, I have become accustomed to asking dumb questions, and I always marvel at how much of the time the questions really aren't all that dumb. Coming to classical music late is, I think, a bit like coming late to golf. If you start when you're fifty, it's unlikely you'll wind up a scratch handicap, but you will learn something new each time out so your game will get better and you'll have more fun, while those who started young see their games deteriorate. Like the fifty-year-old beginning golfer, as time passes I improve both my comprehension of classical music and my library.

In one way, however, my position is much more troublesome than a veteran classics lover. The newcomer yearns to get started so a path to some sort of definition of what music is all about will become clear. I've reached the point where I not only know that I haven't a working definition but have come to believe that there is no definition available unless one arrogantly assumes possession of the ability to determine what sorts of noises are good noises and what are not. I suspect that those who say they understand what is "good music" and what is not are often snobby humbugs. But they have the advantage of knowing just what they want and just what they don't want. Like lawyers and priests, they speak a different lingo than you and I do and can make us feel awfully small and stupid.

To them, the classics are music, the rest (being what they consider outside the pale) is rubbish.

I suppose all plebeians say this, but I rather enjoy my ignorance. I've come to understand that the Beatles were as much musicians as was Arthur Rubinstein. Whether they were better musicians than the great man is debatable but they sure as hell sold more records and left more tunes as their legacy. Don't get me wrong. I don't say that everyone who makes noise that sells is a musical genius or that when it comes to blowing or banging things that everyone is an equal. I don't for a moment contend that a Jascha Heifetz and the fiddler at the rural ceilidh on the Isle of Skye are of equal talent or musical importance. What I do say is that the argument is an idle one, a matter of snobbery rather than importance. Sir Thomas Beecham once said that "the English hate music but they love the noise it makes." If true—and I happen to believe it is true for most of us—the great conductor was telling all of us to make music as we will, but more than that, he's saying (though this may not be what he intended) we should listen to as much "noise" as we can and take from it what we will.

If that's not what Sir Thomas meant, it sure as hell is what I take music to be. Be it Satch, or Ella, Gershwin or Stravinsky, Cole Porter or Stephen Foster, Beethoven or Mozart, Jenny Lind or Eva Cassidy (if you don't know who she was, find out) or even boogie-woogie or Strauss, pere et fils, it's great noise for all of us to enjoy in our own way and too bad for those who think that acceptance of one brand of noise means rejection of other brands. The coolest cat I've ever met in the musical world is Bramwell Tovey, conductor of the Vancouver Symphony Orchestra and a wonderful jazz pianist. When all's said and done, my regret is that Beethoven, Mozart and J.S. Bach never met Nat, Ella or Louis. I think they would have enjoyed each other's talents.

PART EIGHT

Troubling Times, Troubling Questions

The Welfare State—The Philosophy

Most experts are clear that somewhere between 15 and 20 percent of Canadians live in poverty. In a country as rich as Canada this is appalling, indeed disgraceful. And it is as bad or worse in the United States, supposedly the richest country in the world. What is required, say many on the left, is a "welfare state." Well, I agree, but I must also point out that we already have one but its funds are short and its targets often missed.

The welfare state was not invented by the left. A succinct history of the welfare state is stated thus and usefully in the *Wikipedia Encyclopedia*:

> Modern welfare states developed through a gradual process beginning in the late 19th century and continuing through the 20th. They differed from previous schemes of poverty relief due to their relatively universal coverage. The development of social insurance in Germany under Bismarck [who was hardly a wild-eyed revolutionary—my note] was particularly influential. Some schemes, like those in Scandinavia, were based largely in the development of

autonomous, mutualist provision of benefits. Others were founded on state provision. The term was not, however, applied to all states offering social protection. The sociologist T.H. Marshall identified the welfare state as a distinctive combination of democracy, welfare and capitalism.

Examples of early welfare states in the modern world are the Sweden, Netherlands and New Zealand of the 1930s. Changed attitudes in reaction to the Great Depression were instrumental in the move to the welfare state in many countries, a harbinger of new times where "cradle-to-grave" services became a reality after the poverty of the Depression. In the period following the Second World War, many countries in Europe moved from partial or selective provision of social services to relatively comprehensive coverage of the population.

Though the term "welfare state" is usually taken to mean government handouts, it must be remembered that much welfare is privately run and distributed and more and more we see partnerships between governments and the private sector. Those of the far right persuasion, however, treat the term as if it was consistent with treachery, often seeing it as a denial of God's teaching. Their Protestant ethic teaches that all can be like Horatio Alger and by working hard can achieve wealth and happiness ever after. The flip side of this is that those who don't achieve or underachieve should simply live with the consequences. This philosophy translates into slogans like "The government that governs least, governs best," the implication being that welfare bums and the bureaucracy that succours them are keeping the country (and themselves, of course) from the prosperity they deserve. They cry out for tax relief, saying that the money put back into taxpayers' hands will immediately restore the economy. They tell the poor that "a rising tide lifts all boats," which any person of the sea will tell you is nonsense if the boat has too heavy an anchor, which many of the "poor boats" in our society have. Perhaps the more accurate statement is that tax cuts for the rich provide a rising tide that raises all *yachts*.

Interestingly, the term "welfare state" is an old one, and the pioneer was that hard-line Prussian himself: Otto von Bismarck. Indeed, the German model of welfare was what inspired David Lloyd George and Winston Churchill to bring their welfare package into Parliament in 1910. Churchill a welfare state man? The answer is yes, and it was he who brought in the first workers' insurance legislation and labour exchanges. Around the same time, he also brought in massive prison reform. And it was Churchill's World War II coalition government that commissioned the Beveridge Report that, under Labour after the war, morphed into the National Health Service. All credit to Clement Attlee's government for doing this in light of the terrible financial strictures on the UK at the time. Of course, this brought about a doctors' strike and an exodus of doctors, many to Canada, but the system survived and health care for Britons improved dramatically.

In the latter half of the nineteenth century and up until the start of World War I, the world had been, in Winston's terms, "for the few and the very few." It's useful, I think, to remember what Britain was like in those days—and indeed still is today though to a much lesser extent. The rich were very rich and much of the poor were dirt poor. Those even worse off were in the coal mines where, if the coal dust didn't get their lungs, the accidents buried them. The rich based their wealth on land taken into their ancestors' hands by force and passed down from generation to generation. A lovely story tells the tale: a landowner, having apprehended a poacher on his vast estate, told the trespasser, "This is my land. My forebears fought for it nine hundred years ago." To which the poacher said, "Right, then I'll fight thee for it now." It has always amazed me that in a country where so few control the land merely by accident of birth there has never been a major revolution.

Societies must ask themselves what they want to be, the available options ranging from freewheeling to full communism. Does anyone seriously doubt that Canada opted long ago for something in between? In fact, the US, Canada and Britain have all had major social upheavals that hurried change along. World War I saw young men from the lowest order of society facing major bloodshed "For King and Country," and there was no way they were going back whence they came. During the Great Depression for a lot of the unemployed the "miracle" of the Soviet Union had great appeal. Then, when World War II happened, the US, Canada and Britain had to make a place fit for heroes to return to. In the United States and Canada this meant making free education available for service men and women; it meant making land available and mortgages to build new houses. In Britain it meant the National Health Service and massive house building. Along the way, pension plans and other benefits were added. By 1945 it was too late by far to deny the right, indeed obligation, of the government to bring services to all, not just the needy.

Although women had been "rewarded" with the vote after World War I, both world wars saw such huge contributions by women to the war efforts that their political ambitions could no longer be denied. With the 1960s came the Women's Movement and the steady addition of women to the permanent work force. Of course, there was more than the Women's Movement involved; couples found that they needed two incomes, sometimes just to survive. This created a new social problem: how to see that the children were cared for. It took a while but eventually governments saw that some sort of daycare was a social benefit whose time had come. Unfortunately, daycare connotes two problems: if you give to everyone regardless of need, poor people will get less than they need. And to avoid this problem would require a "means test," which is, to say the least, unfashionable these days.

The problems that faced the Lloyd George–Churchill team remain with us today though perhaps in different forms. We still have poverty alongside wealth even though we have welfare provisions, a "free" healthcare system and public pensions. We still have the homeless in the streets, unattended sick people (often with mental health problems), drug (very much including alcohol) abuse way beyond anything seen before, almost epidemic juvenile crime ranging from car racing and drugs to gun battles. All of this means that the philosophical debate about the "welfare state" in its broadest sense continues. "Why," the right asks, "should these people suck off the public teat, namely my tax dollars?"

I am somewhat taken aback by this backlash of neo-conservatism, but it has to be dealt with. We live in a society. Not a brilliant observation, I grant you, but it means that we are all in a social organization, and the question is not whether we should have such an organization, but what it should look like and how it should operate. It begins with the children. Poor people have children. Even if we were to turn our backs on the adults, surely no one thinks that these children are economic sinners. That being said, it's pretty hard to help these children except through the adults in whose charge they are.

I go back to basics and say this is how I think we should guide ourselves:

First, we must accept that the welfare genie will not go back into that bottle. The programs we have, except as they are amended, will not go away.

Second, we must understand the world of today. The ability of people to prepare themselves for life has changed dramatically. No more does a profession attained guarantee a lifetime of work; there are no more secure jobs at the mill, at least in part because more and more of these jobs are being "outsourced" and performed in low-wage countries. Society, meaning our national club, must look after those who are sideswiped by events beyond their control.

Third, we have to understand that every society has its cheats and there will be fraud and that, when it happens, it will be blown out of all proportion by the media. We also have to understand that on one side there is the single mom harried and perhaps jailed for fudging on the system while the rich make out their highly fictionalized, expenses-laden tax returns. So exactly how big a problem is welfare fraud compared to, say, the lunches, dinners, vacations and all other entertainment (usually including the business person as well as the client) that are written off against taxes? I agree two wrongs don't make a right; I only say that, when looking at fraud upon the tax department, we should look everywhere, not just at the poor.

I believe that a caring society takes on the following obligations:

> 1. Every person must have decent shelter. I'm always amazed at those who would eliminate care for the homeless, wanting them instead to be pushed aside and out of sight.

> 2. Basic health care, *including for mental illness*, must be provided every citizen.

> 3. Every citizen must have decent food every day.

> 4. Every citizen must have enough funds available to meet the minimum requirements of life.

> 5. Every citizen is entitled to state-funded education.

> 6. Every citizen is entitled to counsel when he is charged with a crime that might mean punishment by a prison sentence.

What is interesting about the foregoing is that it will bring screams of anguish and suggestions that Mair is a limp-wristed liberal at best and a neo-communist at worst. In fact, all of the foregoing *are* already in place. It's just that sufficient funding has always been lacking.

The funding of "welfare"—and here I use this word to describe what a "welfare state" provides—is what provokes white hot anger in many of our better-off citizens. To start with, they count themselves as better citizens because they have *become* better off, although I must say this phenomenon seems to describe those with inherited money as well. What is also a bit odd about the prosperous is that they often bad-mouth immigrants who have come to this country, done jobs no one else wanted to do, and have prospered. I congratulate those who have prospered, especially those who had a disadvantageous start to life, but it simply is not everyone's lot to have been born with what it takes to be a financial success. Many, perhaps the majority, of people come equipped with skills that limit their ability to make money in any way but by working for someone else, and thus they have their prospects tied to someone else's success—or lack of it. A large number of these jobs are seasonal; many are being sucked out of the country by industry outsourcing.

As a consequence, these people remain poor, and being poor means begetting children who start out poor. This situation flags a huge problem because poverty not only breeds more poverty, it breeds all manner of social problems including crime. This is not to say that social problems including crime are confined to the poor, but it does say that a disproportionate amount of those problems are with the less well-off in our society. The obvious conclusion is that if people are well fed, sheltered and so on by the welfare state, that state will save untold millions dealing with the social problems that cling like leeches to the lives of the poor. In short, the business community and professionals ought to be first in line supporting a welfare state because, while their taxes will pay for the up-front part, they will save money as the social problems decline.

One of the self-serving points the business class makes is that the "welfare state" is so expensive that it raises taxes and thus discourages new entrepreneurial money from coming into the country. There are two answers to that. First, if it's true, it's a scathing indictment of our system because it means that business incentives are provided on the backs of the poor. Second, it betrays an inability of capital gatherers to point out to offshore investors that while the taxes are higher, so are all the benefits, not least of which is health care. These are benefits employers must pay for where these investors come from but which are provided by the state in Canada.

Let's now look at the element of luck. All of us who were born on the "right side of the tracks" started off with an enormous advantage. Our contacts, be they family, friends, schoolmates—the list goes on—have a couple of legs up on the rest of the community. The better off despise the notion of "affirmative action," which they see as being unfair because it sometimes gives an advantage to a less qualified person. While I don't want to get into the endless debate about affirmative action, I want to make two points. First off, were there no affirmative action rules, blacks in the southern states would still not be able to get work in many of the companies doing business with government. Second, no one had a bigger dose of affirmative action than I did. Born into an upper middle class family, with parents who stayed together, with friends and schoolmates that included the sons and daughters of the wealthy and powerful set in Vancouver, with an education in part in a private school, I went into adult life with uncountable people I could call on to help me with my career. I did nothing to deserve that. I was just born to the right parents. I worked hard and was and perhaps am one of the top broadcasters in the country. But aren't there tens of thousands out there who had much greater talent than I who were just—often because of the accident of birth—never in the right place at the right time? And never could have been there?

I'm going to make one final point that will no doubt make me seem like Lenin. When you drive around Vancouver and its suburbs and see all the million dollar-plus homes, when you look in the driveways at the expensive cars, when you look at the marinas and yacht clubs and see the hugely expensive boats, can you really honestly say that there is not enough money to go around a little more equitably? I guess the answer to that is going to depend on whether or not we think we are our brother's keeper.

To me the answer is yes, even if the price of that commitment leads to the welfare state I've outlined.

Corporations or Countries?

There are abroad in this land—and I suspect around the world— some misconceptions about corporations.

First off, when the average person sees "Ltd." or "Inc." after the name of a company, he has a feeling of security. In fact, he should really be worried because those words mean that the liability of shareholders is limited to the value of their shares. The company is responsible but probably not the people who run it. Let us take, for example, the Ajax Widget Company, which has been operating as a proprietorship of Mr. John Ajax for some years. The business having prospered, Mr. Ajax wants to turn it into a company so he can raise money by issuing shares or perhaps because he wants to give shares to his children. His accountant agrees that it would be wise from a tax point of view, so Mr. Ajax takes himself to his lawyers, Scrooge and Company, who draw up a memorandum of agreement and a set of articles of association for him. Ajax Widgets Ltd. is formed with all the assets of the old proprietor being transferred in consideration of most if not all of the shares going to Mr. Ajax.

Say you've been dealing with Ajax Widgets for years, always marvelling at the workmanship in every widget sold. You hear that old

John Ajax has incorporated and it makes you feel even more secure in your widget supplier. However, before Mr. Ajax incorporated, he and his wonderful house, his three cars and his summer home as well as any of his other assets could all be attached if you sued his company because his faulty widgets buggered up your cadiddles, causing huge damage. If the same happened after the company's incorporation, in the absence of a personal guarantee from Mr. Ajax himself, you could just sue the company, which is probably mortgaged to the hilt to the bank. Corporations are, then, beings of their own in the eyes of the law and from the point of view of the owner(s) of the incorporated businesses are their security against being personally liable for any bad things that happen because of the company's fault. For the owner of the business, incorporation is, therefore, usually well worth the legal and accounting fees paid.

The public in general has another misconception about companies, especially large ones. For example, perhaps we are told that Ajax Widgets International Ltd. is a "good corporate citizen." I hate to sound cynical, but even the baseball uniforms with the Ajax logo on them are for the purpose of public relations; they are not to get old John Ajax into heaven when his time comes but to make more money for the company. There are no such things as "good corporate citizens," just companies that aren't as bad as they might be because if they *were* as bad as they might be, customers might stay away.

Another ongoing capitalist mantra is that corporations create jobs. It is true, of course, that when things need to be done, people will be employed to do them. But any job is permanent only as long as the employee is needed. Become redundant and you're out of there! In fact, the company's generosity to a redundant employee depends upon an agreement, the law or a custom. If the custom doesn't allow enough, the employee can and will sue, and usually the judge, knowing what corporations are really like, will raise the custom to a new level. Whatever the settlement, it does not reflect the generosity of a good corporate citizen.

What is very wrong is to blame corporations for high unemployment *or* to give them praise when employment is high. It is not the responsibility of corporations to keep employment high though many on the left believe that it is. The mandate to alleviate the horrors of unemployment rests, if it rests on anyone, on the state. I agree with economists like the late Maynard Keynes and the late John Kenneth Galbraith who believed that the state has the obligation to undertake needed public works when times are tough. Milton Friedman thinks otherwise. To him and his ilk, lowering taxes on the rich will bring more investment and thus employment will rise; the money that the rich save by their lower taxes will in this way "trickle down" to the poor. All I can say is that while that might be so in theory, there is no evidence it works like that in the real world.

The marketplace will, of course, affect wages and conditions of work, but as in many other areas of human endeavour, the marketplace often has a "hidden hand" that drops the ball when the game gets rough. Much more than market forces, unions and the law will invariably provide the benchmarks. But wages and conditions for senior executives are also, it is said, determined by the marketplace. The reason we pay Bloggs $10 million a year to run our company, say the directors, is that this is what he's worth in the marketplace — as if someone making, say, $500,000 per couldn't do just as good a job. The reason he couldn't is because he doesn't have to. This pernicious practice of hugely padded salaries is usually accompanied by huge bags of stock options. It works this way: Bloggs is hired for $5 million per year and given options to buy $1 million worth of shares at the current price of one dollar per share. If under his jurisdiction the stock drops to 50 cents, it doesn't cost him a nickel. If, however, the stock goes to $5 he can exercise his option, pay $1 million for his shares and immediately sell them, pocketing a net $4 million. Note that in large companies the options and rewards are often much higher than in my example. It should also be noted that the directors of these generous companies get stock options, enormous fees for meetings that are often held in sunny, warmer climes during the winter months and prestige. And in addition to their directors' fees, they are also on the receiving end of huge salaries from somewhere else.

Stock option abuse can be horrific. For example, suppose old Mr. Ajax, having taken Ajax Widgets public, has provided himself and his board of directors cronies with a great many stock options. They then incorporate a "straw company" that agrees to buy a million widgets from Ajax Widgets Ltd., whereupon Ajax issues a public release on this huge piece of new business, and the news causes the stock price to double. Ajax and his friends take up their options, sell them at the huge new price, pocket their money and then solemnly and sorrowfully announce that the company that placed the order for all those widgets has just gone broke.

A far-out scenario? Not if you read the story of how George W. Bush made his money. In fact, this is one of the oldest games played in the mining market. Leak out a rumour that you have just struck an amazing ore body, allow this news to drive up the stock, take up your options then express regret that the ore, after all, was not that great.

The one place you can be guaranteed that corporations will not be good corporate citizens and are, in fact, lousy members of the community is in the area of the environment. I once had an argument with Dr. Michael Walker, then CEO of the right wing think-tank the Fraser Institute—a healthy debate it was, too—as to whether our rivers should be owned privately or publicly. It was his position that the private owner of a river, after finding that fish were the river's main asset, would do nothing to disturb that asset. Fortunately for my side of the argument, I had some "for instances" at hand, many of my examples being from England where, from the industrial revolution on, the best use industry (including farming) could make of rivers was to make them waste dumps. I asked Dr. Walker what recourse the downstream owner would have on his privately owned river if his upstream neighbour put crud in the water, and his answer was that his remedy would be in the courts. The trouble with this remedy is that even if it were financially practicable to sue, the injured party would invariably be a "little guy" fighting large, rich upstream industries that would stall, appeal, and use all the other dodges employed by the wealthy to delay, thus driving up the cost of the lawsuit so that the plaintiff would be "money-whipped" into submission.

Environmental safeguards have never come voluntarily from corporations. They have always come from government orders after great public pressure. Even then, corporations will cheat every chance they get then go into denial after surrounding themselves with public relations flacks. This happened in Bhopal, India, where Union Carbide killed thousands and has since then fought every cent of compensation tooth and nail. But if you listened to the stuff coming from Hill & Knowlton, one of the world's largest PR companies, you would think that kindly old Union Carbide had conferred a benefit on the good burghers of Bhopal. (Hill & Knowlton has also advised the BC fish farming industry.)

Having said these bad things about corporations, I must explain why these things happen. A real person is concerned about survival. He must eat, breathe and so on, or he dies. Therefore, he does everything, often desperate things, to keep himself alive. He even takes part in bloody wars for self-preservation. The corporation, on the other hand, has a single indicator of survival. It is called profit. It is the sole reason for the company's existence.

Just imagine if our friend Mr. Ajax, the CEO of Ajax Widgets Ltd., came before the annual meeting of shareholders and said, "We are, of course, under no legal obligation to install scrubbers at our plant and thus make our discharge into the river harmless, but we are such nice people here at Ajax, such super environmentally conscious people, such a good corporate citizen, that I have decided to put $50 million worth of scrubbers in the plant. Consequently, there will be no dividend this year, but I am sure you will be glad to sacrifice that dividend you were expecting because we put corporate good citizenship ahead of profit." Need I tell what would happen to Mr. Ajax and his board of directors? Shareholders want dividends, not medals for good citizenship! There is your corporation—heartless, unheeding of the public weal, concerned only about profit for the shareholders.

Because the "bottom line" is the sole litmus test for corporate success, companies are constantly looking for new ways to compete. Now it must be observed here that corporations regard looking ahead years and decades for business reasons a good thing; on the other hand, they have no need at all to look ahead for employees and make provisions for them to survive and prosper because the convenience of employees has nothing to do with corporate decisions unless the corporation is unionized. Even then the employees' interests may have little bearing on events; just check out the employees of the automobile industry. (I should add that *healthy* competition in business will provide alternate sources of jobs and create a market for wages.)

Although ten or fifteen years ago services such as billing clients were all done by Ajax Widget's own employees, old Mr. Ajax has now found a cheaper way to do these things because of the lightning speed with which money and services can be moved around in this age of globalization. He "contracts out" to a foreign low-wage bookkeeping company, saving a bundle. Who cares about the Ajax employees put out of work? He outsources other jobs to places like India and Thailand where wage costs are a tenth of those at home. So today when I place an order with a Vancouver pizza company, my order is taken in Winnipeg and my American Express account is dealt with in India. I get telephone information from some place in Texas making it useless for me to explain that the Mr. Bill Jones I'm trying to reach lives in Kitsilano and should have a phone number reflecting that.

If North American companies were outsourcing only menial tasks, it would be one thing, but we're committing economic suicide at the highest level. As Thomas L. Friedman points out in his perceptive book *The World is Flat*, the US takes students from India, trains them at Harvard or MIT, gives them hands-on experience at, say, IBM then watches them take all this American-paid-for expertise back to India. Even though this person could make much more in the United States, he is comparatively much, much better off than other people in India and that's the country he wants to live in. From India he does for $25,000 a year what it costs IBM in the US $100,000 a year. And because places in US universities are being occupied by foreign students and jobs in the formerly profitable industries are going overseas, American kids are no longer taking the technical courses at Harvard, Stanford or MIT—or anywhere else for that matter—because the upper levels of many companies now have fewer and fewer, if any, high-paying jobs.

Some of the questions society now has to face are: What's going to happen to our workforce and indeed our society? What's going to happen to our economy? Is every service we require and every product we buy going to come from India, Thailand or China? If Ajax Widgets Ltd. can only operate by outsourcing, aren't we the people in the same fix? Taking it further, if all the goods and services are bought overseas and all technical work is also done in the Far East, how are we to exist—by taking in each other's washing? (A quick anecdote: Wendy and I took a fourteen-day cruise in the Caribbean in March 2006. At every island I bought a baseball cap as a souvenir, twelve in all. Every one of them was made in China!)

So how do we fix this situation? One's first reaction is, of course, to deal directly with Ajax Widgets and make them do more if not all their stuff at home. But how would you do that? What are your means of enforcement? And if you dump on Ajax, aren't you likely to give an offshore company that is not subject to your rules and is entitled under NAFTA to compete in Canada a big competitive edge? The government would have to deal with all corporations, big and small, in the same way. How in hell can a government do that? And if it did, how would it get around all the trading laws that groups like NAFTA and the WTO have agreed to?

We can see this more clearly with an example closer to home. When your neighbour loses his job to outsourcing to a foreign company, you are angry. However, when this outsourcing drives down the cost of things you want, globalization doesn't look all that bad. Why would you pay substantially more for strictly homemade goods and services when you can buy them for one quarter the price from somewhere else—even if it did cost your neighbour his job?

Because I was contracted to the Jim Pattison organization twice and know Jimmy well, I was always amused when callers to my show would berate him for threatening to take his business to where it was cheaper and more profitable. My answer was always a question: Why do you go to Bellis Fair across the border to shop and to American gas pumps whenever the price of currency makes it profitable? There was usually a silence. The truth is that Jimmy does just what the ordinary citizen does but on a bigger scale.

The questions abound, and because the animal is so strong and elusive—I speak of the large corporation—there doesn't seem much we can do about him except by international cooperation. All you need do is look at how the US on the one hand and France on the other deal with their agriculture industries. The United States subsidizes the hell out of its farm produce and doesn't give a damn what the international community says or, indeed, what the international trade laws are. France goes one better. It subsidizes its farms out of EC funds so that other agricultural countries in the Community, like the UK, can't even compete in their own market!

If you have countries so unwilling to play the game when their favourite product is involved, how do you expect international rules to protect countries like Canada from what is, essentially, dumping cheap services across the border? Let me explain that last remark: if the Canadian government were to subsidize a widget industry then dump those widgets on the world market cheaper than other countries can produce them, it would be called "dumping," and dumping is against all trade rules. So what is the difference between that and service providers in, say, India doing all the billing, collecting, legal work and accounting services for a Canadian widget company at, say, 10 percent of the Canadian cost? The only difference—and it is really little more than a distinction—is that in one case we are talking about goods and the other about services.

Of course, the issue is more complicated than that. In the airplane business Canada, along with other airplane producers, does some pretty neat dumping of its own and gets away with it. My point is simply that if we do not come to grips with the outsourcing and other methodologies of the global market we're in, a lot of Canadians are going to be hurt—badly.

Supply Needs More Than Demand

Conservatives believe that Adam Smith's hidden hand does indeed guide the marketplace, but does it? There are some parts of the market that, if left to supply and demand as the only prevailing forces, just couldn't survive, an obvious example being perishables. While it's not my intent to defend all marketing boards, if things like milk and eggs were sold by farmers in open competition for consumers, there would be either a lot of rotten eggs and rancid milk or not enough fresh stuff for the demand, driving the price up dramatically. It might be argued—and is—that less perishable agricultural products may need less help, but there is no way in the world that stuff with a short shelf life could sustain an industry that wasn't sheltered by controls.

However, it's always a good question how much control should be exercised because farmers are indeed a strong political lobby and consumers are not. I would argue that there are areas where the government has a right, if not a duty, to be in the market because these areas are not suited to raw free enterprise. For the most part, I'm talking about industries that don't lend themselves to competition and tend to be monopolies. Power, water, and railways often fall into this slot. There are many who argue that BC Hydro ought to be privatized and competition allowed. At the lower levels this may make sense and indeed British Columbia governments have gone some way towards encouraging small power companies to feed into the main grid.

Private companies such as Alcan have been doing this for years. The problem comes when major power sources must be built. This is when it is not only the type of power—hydro, fossil fuel, nuclear and so on—that must be questioned but also the environmental, economic and social considerations. If, for example, private power companies were encouraged to build a big dam on any river they chose, undoubtedly they would pick the Fraser or the Skeena and to hell with fish and other concerns. Every kind of power generation, even wind and tide, carries with it environmental considerations as well as technical ones. Therefore, to put the main generation of power into the hands of capitalism is to abandon the public to the bottom line and to remove from government the ability to effect public policy through energy development.

Water is soon to become, in my view, as thorny an issue as power because US thirst can no longer be slaked by that country's own supplies. Clearly it's a matter of public policy as to whether public waterways will be used to supply export water. Would anyone support the notion that private companies can come into British Columbia, choose locations of supply without hindrance and take as much water as they can sell? Of course not!

I also mentioned rail because of our present situation in British Columbia. Nearly sixty years ago W.A.C. Bennett took over the Pacific Great Eastern Railway, renamed it BC Rail and used it as a development tool. The present government sold BC Rail to CN. You will note I call it a sale because surely no one apart from Premier Campbell is going to call a 999-year lease anything other than a sale. To show how long that is, if you went back that far in history, England would be under the reign of Ethelred the Unready. Both Bennetts, Dave Barrett, Bill Vander Zalm and the

NDP premiers of the 1990s saw BC Rail as a tool for government-led expansion and economic development. Indeed, it could and often was run at a profit—except for the times it was ordered by the government to blaze trails that would only make money perhaps decades down the road.

There is no reason to think that CN will invest a penny in the development of our province unless it advances that company's own economic interests, which may or may not coincide with those of British Columbia. To illustrate what I mean, the government of the day put a lot of money and effort into Expo 86, and without question it made millions aware of BC who otherwise would not have been. The payback was enormous and continues to this day—in fact, the benefits are impossible to compute. But no private enterprise would have taken that chance without a cash profit being guaranteed. Only a government could say that it was a good idea, that it would cost money up front but we are satisfied to take the benefits much later.

Let us suppose that our government wanted to make cheaper, more frequent train travel available from Vancouver to Prince George and places in between, knowing that the increase in tourism would eventually offset the cost. Does anyone think that CN, absent such an idea being hugely and immediately profitable to them, would bring in such a service? In fact, they have handed off even the current passenger train service from Vancouver to Whistler into the hands of a private entrepreneur, Rocky Mountaineer Railtours.

W.A.C. Bennett also took over the Black Ball Ferries Ltd. and reconstituted it as a crown corporation called BC Ferries. It is the nature of a coastal ferry system that some runs will make money, some will break even and some will be losers—sometimes big time. Private ferries operate on the principle that if a run isn't profitable, it shouldn't be serviced. Or, if there are public policy reasons for servicing a losing run, government subsidies should support the private company to service it. But the whole point of government involvement is, of course, the social issue of bringing transportation to places no private business would go.

There is an axiom by which private capital lives and breathes: If there is a monopoly, private capital will run it more efficiently than will a crown corporation. This is nonsense and is best proved by the history of BC Tel, which for eons ran a privately owned monopoly. When deregulation was on the horizon, they screamed like stuck pigs that they alone knew how to make telephones and telephone wires work. When private companies making telephones came into the market and provided competition, it was quickly seen that BC Tel had been ripping us off. When other companies got the right to use BC Tel hardware we saw that rates, especially long distance rates, had been far too high. What the monopoly BC Tel had been missing was competition.

There are some traditional areas of business that demonstrate that the "hidden hand" of supply and demand must also take *time* into consideration. For example, automobile manufacturing companies have mostly done their business in the open market. It's hard to imagine a more volatile industry; one or another major car company always seems to be in trouble and looking for a government handout. The current situation shows why. At a time when oil prices are skyrocketing out of sight—a most predictable occurrence—these car companies are awash in SUVs and other gas-guzzlers. There is a high demand for "hybrids" and other fuel-saving vehicles, and not only are the companies unable to meet the demand, they can't unload their stockpile of gas-guzzlers either.

It certainly isn't my position that the law of supply and demand isn't an important part of a market. It clearly is. Governments have found to their horror that when they move into the arena by playing favourites, it is invariably a catastrophe. Monopolies, not having to compete, tend to get fat. However, my question is this: is privatization the right way to go with crown corporations? My answer is sometimes, but never when that crown corporation is responsible for services and economic development where private capital will not go.

The Time Has Come

I wanted to go to Harvard. It was the fifties and the Ivy League look was everywhere. The Kingston Trio and other preppy groups were singing the songs. And besides the football was so much better at Harvard than the stuff at UBC where the Varsity couldn't even defeat the tuppenny-ha'penny junior colleges in Bellingham and Walla Walla. But considering my atrocious record in my early years at UBC—I had failed second year—there was no way my old man was going to pay Harvard prices to educate a beer-slopping gambler, golfer and full-time woman chaser.

Well, I asked, how about Oxford? That, too, was out of the question, and my father, who had been remarkably patient with me, gave me the options of taking law or accounting or getting a job. And that is how in September 1953 I found myself in UBC's law school where, while I avoided the gold medal by a wide margin, I did finish in the top third of the class and graduated with the remarkable Class of 1956 which included the likes of Tom Berger, Ron Basford, Peter Butler, Tom Braidwood and a goodly number of other judges and politicians. We even had a murderess, though in fairness to those who came later she failed first year and graduated with the class behind me. In later years Dean George Curtis, whom my mom knew well, always asked after me, each time observing that I had been one of his brightest students. I never had the heart to tell her that the dean was confusing me with another R. Mair, Bob Mair, a gold medalist who did his masters at Harvard.

Our class recently celebrated its fiftieth anniversary, but I have a terrible confession to make: I have no nostalgia for the University of British Columbia or its law school. I had fun—too much fun—and I made lifelong friends and acquaintances so I feel a special bond with my classmates, but I have none for the institution. Indeed, such is my lack of interest in it that, when a young UBC student who was doing research for the seventy-fifth anniversary of some damned thing or another at UBC asked me for a two-hour on-camera interview, I accepted but told her that frankly I didn't much care about the institution one way or the other. Some ten days or so before the filming was to be done, she emailed me and rather curtly, I thought, told me she didn't need me. It's not, I must emphasize, that I don't like the place, just that I'm indifferent to it.

I am not, however, indifferent to the need for more people to get higher education, whether it be in terms of better apprentice-ship programs or education at the post-grad level at a university, and, I submit, *it should all be publicly funded*. (Incidentally, I do have a small scholarship at the School of Journalism at UBC.)

Before beginning this chapter, I researched as best I could the history of publicly funded primary education, and it seems it pre-dates our entry into Confederation. In the US it had already started by the time the *Mayflower* arrived. Thus, I am sure that a couple of centuries ago there must have been debate on state-funded primary education with one side arguing vigorously that it was the responsi-bility of the family, not the state. The other side would have said it was in the interests of society in general and the state in particular to have the best educated people possible and that meant the public must pay. The rationale then must have been that public money put into primary education was a state investment, and in time this was the accepted norm. I have been around for some years now, and I have never heard anyone argue that kids from grades one to twelve should not have their education paid for out of the public purse. In fact, it's been quite the reverse: the argument has sometimes been made—and partly successfully—that public funds should also be available to private schools. Now, so entrenched is our faith in tax-paid primary education that we never question it and accept that an uneducated citizenry will suffer for its ignorance.

If, then, we agree—all of us—that the state has a major financial role in educating our young people, why does that argument not extend to post-secondary education? What I am suggesting is that we look at our 150-or-more-year-old publicly funded school system and ask ourselves the same question our antecedents did. It's a short question: Do we as a society need significantly greater numbers of higher educated or trained people in the near future? (If you are one of those who doubt the need in the years to come for a highly educated society, you would do well to read both *The World Is Flat* and *The Lexus and the Olive Tree* by Thomas L. Friedman. Ahead of us are very tough times, even for the well-educated or well-trained person. Outsourcing to foreign lands is not going to go away. We are late off the mark as it is.)

Having surely answered the first question I posed in the affirmative, my next question naturally follows: Will that education be denied those who can't afford it or should the argument that prevailed for publicly funded schools now logically extend to post-secondary education?

To say that funding it is up to the parents condemns thousands of young people to the role of the undereducated simply because of who they were born to. Public funding of post-secondary education means that not only will we have a more productive society, we will avoid the catastrophe of not being a well-educated one. But won't such a scheme lead to sex-obsessed gamblers and golfers like Rafe Mair whiling away their time as they feed at the public teat? Not if suitable safeguards are in place to ensure that university seats are available only to those who take their education seriously. Back in the 1950s I put fun before education for the same reason a dog licks his balls: I could. Had I been forced to face up to the fact earlier that my paid education was ending if I didn't take it seriously, it would have been lesson enough. As it will be for most young people. There is, of course, also a legitimate concern that out-of-country kids will flock to where fees are paid. This is one good reason that higher education ought to be funded jointly by Ottawa and the provinces and safeguards put in place to ensure that those outside Canada are required to pay fees.

The solution to the funding of post-secondary education comes down to the will of the taxpayer to send the necessary money to a government with balls enough to spend it on such education. And that unwillingness wouldn't be there if governments would look beyond the current fiscal period and past the term of office they are bound by and try to assess what a well-functioning society must look like in the future.

I believe that taxpayers will, more and more, be willing to help high school graduates get higher and better training and education. But will they make that decision in time? BC, indeed Canada, cannot afford to lag behind as we surely will if we don't address this issue quickly and properly. If we believe society must fund K-12, logic and common sense tells us that the time has come to re-evaluate post-secondary education as our forefathers evaluated primary education.

Is Churchill Still Relevant?

I am a lifelong admirer of Winston Churchill. I am old enough to know what his impact was on Britain and the rest of the free world in 1940 when the UK was alone against Nazi Germany and fascist Italy. I mention Italy because, however much we may laugh at their military inadequacy (one of the smallest books in the world is entitled Italian War Heroes, har-de-har-har), Italy had a modern navy that seriously threatened Britain's lifeline to the east through the Suez Canal. I came of age during World War II and was subjected for six formative years to unbelievable propaganda in favour of Churchill and all he did and stood for. So I was horrified, flabbergasted, when revisionists came along about fifteen or twenty years after the war and criticized everything he did and stood for. How could these people not know? What was it that made them unable to understand?

The neo-Nazi David Irving had a field day. Maybe, said Irving, Hitler was a little rough on the Jews but, if Churchill had only made peace with him in 1940, why Hitler would have beaten the bejesus out of the Soviet Union and we would never have had the Cold War. The fact that Churchill knew that peace with Hitler would have meant German control of most of the oil available to Britain and that Hitler would soon have turned on Britain despite any peace deal, just as he was to turn on the USSR, seemed too difficult for the revisionists to grasp.

During the revisionist period—which has petered out but is not yet gone—I remained loyal. I waded through the eight-volume, eight-thousand-page official biography of Churchill that was started by his son Randolph. Sir Martin Gilbert wrote the last six books. Reading them gave me the chance to deal with my hero virtually day by day. As the process of my own aging continued and as more Churchill evidence poured out into the market, I realized that Churchill had made mistakes—big ones. I read everything there is to read on Gallipoli, which his political foe Clement Attlee called the only innovative suggestion of World War I, and I saw the impetuousness and the power of persuasion with which Churchill had backed it up. Yet I saw, as Attlee did, that it was often not the idea that was at fault but its implementation, most of which was out of Churchill's hands. Had Gallipoli worked (and thanks mainly to Lord Kitchener it *was* badly implemented), the slaughter in the trenches of France and Flanders might have been considerably shortened.

I saw that Churchill's position on India was wrong and outdated and that this cost him support when he and the world most needed him to have influence—in the 1930s—and could have cost him the premiership in 1940. I also saw that, though Churchill may have been wrong in principle, he was horribly right in assessing the cost in human life that Indian independence and the Hindu-Muslim split would engender.

He was wrong to stick up for Edward VIII when he tried to keep both his twice-divorced American lady and the throne, but he was true to his friend and what he saw as the threat to the monarchy. His error on this score, however, was mostly because the unpopularity he achieved in and out of Parliament nearly kept him from leading Britain and the free world after May 1940 when all hell broke loose in France and the Low Countries, and when Germany smashed all resistance and stood on the beaches of France with only the Channel lying between Hitler and Buckingham Palace. But while the revisionists made me think and be more critical, they also confirmed for me that Churchill was indeed the outstanding statesman of the twentieth century—by a mile.

But has he any relevance today? When hoodlums defaced his statue in Parliament Square a couple of years ago, the nation arose as one in indignation, but did that really mean anything? Many modern-day politicians invoke his name when opposing what they see as appeasement, but they ignore the fact that Churchill favoured appeasement of legitimate claims, only condemning it when it postponed the inevitable and gave tyrants like Hitler that to which they were not entitled in the first place.

What of the Churchill who, out of office but clearly not out of power, spoke in Zurich in 1946 of the unthinkable: bringing Germany and France together in order to eventually bring about a United States of Europe? What of the Churchill of the same year who in Fulton, Missouri, (to the horror of his host, President Truman) talked of the "Iron Curtain" that had descended from "Stettin in the Baltic to Trieste in the Adriatic"?

Does Sir Winston Leonard Spencer Churchill (his proper moniker) have any relevance in the first decade of the twenty-first century? I invite you to visit the new (opened in February 2005) Churchill Museum at the Cabinet War Rooms next to Horse Guards palace and just around the corner from the Houses of Parliament. It is a brilliant museum complete with old footage, speeches remembered and forgotten (some best forgotten) and terrific user-friendly, touch-to-operate exhibits. Wendy and I spent nearly four hours there in August 2005 and as much again that November, and both agreed that we had barely begun. He is all there, warts and all. This is simply the best—far and away—museum of its type I have ever seen. And it answers the question, "Does Churchill have relevance?" with a resounding yes! If you go to learn, not just to confirm prejudices one way or another, you will meet the man who served his country and the world such that without him the Nazis would have won the war with God-only-knows-what consequences. You will see real leadership by a man who was scarcely beloved of the country when he took office. You'll see a man who not only had the necessary words but backed them up with deeds, a man who not only spoke of courage but had his own superb personal and political courage. You'll see the man who, when France had fallen and the evacuation of Dunkirk had left the army without equipment and the air force was dramatically out-manned and out-planed by the Luftwaffe, and an invasion was all but sure, could say this: "Let us therefore brace ourselves to our duty and so bear ourselves that if the British Empire and its Commonwealth lasts for a thousand years, men will still say this was their finest hour."

Soldier, journalist, painter, Nobel laureate for literature, world leader who saved western civilization, prophet. If we have become so jaded that the things he did, the principles he stood for and the words he spoke no longer matter, if we have reached this stage of the world's progress—if indeed progress it can be called—that we are no longer thrilled, touched, moved and inspired by this sort of example, we're likely on a downslope that leads to a bottomless pit.

For this indeed was a man.

Who's to Blame?

It is over sixty years since the discovery of the Nazi extermination camps and strange things are happening, strange and bad things.

The late Elie Weisel, the well-known survivor of the death camps who from 1945 until his death devoted every waking moment to locating Nazi war criminals and bringing them to justice, was invited to address the United Nations on the sixtieth anniversary of the liberation of the camps. However, barely half the delegates did him, the dead, and the millions who were physically and emotionally impacted the honour of attending.

Now we begin to hear it in the pubs and restaurants, over coffee and the newspaper in the morning—we've all heard it—why can't those damned Jews let it alone? After all, it's been sixty years and it wasn't *our* fault. Besides, Stalin, Mao and Pol Pot were as bad or worse than Hitler. And who says it was actually six million, anyway?

This is part of an anti-Semitism that has gone on for two thousand years. In spite of the overwhelming information, there are still those who deny they are anti-Semitic while at the same time they raise such hoary, discredited arguments as the fraudulent *Protocols of the Learned Elders of Zion.* The "I'm-not-a-bit-anti-Semitic-but . . ." folks and, of course, the "Some-of-my-best-friends-are-Jews . . ." people have not gone away.

I believe it is not open to us to compare the Holocaust to other horrors and thus minimize what the Nazis did. At the same time it is not open to us to cut Germany off from the herd and pretend that the responsibilities ended at the German borders. The fact is that we are all to blame, and in a big way, not just in some symbolic sort of fashion. We in the comfortable west look at Stalin's crimes, the atrocities of Pol Pot, the mass murders of Mao, the horrors of Rwanda and so on and conclude that these were acts of barbarian societies and had nothing to do with us. We ask why we can't just say that the Holocaust was German and thus had nothing to do with us.

Yes, the Holocaust was German, but it could not have happened without a deep-rooted anti-Semitism not only in Germany and Austria but throughout the western world. It is to the eternal shame of all of us—a big stain on our societies—that we turned aside Jewish refugees at our borders, thus forcing them back to certain death. Our western societies, so ready to embrace Beethoven, Mozart and Goethe, forget that the anti-Semitism of Wagner and others came with it. But it goes much further. The authorities in Vichy France, the part not under Nazi occupation, and indeed French authorities on both sides of the line that separated occupied and non-occupied France, enthusiastically delivered up an estimated seventy-six thousand Jewish fellow citizens to the Nazi death camps. This perhaps shouldn't surprise anyone because France, though considered a cradle of democracy and culture, was simply reinforcing the fact that the same virulent, deep-seated anti-Semitism that had wrongly convicted Alfred Dreyfus of treason in 1894 and sent him to Devil's Island was alive and well.

Would Britain have been any different had Hitler successfully invaded and put Jews at the tender mercies of Sir Oswald Mosley and his Blackshirts? Of course there were acts of courage—Holland,

Denmark, Poland and Czechoslovakia come quickly to mind—but the fact is that European civilization—all of it—stands accused and condemned of an anti-Semitism without which a Holocaust could not have happened. I don't say that today all Germans, French, Britons or anyone else must take personal blame for what happened. Even if, as has been suggested, many Germans had to know about the slave camps and exterminations, most alive today were not even born then.

And from our comfortable perches we must in fairness also ask this question: What would we individually or collectively have done in their place? Indeed, it is the answer to this that exonerates most individuals from direct blame but at the same time condemns a culture—*our* culture—where such atrocities could be committed by those in authority and ignored by the rest of us. Who is the more culpable, the French prefect who sent Jews to Auschwitz or the Canadians and Americans who sent them packing from their shores in full knowledge of what Hitler was all about? Okay, when we turned those refugees away, we could not be sure they would be murdered, but we all knew about the Nuremburg laws, we all saw the pictures if not the actualities of *Kristallnacht* where Jews, already victims of the worst pogrom in history, were being forced to pay for the damage done by their persecutors. It was no secret that Jews by the thousands were being turned away from safe refuge in western countries and robbed and imprisoned in increasing numbers.

It is here, I think, where we are missing the message of the late Mr. Weisel and others. It's not a question of accepting personal blame for a horror that in the hands of a government such as Hitler's was probably impossible to stop; rather it's a question of understanding that the Holocaust relied upon the Jews of Europe being privately vilified and, in a wider sense, friendless. The thousands who participated in running the death camps weren't under any compulsion to do what they did. Under the rules they could have opted out, but the theory was that they were a part of a host society where the vermin of anti-Semitism could prosper. The steps from blaming Jewry for the loss of World War I to considering them subhuman vermin without the right to live could only be taken in a culture that made those steps possible.

We in Canada denied Jews the right to buy houses in certain areas and the right to belong to most clubs. Neither of these caused Hitler or the Holocaust, but it was the underlying anti-Semitism in our society that blunted the message and made it easier for Hitler and his henchmen to get away with this massive crime.

No, when we talk about the Holocaust—and we should do that a lot—it is not a time to revisit the questions of blame. It is rather a time to remind ourselves that anti-Semitism is alive and well in this country and elsewhere, and that without deeply rooted anti-Semitism in our western European-style society, the Holocaust could not have happened. For when we stood on the sidelines and turned our eyes away from the scene, we too played a role.

An Act of Plunder

Last spring two things happened to me that took me into a small corner of my brain that I don't like visiting. First there was an email from a sometime editor of mine telling me that efforts were being made to save the childhood home of internationally acclaimed writer Joy Kogawa, a house located at 1450 West 64th Avenue. Then on the weekend I read a review of the autobiography of Dr. David Suzuki.

Allow me to paint a picture of British Columbia in the early months of 1942. On December 7, 1941, the Japanese had attacked the US naval base in Pearl Harbor, causing large-scale damage to the ships there and death to many Americans. This devastating attack drove a stake of fear into the hearts of Americans and Canadians living on the West Coast. But it was more than just Pearl Harbor that had done it. Japanese soldiers had committed horrible atrocities—perhaps too mild a word—in their undeclared war in China. Between December 1937 and March 1938 approximately four hundred thousand Chinese civilians and prisoners of war had been slaughtered by the invading troops. An estimated eighty thousand women and girls were raped, many of them then mutilated and/or murdered. This massive atrocity went into the history books as the Rape of Nanking. The prejudice against Japanese Canadians was also part of the prevailing mood and social fabric. "Japs" or "nips," as they were always called, kept to themselves and were obviously not to be trusted. Long before Pearl Harbor, politicians and newspapers were warning of "The Yellow Peril."

In 1942 I was in the eleventh year of my life, while David Suzuki, a third generation Japanese-Canadian, was six. Joy Kogawa, a year older, was second generation. They, along with all Canadians of Japanese origin—among them a little girl from my class at Maple Grove Elementary, Michiko Katayama—were transported to concentration camps, mostly in the interior of BC, where they remained interned until the war ended in August 1945. But there was more to it than just internment. A "trustee" was set in place to manage all the internee's holdings, and he sold them all for as low as ten cents on the dollar, with the money collected going for the upkeep of the prisoners. And here is where I'm forced into the distant recesses of my mind because my dad bought a paper box company from the trustee at a 90 percent discount. Thus, it is fair and accurate to say that I was fed, clothed and educated on assets literally stolen from the true owners. This is a part of me that I can never be rid of. My dad would have been one hundred this July, my mother the same age in November, so I feel I can finally talk about this without opening old wounds.

It must be clearly understood that my dad didn't do anything wrong by the standards of that day. Indeed, this sort of thing was seen as a form of patriotism since it got even with the Japs and kept people working. And that is a key point: with the exception of the Winches, father and son of the CCF (later called the NDP), few expressed any horror at what had been done. Indeed, it was quite the reverse. Government MPs from BC badgered Prime Minister Mackenzie King, who had been told by the commissioner of the RCMP that the Japanese-Canadians posed no threat, to go along with the internments. The local newspapers egged the politicians on. It also must be stressed that while the Japanese forces were horribly cruel to their prisoners—Canadians will always remember the brave soldiers who fought such a hopeless battle in Hong Kong—the people we interned and from whom we stole goods were Canadians. Indeed, there is a memorial column in Stanley Park in remembrance of Canadians of Japanese descent who fought and died for Canada during World War I.

In a curious twist, at the conclusion of WWII the federal government offered all these internees a one-way passage to Japan, a country few had ever seen. Many, however, chose to come back to the West Coast to start again from nothing, and while Joy Kogawa and David Suzuki are shining examples of forgiveness and achievement, they are by no means the only ones who returned to live useful lives here.

It is difficult for us nearly sixty-five years later to assess the situation and make judgments. We must be careful not to substitute the mores of today for those of 1942. Although I was just starting my teens, I can still vividly remember the fear in the eyes of my parents, especially after an air raid drill. But even without the fear of war, this was a racist time. Jews were "kikes," Catholics "micks," Chinese "chinks" and blacks were "niggers." This wasn't just the talk of the beer parlour but of the highest society as well, not to mention the newspapers. Titles to land carried "restrictive covenants," meaning that you couldn't sell your home to minorities. Most minorities, including Native Indians, couldn't vote. Still, people at the time didn't see their society as racist but "normal."

But it was wrong, terribly wrong. It was mob rule with nearly all the white citizens as part of that mob. That wrong was eventually dealt with in part, and thus acknowledged, by the government of Canada paying token damages to survivors of the people imprisoned. It's interesting to note, however, that both the supreme courts of Canada and the US have heard cases putting this point in issue, and in each case the government won.

A lot of time has passed. The generation old enough to vote at that time are almost all gone. The progeny of the imprisoned people have simply blended into the overall community. But the legacy is still there, the stain on the escutcheon still visible. And the legacy and stain will remain.

The positive consequence is that we have changed—not away from prejudice, for that exists in great abundance in our communities—but to the extent that we, officially at least, condemn bigotry and racism. We collectively know it is wrong and our laws now reflect that. Much of that change is because of people like David Suzuki and Joy Kogawa because their legacies will be with us and our community long after they and we have gone—and for that we must all be eternally grateful.

PART NINE

Still Travelling

In Which the World Traveller Goes to the Big Apple—Finally

I have been to all continents but Antarctica and have been as close to that as I wish to be. I have visited London more than eighty times and have seen most of the great capitals of Europe, yet until March 2006 I had never been in New York City except to change planes. I don't know why this is so. Everyone I spoke to told me that New York was a wonderful place but somehow I shied away from it. Perhaps, deep down I was a little scared to go. It seemed so overwhelming in the contemplation—huge, very tall buildings, cranky taxi drivers, violence on the subway and in Central Park.

Wendy and I had long planned a Caribbean cruise and saw an ad for what we wanted for early March. As I checked online for the best routes to San Juan, Puerto Rico, whence the cruise began, New York seemed to be in the way. It would be a bit of added expense but what the hell! I booked us home via New York and blocked out four days for a stay.

I belong to the Vancouver Club, which has privileges in several New York clubs, so that seemed to be the best way to go. Except I couldn't do it that way. I could hear my late mom whispering, "Son, it's the Algonquin you must stay in—no ifs, ands or buts!" It was a little more expensive than a club but, obeying the voice I had always loved to hear, I booked us into the Algonquin Hotel on 44th Street, a couple of blocks away from Times Square. I knew I was going to a shrine more than a hotel. When I was growing up, there was always a copy of the *New Yorker* lying about—intentionally, I later learned from my mother. I was deliberately weaned on articles and cartoons by James Thurber, by the biting wit of Dorothy Parker ("If all the debutantes at the Yale Ball were laid end to end I wouldn't be at all surprised") and the milder but just as funny Robert Benchley ("I think I'll get out of these wet clothes and into a dry Martini") from whose loins sprang Peter and Nathaniel. There was the biting wit of Alexander Woollcott, George S. Kaufman and Franklin P. Adams. There was the great playwright Edna Ferber, comedian Harpo Marx and the still highly readable and amusing "poet" Ogden Nash, (the quotation marks are there so as not to offend real poets), he of course of the "candy is dandy but liquor is quicker" fame.

The above wits of New York writing—and sometimes the creator of the *New Yorker* magazine, Harold Ross—had repaired daily during the 1920s, '30s and '40s to the Round Table in the Algonquin Hotel's Oak Room to have lunch. Thus, since this was where the writing elite of New York had come, it had to be the Algonquin for us. Happily there was a bargain price available and even more happily they had room for Wendy and me for four nights.

We arrived at Newark airport just after 8:00 A.M., having arisen in time for a 4:45 A.M. flight out of Puerto Rico. Now I can remember when getting home at 2:00 A.M. was not an uncommon occurrence but those days are long behind me. Tired though we were, somehow arriving in this awesome city made us feel as if we'd had plenty of sleep.

The city came into view not long after we left the airport. There she was in all her glory, and towering above her rivals stood the Empire State Building. We were too early for our room to be ready, but we learned from the concierge that a tour bus left Times Square every half hour. As Wendy and I love tour buses—even in London where we visit so often—we immediately booked and set off on foot. Then, good grief, there we were in the most well-known square in the world, gawking at the big buildings and the large signs as though just in from Prairie Dog, Saskatchewan!

It was cold as hell that day—the temperature was 30° F with a wind chill factor that sent it at least 5 degrees colder—thus a considerable sacrifice of comfort was required as we boarded the bus and went to the top. But what fun it was. Our guide, Susan, had that New York Jewish accent that Ann Bancroft portrayed so well in *84 Charing Cross Road*—and she was delightful. Amusing unto funny, she was one of the best guides I've ever known. And the places whizzed by: Times Square, Ground Zero, the Rockefeller Centre, the United Nations and General Assembly buildings, the ever-present Empire State Building, Saks Fifth Avenue, the Trump Building, Madison Square Gardens, Herald's Square, Macy's, Greenwich Village, Wall Street. On and on it went.

However, having just arrived from the tropics and having no access to our suitcases, we had embarked on this expedition pretty sparsely dressed. Fortunately, the helpful concierge had advised us that we could buy scarves and mittens on street corners for modest sums, and she was very right. I got a pair of lined gloves and a serviceable scarf for $8 all told! Despite this, when we completed our bus circuit, I was shivering so hard I literally couldn't talk. But it was into a local bistro for the customary restoratives and we managed, just, to fight off hypothermia! Back at the hotel we added a few layers of clothing and were ready to go at it again.

Wendy and I always cover a lot of ground just walking. One day we walked from the hotel to Pier 78 for the harbour cruise and the Statue of Liberty. (I digress to point out that here was a statue offering help to the "huddled masses" while the US government was now deporting the "huddled masses" in large quantities. How times change!) When we got back to shore we walked and walked and walked some more until we had pretty much covered Greenwich Village and wound up in lovely Washington Square, where the hippies of the sixties performed, and met Rex, a chocolate Lab, who reminded us of Chauncey and brought a tear to the eye.

We were going to take the subway back to the hotel, but after seeing how confusing the routes were, we decided to walk, which we did, but not before visiting the Strand Used Book Store which bills itself as the biggest in the world. I believe it! Wendy, with her eagle eye for bargains, found Studs Terkel's first little book, now reprinted, on jazz—a little gem. On the way to Puerto Rico I had lost the Peter Ackroyd biography of Shakespeare I was reading, and damned if Wendy didn't spot a copy, still in its cellophane, at half the retail price and signed by the author! This store is unbelievable and for a book lover a place to spend hours, nay weeks.

It was, of course, obligatory that we see a Broadway play and we settled on *Spamalot*, an adaptation of the Monty Python skit on Camelot. I thought I would laugh to death. The rest of the audience loved it too and gave the cast a welcome and deserved standing ovation. Another highlight was a horse and buggy ride through Central Park. The best part is that the horse didn't fart—which they usually do when I'm in a horse-drawn buggy. We went to the Empire State Building, of course, and the more plucky of us went to the top while I had lunch and waited. Wendy was enthralled by the experience. (Incidentally, there is now a charge to go to the top.) We didn't really dine out as one would usually do in the Big Apple. I have trouble not only meeting the prices of famous dining rooms but, being diabetic, usually wind up wasting the money. We did find a nice Irish Pub around the corner that served just what I needed to go with the occasional flagon of draft beer.

I have, for most of my adult life, indulged myself with good clothes and shoes—my suits and jackets are almost all from Gieves & Hawkes of 1 Savile Row, and my shoes are also British. But as Wendy and I were walking down Fifth Avenue, we saw Brooks

Brothers and, to get right to the point, I now have a Brooks Brothers suit, a seersucker, to join the Gieves & Hawkes ones.

Some things about New York did surprise me. For one thing, there was at least one and often several policemen on every street, and I was told that this was part of former Mayor Rudolph W. Giuliani's war on crime. I was also surprised at the relative cleanliness of the city. And I was most agreeably surprised at the people whom I had expected to find surly and unhelpful. It was quite the opposite. It seemed that as soon as I got my map out there would be someone there to help me out.

Four days is scarcely enough time to even begin to see New York, but it's enough to get one hooked on the place. I now understand why friends have found it remarkable that I had never been there. We shall return!

Travel Vignettes

I first went to Germany in 1964 by accident. I had to go to Britain and Ireland to settle a lawsuit against a client, and the economics of that time were that it would be cheapest if I took a fourteen-day airfare instead of the lesser time I required. Because I didn't have a passport, I had to fly across Canada and pick one up as my journey hit Montreal. This stopover meant that I had to fly Vancouver-Edmonton-Toronto-Montreal via Air Canada, thence to Amsterdam by KLM and then to London via British European Airways (now part of British Airways).

The second half of my business adventures were to take place in Letterkenny, County Donegal, Eire, so I flew to Belfast and hired a car for my first adventure on the left-hand side of the road. It wasn't too bad but that's probably because there wasn't much traffic in Northern Ireland. It was lunchtime when I got to Derry (Londonderry if you're a northern Protestant), so I stopped for a beer and sandwich at a pub. Being noon it was jammed but as I walked in the door the place went silent. I couldn't believe it! Everyone was looking at me and the looks weren't all that friendly.

I went to the bar and asked if I could have a Guinness and

perhaps a cheese sandwich. The bartender then announced to all and sundry, "It's all right, lads. He's a Yank." I have no idea what it would have meant had I been whatever it was they didn't want to see, so I slunk to a table, quaffed my ale in silence and munched my sandwich. Such was my introduction to a country, north and south, that I've visited many times since and have come to love so very much.

Having concluded my business in Letterkenny, I left Dublin for Amsterdam but with three days still in hand before my flight home, I decided to rent a car and go to Copenhagen. I remember driving along the new highway enclosing the Zuider Zee singing "Wonderful, wonderful Copenhagen," but by the time I had reached Bremen it was pretty obvious I wasn't going to Denmark. Thus, I turned right and went to Hanover, somehow finding a tiny hotel for the night. Unusually, neither the herr nor the frau knew English and I had no German, and I was hungry enough to eat a raw cat. This was a message we all understood and we also got on common ground that it was a sandwich I would like. But what kind of sandwich? I thought chicken would be nice and, after flapping my wings and getting nowhere, I went "cluck, cluck, cluck." The frau's face lit up. "Ja, ja," she said and disappeared into the kitchen. She emerged a few minutes later with a huge cheese sandwich! Evidently chickens in German don't cluck and cheeses do!

I very well remember my first trip to New Zealand in 1981. My wife and I were doing some promotion work for Air New Zealand and the company provided us with a tiny car. On day one as we drove up to our motel in Rotorua I heard a hissing sound. "Dammit, I've got a flat," I said. "I'll check us in and then change it." When I'd finished checking in, I came back to the car to find that the husband, who'd been working in the garden when we arrived, already had the bad tire off and was about to bolt on the spare. This was how I learned about the famous New Zealand hospitality, which over the many years I've been visiting the land of my father became ever more evident.

A listener of mine phoned me not long after I had related this story on-air to tell me about his own New Zealand experience. He and his wife were travelling by public bus, stopping for a while wherever it suited them. One day they were walking in a small farming village on the South Island when they started a conversation with a local farmer. When it transpired that my friends were just looking around, the Kiwi announced, "You can't see this place that way!" He took them home, put them up for three days and gave them a car to use!

One other little vignette about New Zealand: On my first trip I took a couple of old friends to dinner in an Italian restaurant in Auckland. When the bill came, I asked my friend how much I should tip. "Nothing," roared my pal. "You damned North Americans are spoiling people with your throwing money around. If you've got some loose change, leave that but *no more!*"

The next day I was driving towards Turangi on Lake Taupo when I saw a sign on the side of the road saying "Refuse Tip." What the hell is this? I thought. This is like North Korea with its signs saying "Love Your Leader!" They really do take this tipping bit seriously in this country. A few miles along I stopped at a service station. (In the years ahead the proprietors, Pete and Stella Gordon, became great friends to Wendy and me.) I asked Pete about this sign. Was tipping really all that big a deal in New Zealand? He started to laugh. "No!" he said. "Here we call a garbage dump a refuse tip!" Ah, the handicap of a common language!

There's a story about Japan I've been told and have no reason not to believe. A BC cabinet minister that I will call Jones was visiting Tokyo on a mission. He was accompanied by his wife who used her unmarried name, Smith. When they got to the hotel, the minister found he had been given a room in the name of Mr. and Mrs. Jones and, very conveniently, a room next door assigned to Ms. Smith. The Japanese are very discreet about these things!

When I made my own first trip to Tokyo in 1979 as a minister in the BC government, I was given a luncheon by the Canadian ambassador. After lunch we walked out onto the embassy patio, which had a marvellous view of downtown Tokyo, and the ambassador asked, "Does Tokyo look a bit strange to you?"

I said that it did and my colleagues and I were trying to figure out just what it was.

"Well," said the ambassador, "with the exception of the palace, the Imperial Hotel that General MacArthur wanted as his headquarters and the Diet that he wanted to symbolize democracy, the whole city was flattened during the war, which means that every building you see is the architect's first try!" Of course he was right. As Tokyo was rebuilt, there were no tiresome city councillors to nitpick about how buildings should look.

He made another interesting observation. "Have you seen the Ginza (Tokyo's famous main drag) at night?" Indeed I had. "And what did you think of the massive, multi-coloured neon signs?" I said that they made a fascinating spectacle. "What," asked the ambassador, "would you have thought if the signs had all been in English?" And of course he was right again. It would have looked like any North American city, but because all the signage was in Japanese characters, it had a distinctly artistic look about it.

I found that everywhere I went in Japan young people wanted to try out their English on me. One afternoon in Osaka a number of young girls came up and asked me what time it was. "The same time as on your watches," I said, laughing. They giggled and the next thing I knew we were all talking up a storm. One of the lasses took a bunch of pictures and sent me copies. Nice feeling.

In 1988 I was in Budapest with a tour I was leading. This was, of course, before the Iron Curtain fell, but you could already sense that things were not all that great for the government because in the main square, money changing—a nasty capitalist business—was being done right in front of policemen. On a Sunday stroll I window-shopped downtown and couldn't believe my eyes. There in the store windows were expensive name brands galore, all with unbelievably low price tags. I made up my mind to come back the next day when the stores opened to buy my brains out! Except on Monday all the clothes and magic prices had disappeared, and the same drab stuff was back. I don't know who the government thought they were fooling, but as I found out two years later, things were the same in the Soviet Union.

When I went to Moscow in 1990 the official exchange rate was one ruble for one American dollar. At my hotel you got seventeen rubles for your Yankee buck, and in Red Square you could get thirty rubles to the dollar!

When I left the country, I had time to look around the duty-free store in the airport. Technically one was not supposed to have any rubles when leaving the country, but I still had several hundred. I saw a fantastic camera, brand name and all, for sale at 250 rubles. I proffered the appropriate amount to the clerk, who said matter-of-factly that the price was US$250. "But," I stammered, "the sign says 250 rubles!" And he replied, "That's what it costs, sir. The ruble is the same price as the dollar but we only take dollars!" The Soviet Union itself wouldn't accept its own money! And there was no arguing with Soviet officialdom!

Another interesting thing about the Soviet Union related to taxis. There was a taxi rank right in front of the National Hotel on Red Square where I was staying. I was in the city to do a radio show and my producer and I needed a taxi to get to the studio, but one after another the taxi drivers looked up from their newspapers and said, "Nyet." Then we remembered what we had been told: offer a package of Marlboro cigarettes. It worked like a charm. The answer was pretty simple: the taxi drivers were paid by the state whether they drove or not, and all fares went to the government, so why drive?

Every November Wendy and I go to London for three weeks but break the visit up with a three- or four-day visit to a European city, usually staying in a two- or three-star hotel that provides a continental breakfast. About five years ago we chose Paris, a city we had both visited before. It is, of course, lovely, but Parisians are rightly reputed to be bloody-minded. We took the Chunnel train from Waterloo to Gare du Nord. It appeared that our little pad was only about a one-mile walk from there so, it being a lovely day, we elected to hoof it. The first street we had to cross was a through street so we waited on the curb for a taxi to proceed. Instead, he slowed down and blinked his headlights. We assumed this meant we were to proceed, but as we stepped off the curb, he hit the gas pedal, narrowly avoiding us and shouting what I could only assume were French swear words. We decided what we should have known before: if Parisians are indeed bloody-minded, the most bloody-minded of all drive cabs.

Paris is also known for its pickpockets. Many years ago when my then wife, mother-in-law and two stepchildren took a trip there, I took the kids to see Napoleon's Tomb at Les Invalides while the ladies went to shop at the very toney Rue Rivoli. When we met up again, I learned that the ladies had been robbed. Several little kids, all neatly dressed, had come up to them. While one kid distracted them, the rest had picked them clean. It only took a few seconds.

I arrived just minutes after it happened, and after locating the nearest police station, went there only to be told that they didn't do street crime and that I should go to the one across the street from the Louvre. "What! Do you have special police stations for different crimes?" I asked. Getting a blank stare, we went to the proper station where we found a long lineup of people similarly robbed. When I made it to the wicket, I asked, "Parlez-vous Anglais?" To which the sullen reply was "Non." In fact, everyone in Paris speaks good English but they simply refuse to do so. Fortunately, the lady behind me could translate and helped me give my vital statistics. When it came to the "how did it happen" section, the policeman quickly wrote down "jeunes Yugoslavs," which is evidently the phrase used for gypsies. When I asked if he wanted to know where and how it happened, he said an abrupt "Non" and waved me aside. When I got home, I told this story on-air and received, off air, an irate call from the French consul who said in effect that this happened in all big cities. I replied that maybe that was so but at least other civic police forces act as if they cared just a little bit.

The story had an amazing sequel. A month or so later Patti and I were sitting by our pool when a courier came up the driveway, and what do you suppose he had? Patti's purse and the little purse within her purse where her important stuff had been stored. It was minus the money, credit cards and the lot, but there was her purse. No note, no indication of where this had come from but there was her purse! The only explanation I can think of is that the police were into this business up to their eyeballs, and after the French consul got busy, the top cop got hold of the top gypsy and said "We're getting heat from the consul so give us the purse back." Paris is a jewel but keep your money in your fist inside your pocket. Oh, and one thing more: when you get the bill at a restaurant, do check it carefully. Restaurants are known for sloppy addition and it is always, for some reason, in their favour!

One of the loveliest cities in the world is Prague. Basically untouched by wartime bombings, it is a medieval city in the twenty-first century. The "New Town," for example, was founded by Charles IV in 1348! It's a wonderful walking town, with old cobblestone streets, super old buildings and the wonderful Charles Bridge over the Vltava River, a stone Gothic bridge that connects the Old Town and Malá Strana. It's a city to get lost in because the streets look as if they were laid out by a spaghetti maker! But being lost is a temporary thing rather like being in a maze. One night after Wendy and I had a hot drink in the Old Town Square, we set out for our hotel but somehow never got there and kept winding up back in the square. As we were laughing about it, a lady standing next to us asked if we were lost. We replied "a little bit" and told her where our hotel was. She, it appeared, lived right across the street from it. Then it transpired that she was married to a Canadian and lived only a few months each year in Prague, the rest of the time living in North Vancouver where Wendy and I then lived. Indeed, it is a small world!

And speaking of small worlds, one day some years ago while flying from London to Vancouver, I sat next to a fellow from New Zealand. It turned out that he lived in Paihia in the Bay of Islands where the Mair family hails from. "A great place for sailing," I observed, and the stranger agreed, saying that he was a sailor and was on his way to Auckland to look at a boat.

"Oh," I replied, "I've sailed quite a bit in Hauraki Gulf, the Barrier Islands and so on."

"What kind of vessel was it?" he asked.

"A forty-two-foot motor-sailor," I said.

"Well," said my companion, "I just happen to be going to look at a motor-sailor myself."

I had the funny feeling that sometimes comes when you anticipate the improbable. "What's her name?" I asked.

"The *See Vogel*," was the answer. For the love of Mike! I was sitting next to a man about to buy my friend Sir Earl Richardson's boat upon which I had spent so many happy days! Small world indeed!

One of the nicest cities to visit for walking, shopping and atmosphere is Copenhagen. In 2004 we started and finished a Baltic cruise there, and on our return elected to stay a bit longer before going back to London. We'd been there before and loved it so this was a time to do some touristy things we hadn't previously done. So it was we took a guided cruise of the harbour.

Now, I must tell you that I'm the bane of tour guides' existence for I'm always correcting them. We had a lovely young lady guide and, among other things, she told us how Admiral Horatio Nelson had beaten the Danish navy at the Battle of Copenhagen in 1801 (he did) and then again in 1808. As sweetly as I could, I said, "What a remarkable feat since he was killed at the Battle of Trafalgar in 1805. He was obviously an even more amazing man than I had always believed." The lady got huffy and insisted I was wrong. I gave her my card and asked her to email the results of her new research. I received no email from her.

Speaking of warships, Sweden provides a wonderful tale of

plans gone awry. Here's how the Vasa Museum, which Wendy and I visited in June 2004, tells the story: The *Vasa* was built at the shipyard in Stockholm by Henrik Hybertsson, an experienced Dutch shipbuilder, and this experience was much needed as this warship was to be the mightiest in the world, armed with sixty-four guns on two gun decks. Sunday, August 10, 1628, was the day set for the celebration of her maiden voyage, an act of propaganda for the ambitious Swedish king Gustavus Adolphus, and the beaches around Stockholm were filled with spectators, among them foreign diplomats. The *Vasa* set sail and fired a salute. But after only a few minutes of sailing the ship began to heel over. She righted herself slightly, but heeled over again and water started to gush in through the open gun ports. Then, to everyone's horror and disbelief, the glorious and mighty warship suddenly sank! Of the 150 people on board, 30 to 50 died in the disaster. When the *Vasa* was salvaged in 1961, archaeologists found the remains of 25 skeletons.

Former Premier Glen Clark can console himself with the evidence that government bungling certainly didn't start in our time. The fast ferries fiasco had plenty of ancestors!

One day many years ago I decided that I would take a tape recorder with me on a taxi tour of London and, as luck would have it, found just the right guy—a Cockney who had spent all his life in London. Radio is, of course, theatre of the mind, and the results were wonderful as he described all the sights, many of which are not on the normal London tours. After we crossed Tower Bridge, we approached St. Paul's Cathedral from the east along Cannon Street. We stopped and spent several moments just looking at that magnificent dome, 365 feet high—one foot for every day. This is the Sir Christopher Wren masterpiece built on the site of the old St. Paul's that was destroyed in the Great Fire of 1666. The "new" St. Paul's was itself subject to heavy bombing during the Blitz of 1940–41, and my driver's voice broke as he said, "There she is, the grand old lady. She sat there, unable to move but shaking an imaginary fist and saying, 'You'll not get me, 'itler! Do your worst but you'll not be getting me!'" Here we were at the foot of English Christianity weeping, a Canadian and a Jewish Cockney from Whitechapel. There's now a wonderful memorial statue of the St. Paul's Fire Brigade who saved the grand old lady that night.

Airlines provide a special sort of memory for me, mostly bad, but I think that is in part because they make such nice big targets. I have two memories of British Airways, an airline I've done a fair amount of business with over the years. They have been very helpful when I have needed a pass to do a travelogue, for example, and they're a good airline. In 1990 I was on one of their flights from Moscow to Auckland, New Zealand, travelling business class. BA still had smoking sections in those days, but my part of the cabin was non-smoking, which meant that the loos were as well. I haven't smoked for forty years and, like most ex-smokers, am a bit of a pain in the ass about it.

Somewhere between Abu Dhabi and Singapore my constipation ended, and I had to go to the biffy. I did so and had just settled nicely into having a relieving bowel movement when there was a banging on the door. "Come out at once, sir" was the cry. "You're not allowed to smoke in there!"

"I don't smoke," I replied.

Whereupon the voice said, "Open up *now!*" I was in no position to obey the order, so "Whap!" the door was flung open, exposing me in my embarrassment to all who had become curious at what was going on. There was a rustling of trousers and hearty apologies from the cabin attendant, the door was closed and I was allowed to resume my mission. It turned out that the smoke alarm was faulty, a fact that was known to the purser who just forgot to tell anyone!

On another occasion I was flying British Airways from London to Vancouver, and in those days the plane stopped in Seattle before doing the remaining short hop to Vancouver. BA had asked me to take a tape recorder and ask passengers in the economy section how they were enjoying their flight. (In those days the airline's competition came in part from Air Canada but even more from Wardair, which was an extremely popular charter company.) All might have gone well except the cabin crew asked that I not disturb passengers en route but wait until I got to Seattle when everyone was awake and pissed off that they had to wait to make that short hop to Vancouver.

"How have you enjoyed your flight with British Airways?" I would ask.

To a person the answer was "Pretty good, I guess, but nothing like the wonderful flights you get on Wardair." Somehow I don't think the advertising people at British Airlines got too many clips suitable for advertising out of my efforts!

The scariest flight I ever had was on Air Canada travelling from Vancouver to Toronto back in the seventies. Being a minister of the Crown, I was travelling first class—couldn't let the voter down, you know—and next to me was a lawyer friend from Victoria, Cec Branson. We chatted along as seatmates will, and I remembered that he had once experienced a little excitement travelling on Air West, the seaplane port-to-port carrier between Vancouver and Victoria. (We who used the company a lot called it "Scare West.")

"Oh yes," Cec reminisced, "I was on that plane that crashed on Saltspring Island."

"Jesus," I said, "and I'm riding with you!"

Just then we heard a funny sound that was followed by the captain's voice on the intercom saying, "I don't want to alarm you (which he sure as hell did) but we've just lost one of our port engines, and we're making an emergency landing in Winnipeg in half an hour or so."

I turned to Cec and said, "I had made a vow not to have a drink on this flight so that I'm not half in the bag when my son picks me up in Toronto but to hell with that!"

As I recollect it, we spent a couple of hours playing gin rummy in Winnipeg accompanied by a bottle of Scotch courtesy of Air Canada. I'm usually prepared to keep my pledges, but I can tell you that if fear is an excuse, I had it—and I made the most of it!

Some Thoughts of London
on August 25, 2005

I have two loves of my life (three if you count Chauncey): Wendy and London. I've written about them all in the past, but I want to give you some of my thoughts as I sit in our room after a typical day in London, August 25, 2005. This is the first of three visits planned for this year; we will be here again in November and, if Wendy gets our taxes in hand and I have enough points for a couple of tickets, we'll be here for my birthday on New Year's Eve. [Those trips did indeed come to pass.]

Today I noticed that Tube prices in Zone 1, Central London, are now two quid. [In January 2006 they went to three pounds!] Here's where the marketplace comes into play. With two travelling companions, Bob and Edith, it now nearly pays us to take a taxi into downtown; you can travel a fair distance by cab for eight pounds. There is always the other consideration, though; the Tube doesn't get into traffic jams. What we've noticed on the Underground is that it's much cleaner than it used to be and much more efficient.

This city is no place for a bookaholic. As usual, Wendy brought a duffle bag along to take home the books I would purchase. "Waste of space, honey," I said. "This isn't really a good year for books and, besides, I have over forty new ones at home I haven't read yet." Now with a week still to go I have twelve books, the duffle bag is full, and Bookthrift, just around the corner, is having a sale. Just a little hint for other bookaholics: if you want to throw your mate off the scent, tell her, "Let's take a little walk along the South Bank, maybe even take a ride on the big Ferris wheel they call the London Eye, then walk through to the Millennium Bridge and up to St. Paul's." If he/she agrees, and it happens to be Saturday or Sunday, you'll pass right through a huge open-air book sale where there are often some very good buys. And while I know I shouldn't be an enabler and encourage your bad habits, I must tell you that Quinto, a good used bookstore on Charing Cross Road, now has a new and even bigger one on Great Russell Street opposite the British Museum.

Eating in London is hugely expensive. A nice Italian dinner for two with wine will run you CDN$100, though, oddly, it's not much higher in a hotel restaurant unless we're talking the Ritz, the Chesterfield or Claridges—which I certainly am not. The best way is to forget about it, charge it up and enjoy. Of course, the day will come when the bills arrive, and that is when you and your love swear an oath not to go to London for a while, (for us this lasts until Wendy gets the pictures developed) and if we do, we'll force ourselves to eat every third meal in a fast-food restaurant (which we won't). Lunches are also very expensive here unless you have a sandwich at one of a zillion Pret a Mangers (which, for the language-challenged, means "ready to eat") and they are quite reasonable. They have a very large selection of very fresh sandwiches and assorted other goodies. There are even more Starbucks—there's actually a plague of them in London and they are very popular. If, like me, you must avoid sugar, you should avoid Starbucks because you'll be sorely tempted to eat their sugar-loaded muffins; they are good but guaranteed to drive that old blood sugar to the moon! Some serve sandwiches but they're not as fresh as at Pret a Manger. There are quite a number of coffee places much like Starbucks—Costa and Esquire come to mind—but I have the same complaint as with Starbucks and now nearly always eat lunch at the Pret a Manger. However, today Wendy and I ate in the Café 400 in the basement of Selfridges department store where—are you ready for this?—they do the best pizza in town!

Staying in London is very expensive but there are good deals available, especially off the internet, always remembering that if it doesn't work out there is no "Mr. Internet" to complain to. There is also the option of renting a flat by the week or more, especially if you're travelling with another couple. There are, of course, lots of things that add up the rent, but a rule of thumb is that things get cheaper the further you move out of the centre of town.

While God knows we're no upper-crust snobs, the theatre is one reason we love London, but it too is expensive as hell. There are cheap tickets available at, for example, Leicester Square, but they're not for the big shows. To see one of them, expect to pay between CDN$75 and $100 per ducat for good seats. Again, if you have patience and are good at that sort of thing, you can often make a bit better deal yourself online. Of course, the less attractive the seat, the less you pay.

Sitting as we have, in a pub with a pint, one thought prevails: when are we coming back and how will we get the money to pay for it?

PART TEN

Mortal Thoughts

The Good Old Days

I suppose every generation looks back at their younger days wistfully. Those were the days! High school romances. Summer loves that would last forever. Dad's car. The easy life when you could leave your house and car unlocked and where everyone knew their place. For me it was a time when all kids hitchhiked and were always promptly picked up and dropped off without being attacked sexually or robbed. Traffic was lighter and drivers more courteous. There was no crack, crystal meth or cocaine. It was the time of the Saturday night dance at the church hall where you hoped you would dance the home waltz with that neat chick you'd had your eye on. Your mom and dad stayed together, and if you had a black dog it was probably named Nigger or Darky and nobody thought anything about it—though they sure should have. Television had good stuff on it: variety shows and excellent plays. It was a hell of a good time to be young.

But how good was it really? Every summer there was a polio epidemic that scared everyone and hit far too many. Women were second-class citizens at best. They stayed home and did all the crappy things while the husband often acted as if he wasn't really married at all. Men knew it was a case of "drop one dish and one baby and you'll never be asked to touch either one again." Women in the workplace were paid substantially less and rarely were they permitted to compete with men. In fact, many people saw working women as taking a breadwinner's job away from a husband and father. A woman couldn't get credit without her husband's signature. She dared not divorce a straying or, as often was the case, brutal husband because of the stigma attached. Women who got divorced had their names in the paper for all to see. Policemen, on arriving at a house where the old man was kicking the shit out of his wife, simply restored order and went on their way, marking it down as a "domestic dispute."

Racism was rampant and not only in the southern United States. Jewish, African and Asian Canadians couldn't buy property in many areas of Greater Vancouver and were not allowed to join many private clubs until the 1970s. Women waited to get into the Vancouver Club, the province's most prestigious, until 1995. Native people and Asians didn't get the vote until after World War II. Visiting black performers knew which Vancouver hotels would take them and which would not. The "better" ones would not.

If you wanted an alcoholic drink or a glass of wine when dining out, you had to bring your bottle to the restaurant inside a paper bag and keep it hidden under the table. The Penthouse nightclub had slots built under their tables where you could stow your bottle in case of a police raid, the timing of which was usually known to the management. The only place you could get a beer was in a "beer parlour": cavernous, unfriendly dumps where men sat on one side of a partition and "Ladies and Escorts" sat on the other. There was, as you would imagine, much illegal trolling of the Ladies and Escorts side by swains on the make.

The pill hadn't been invented yet so in most cases wooing had an unattainable ambition attached. A female who got pregnant was an object of shame, whereas the boy pretty well got away with it. There were a lot of shotgun marriages. Young people never lived with one another or even travelled together as one of my daughters and her boyfriend did in 1979, which was about the time the new morality took hold. Homosexuals were not only discriminated against, but homosexual practices were against the law, and gay people were jailed.

There are indeed many things wrong today, very wrong. But it wasn't all peaches and cream back then either.

Growing Old
Is Not for the Faint of Heart

It's not easy to tell when it happens. For example, when I started to get what the Brits call "concessions," it was pretty clear that they thought I was old—or perhaps older. Since concessions start at sixty in the UK, I was able to pretend that it wasn't me getting older but just the generosity of the British version of the welfare state that made it look that way. I just didn't feel old.

I must confess I did have some ongoing signs. When I grew a beard in 1970 at age thirty-eight, it was dark in colour. Over the years, as I got it trimmed, I saw some grey whiskers on my barber's apron. I joked about it because it was only just a few. Then before I knew it the hairs falling onto my lap were grey with only the very occasional dark one. But what the hell! One of my grandfathers was grey when he was eighteen.

Becoming a grandfather in 1980 at the age of forty-nine shook me. I got the news at a hotel in Richmond where my wife and I were staying, and it being a beautiful summer evening, I sat on the balcony and solemnly drank most of a bottle of Scotch as I contemplated this milestone. A grandson, named after me, who will grow up before my eyes though I won't know him when he's my age—a sobering thought. My fiftieth and sixtieth birthdays didn't seem to do much damage to my ego. Hell, I was still playing lots of squash and was reasonably fit. But there was one little thing nagging at me—every once in a while my left knee would give out on me on the squash court and I would hit the deck. But it was no big deal.

In 1990 my mom died at eighty-four and that brought a special sorrow for she was my last link to the past. Her death also acted as sort of a line of demarcation. I had lived past my father's age at death; would I make it to eighty-four?

As I moved through the nineties, I developed a couple of health problems, the more serious being type 2 diabetes, which was only supposed to be for old folks. But these days that is no longer the case as quite young people are being diagnosed. It didn't bother me too much since I wasn't on the needle, but it was another little billet-doux from the Grim Reaper that he had me in his sights.

What did give me a jar was my son turning forty in March 1996, though even worse was Kenneth Rafe III turning twenty-one on July 1, 2001. How in the hell had that happened so quickly? And there were another two grandchildren, Kevin and Ashleigh, not far behind. But the all-time worst was when, on March 22, 2006, my son turned fifty. Now it wasn't my own milestones that bothered me. It was those of my descendants.

Both my knees were starting to get worse, still, I came through the nineties and celebrated my sixty-ninth birthday as the first second of January 1, 2001, brought in the new millennium. Life was good. I'd found real love and peace with my lovely Wendy, I was doing well in my career and finances, and although I wore knee supports, I was still playing some squash.

I took my seventieth birthday in stride, celebrating it with Wendy, and Russ and Jone Fraser at a sidewalk Italian restaurant in Cabo San Lucas, Mexico. Oh, of course I was a bit reflective on the biblical lifespan bit, but what I really began to think about were the years wasted, the time in my life when I always seemed to be on a golf course or playing poker and gin rummy at the golf club. Why hadn't I taken a bit of that time to start doing things? There were truly some years that the locusts ate, and I vowed that from then on I would start writing, thinking, taking up issues that troubled me. Though it was a process that had really started when I was in my early forties and went into politics, it wasn't until I was seventy that the evaluation process set in, and I felt a profound sense of dissatisfaction in myself. I was writing a book a year, doing some pretty good radio—I thought—and some television. Whether I was having any impact on anything was for someone else to answer. What I was doing, however, was pleasing myself a bit more because I was trying to make a difference in the political arena, with environmental causes and in the field of mental health.

But I did have an epiphany at that time: I had discovered the antidote to mental old age. And it was simple. Just continually look at the world through a younger person's eyes and concern yourself with things that will come to pass long after you're gone. If you see the world just through your own eyes, you will get meaner and grumpier as you come close to the end. If, however, you worry and think about what the world will be for your grandchildren long after you've hopped the twig, you will keep the mind alive till the end.

Now, at seventy-four, I wear two knee braces and use a walking stick. There's no more squash. My blood sugar readings occupy much of my contemporary worrying time. But I'm a lucky man: I don't want to retire and I still look forward to Monday, and that's an incredible advantage. Most people don't like their work that much and can't wait for gold-watch time.

And I'm still able to think ahead. This isn't easy because of all the reminders, like when your stockbroker talks in terms of the "long term" and you realize that you don't have a "long term." Or when you apply for work and you see that look of slight amazement that says, "Aren't you a little long in the tooth to be still doing this?" You silently pray that someone giving you a seniors' discount will demand ID, but it never happens. You read the obituaries carefully so that when you run into Charlie you don't ask after his wife only to find that she died last year. You go to a lot of funerals and you begin to see death notices of your kids' friends. That really does shake you. You find that much conversation centres around health problems and dying friends. (In my group we have made a rule: we can talk about health and death for fifteen minutes and then it's onto more cheery things. I think it helps.)

Thoughts of religion become more frequent. I went through most of my adult life uncaring about God or matters of religion although I suspect that deep down I expected to be given enough time to say, "Sorry, God. Please forgive my dilly-dallying and let me in." Now, while like most people I'm scared as hell of dying, I do think that by accepting Jesus's two commandments, love thy God and thy neighbour, I have as much chance at the Pearly Gates as one who believes that each and every word of the Bible is true.

I hope my time is a long way off but that no one knows. I find that as the years pass I do think more and more about death, both the act of dying and death itself. I hope, that as Kenny Rogers sings, I'm lucky enough to die in my sleep. But die I will, and then what? We have considerable evidence from "near death" experiences to know that there is a great sense of peace and that there is a brilliant light involved, but as a religious friend of mine says, that's dying, not death. And there's a big difference!

For obvious reasons we know nothing, except what priests tell us, about the afterlife, if afterlife there is. I'm mindful of the wag who said, "Many who yearn for the afterlife don't know what to do with themselves on a rainy Sunday afternoon." I have, however, often wondered what heaven, if there be one, is like. In Salt Lake City many years ago I watched a Mormon movie about heaven and it showed loved ones in visible form all being reunited. That gave me a start. Would this include my two earlier wives? What about members of my family I'm not speaking to? If I've been very good, do I get to select whom I see? And what about the ones I want to see whose idea of heaven is never having to listen to Rafe Mair again? Are we, more likely, dealing with a spirit world here? Is there reincarnation, in which case the supply of spirits might meet the demand? Or are we, perhaps, going into a perpetual sleep without dreams and without awakening?

The Christian faith has been remarkably secretive on this subject. We hear of heaven and paradise but really have no idea what it means. And if it's so wonderful, and if popes and archbishops are on a fast track to Jesus's side, why do they fight death every bit as hard as everyone else does?

So what does a poor human do? Does he just do the best he can or must he worry about bishop-created catechisms for which there is little or no biblical authority? I believe he does the best he can to lead a good, decent life and tries not to worry about the fate all of us must face. Or as Porky Pine in the classic comic strip *Pogo* said, "Don't take life so serious, son, it ain't nohow permanent!" In the end I guess one really has no choice but to do what the great Scottish minstrel Sir Harry Lauder advised when he sang, "Keep right on to the end of the road."

What else is a poor mortal to do?

On Staying Alive

We all must die. At least that's what we're told, though I'm hoping they'll make an exception in my case. I must admit, however, that on the evidence so far, it's a gloomy picture, so I have made my will and left a list of where I want my Churchill library and mementoes to go.

I decided long ago that I would, if at all possible, die in bed and to that end I compiled a list of the ways I'm not going to die.

I'm not going to die, either from a weak heart or a broken rope, while bungee jumping. Though I carry New Zealand citizenship as well as Canadian, the Kiwis can play their little game without me.

I'm not going to die skydiving. There might be knotted ropes or rot in the parachute, so someone else can have that ride.

I'm not going to be killed by a hitchhiker. Every day as I enter the Sea to Sky Highway at Horseshoe Bay I see hitchhikers. They all seem like nice, decent kids, but if there was a thief or a murderer among them, would he look like one or, more likely, like a nice, decent young kid? If I don't ever pick up a hitchhiker, I'll never be killed by one.

I'm not going to be killed hang-gliding. I see those idiots along the North Shore mountains near where I live and I marvel at what they do. Which reminds me, not having wings of my own, I'm also not going to die because an ultralight packs it in when I'm in bad shape.

I'm not going to be killed doing skiing or snowboarding tricks, nor am I going to be killed by an avalanche. I'm lucky here, though, because I don't like snow in the first place.

I'm not going to die trying to make my motorcycle clear a dozen cars or so, Evel Knievel-style. I won't be tempted to do any tricks on a motorcycle because I don't own one, never have and never will. And the fact that they make cyclists wear hard hats tells me that there must be a pretty high incidence of bicycles throwing cyclists onto their heads. I don't own a cyclist hat.

I'm not going to die scuba diving although I recognize that those who do see a lot of very neat things. But I can see those things in aquaria and in neat picture books.

I'm not going to die by eating that fish prepared by Japanese cooks—you know, the fish that if not properly cooked kills you instantly? Again that's an easy one because I don't like fish.

I'm not going to die in a fall from a ladder or falling off my roof. Wendy and I have a division of responsibilities—I do the broadcasting, speeches, writing and the garbage. Everything else is in her domain.

I'm not going to be killed while racing my car. Considering the idiots who flash by me in their SUVs on the Sea to Sky Highway, which I must drive every day, my chances of being killed there are far too good already without racing.

Why Me?

When I was sixteen, I sat in tears on the dock at beautiful Maple Bay on Vancouver Island. My steady girlfriend had just broken up with me. I loved her so much and there she was up at the dance in the arms of another fella. Why me, God, why me?

In October 1976 my daughter Shawn, my beautiful Shawn, was killed in a car accident. These things always happened to other people. Why me, God, why me?

In May 1984 I was fired from my high-paying radio host job and found that I was stony-assed broke. My mortgage was being foreclosed and it was higher than the house's value. I had no assets and owed over $250,000 to banks, credit cards and the tax department. One morning I learned that my loans at the banks had been called and that the tax department was about to break my kneecaps (speaking figuratively, of course) if I didn't pay up immediately. After talking to the tax lady, I sat by the phone and discovered my heart was beating so hard I could hear it, and I asked, why me, God, why me? (Incidentally, I refused to go bankrupt and paid it all back.)

In 1987 I snapped. I've told the story elsewhere of how I was diagnosed as depressed, but while I waited for the prescribed medicines to slowly bring me recovery, I found myself thinking, why me, God, why me?

When the management of CKNW fired me without cause, having manufactured a case against me and leaving a host of utterly untrue rumours in its wake—rumours and statements that I was utterly unable to contradict because the terms of the settlement prevented me from discussing it—I thought, why me, God, why me?

Now, as I look back, I take stock. I have received all the honours one in my profession could hope to have. I look out the bay window of our small condo in Lions Bay and see a view that is unbeaten in the world. I take our wonderful chocolate Labrador, Chauncey, for his daily swim. As I wait for that tennis ball to be dropped at my feet by a sopping wet dog, I look out at Bowen and Gambier islands and the entrance to Collingwood Channel and watch a sea otter swim nonchalantly by. I catapult the tennis ball as far as I can and see, first to my horror but then to my great pleasure, two seals come up near Chauncey, obviously simply curious. An eagle takes off from behind me and flies past majestically. I think of the wonderful vacation we just took in the Caribbean and New York City, and I reflect that, though by no means rich, we can get by. And I see, sitting next to me, my wonderful and beautiful Wendy, the love of my life and think, why me, God, why me?

Index

Abdullah of Saudi Arabia (Crown Prince), 101
Acheson, Dean, 83
Achille Lauro, 110
Ackroyd, Peter, 266
Adams, Barbara, 182
Adams, Earl, 182
Adams, Franklin P., 264
Adolphus, Gustavus, 276
Afghanistan, 102, 113, 114
Africa, 156, 157
Aga Khan, 112
Agricultural Land Commission, 72, 73
Agricultural Land Reserve (ALR), 71, 72
AIDS, 156–157
Air Canada, 268, 277, 278
Air New Zealand, 269
al Qaeda, 111, 116
Alaska, 26
Alberta, 22, 23, 24, 25, 30, 31, 32, 40, 41, 46
Alcan, 242
Alexander the Great, 102
Alger, Horatio, 224
Algonquins, 16
al-Jazeera, 132–133
Amazon.ca, 207
American Revolution, 34
Anglican Church, 112, 155, 159
Apps, Syl, 18
Armstrong, Louis (Satchmo), 219
Asia, 37, 39, 43, 45, 100, 195, 196; East Asia, 96; Southeast Asia, 108
Asper family, 135, 137, 138, 139, 198
Asper, Izzy, 137, 139
Asper, Leonard, 198
Atlantic Canada, 25, 49
Atlantic Charter, 111
Attlee, Clement, 225, 250
Australia, 113, 114, 214
Austria, 81, 85, 184, 254
Bach, J.S., 229
Baghdad, 108
Baldwin, Stanley, 117
Balkans, 87–88, 95
Ballesteros, Seve, 196
Bancroft, Anne, 19, 265
Bannerman, Gary, 123
Barbeau, Jack, 20
Barnes and Noble, 207
Barrett, Dave, 242

Basford, Ron, 245
Bawlf, Samuel, 182
BBC, 111
BC Broadcast Performer of the Year, 12
BC Ferries, 76, 243, 276
BC Hydro, 242
BC Rail, 242–243
BC Tel, 244. *See also* Telus
BCTV, *see* Global/BCTV
Beatles, 91, 219
Beecham, Sir Thomas, 219
Beethoven, Ludwig van, 217, 219, 254
Begbie, Matthew Baillie ("the Hanging Judge"), 17
Belgium, 84, 85, 89
Bell Canada, 137
Bella Coola, 75
Benchley, Nathaniel, 264
Benchley, Peter, 264
Benchley, Robert, 191, 197, 264
Benelux, 84
Bennett, Bill, 12, 44, 70–77, 242
Bennett, Dan, 191
Bennett, Russell, 77
Bennett, W.A.C., 23–24, 76, 242, 243
Berg, Ray, 210
Berger, Tom, 245
Bibeault, Paul, 18
Bierce, Ambrose, 191
bin Laden, Osama, 103, 109, 111–112, 176
Bishop, Peter, 184
Bismarck, Otto von, 81, 223, 225
Black Ball Ferries Ltd., 243
Black Wednesday, 45
Black, Conrad, 136–137
Black, David, 198
Blair, Hugh, 20
Blair, Tony, 41, 88, 90, 92, 102, 109, 116
Bloc Québécois, 30
Boer War, 82
Bolt, Tommy, 195
Boney M, 213
Book of the Month Club, 207
Booker, Christopher, 86, 88, 91
Boone, Pat, 213
Borders, 207
Boston Globe, 158
Bourassa, Robert, 29, 49
Boyd, Denny, 183
Braidwood, Tom, 245

Britain, 16, 19, 28, 33, 35, 42, 43, 45, 49, 82–93, 95, 113–118, 125, 133, 140–141, 195, 196, 207, 210, 213, 225–226, 249, 250, 252, 254–255, 266, 268, 277, 280, 288. *See also* UK; London
British Airways, 268, 277–278
British Columbia Resources Investment Corporation (BCRIC), 76
British Monopolies and Mergers Commission, 141
British Open, 195, 196
Brooks Brothers, 266–267
Brown, Gordon, 89, 92
Bruce Hutchison Lifetime Achievement Award, 12, 121, 122, 123
Bruchet, Dr. Mel, 55, 56–57
Brussels, 43, 84, 89, 92, 93. *See also* European Community
Bulamatari, Archbishop Dominique, 156
Burke, Brian, 127
Bush, George W., 36, 39–40, 41, 42, 44, 101, 102, 109, 116, 117–118, 153, 175, 176, 235
Business Development Bank, 62
Butler, Peter, 245
California, 19, 26
Cambodia, 107
Cameron, Stevie, 9–10, 66, 128
Campaign for Press and Broadcast Freedom, 140–142
Campbell, Charles, 198
Campbell, Gordon, 62, 242
Campbell, Kim, 175
Campbell, Mike, 197
Canadian Alliance Party, 150
Canadian Association of Broadcasters Hall of Fame, 12, 122–123
Canadian Association of Journalists (CAJ), 136
Canadian Football League, 20
Canadian Jewish Congress, 133
Canadian Mental Health Association, 58, 60
Canadian Pacific Railway (CPR), 17
Canoe (website), 137
Cantrell, Roger, 19
CanWest, 126, 135–138, 140, 197
Cape Breton Island, 16, 164
Carlin, Vince, 137, 138
Carney, Pat, 64
Carroll, James, 98
Carter, Jimmy, 148
Cartier, George-Étienne, 31
Cartier, Jacques, 16
Cascadia, 26

Cassidy, Eva, 219
Catholicism, 95, 110, 112, 148, 155–158
CBC, 17, 18
CFAX, 132
Chamberlain, 91
Champlain, Samuel de, 16
Chapters-Indigo, 165, 207
Charest, Jean, 21, 32
Charles IV, 274
Charlottetown Accord, 9, 29, 31, 49, 67, 124
Chauncey, 9, 21, 167, 190–192, 266, 279, 296
Cheffins, Ron, 49
Cherry Creek Ranch, 187, 188
Chicago Black Hawks, 18
Chile, 71
China, 45, 96, 99, 144, 238, 257
CHOI (radio station), 130, 131
Chopin, Frédéric, 217
Chrétien, Jean, 21, 41, 62, 137
Christian Coalition, 149–153
Christianity, 23, 95, 111, 147–154, 277
Churchill Museum, 251
Churchill, Randolph
Churchill, Winston, 28, 42, 43, 83, 93, 97, 99, 101, 105, 111, 115, 200, 202, 209, 225, 226, 249–252
Civil War, 34
CJOR, 74
CKNW, 15, 121, 122, 124, 127, 214, 296
Clark, Glen, 76, 276
Clark, Joe, 21
Clayton, Buck, 214, 215
Clinton, Bill, 118
CN Rail, 242–243
CNN, 132
Coal and Steel Pact, 83
Coast, The, 138
Cold War, 97, 249
Cole, Nat King, 201, 219
Collins, Michael, 28
Combs, Roberta, 150, 153
Community Agriculture Policy, 42–43, 88
Competition Bureau, 141
Congo, Democratic Republic of, 156
Congress of Vienna, 81
Conservative Party (BC), 23
Conservative Party (Newfoundland and Labrador), 49
Conservative Party (Canada), 126, 149, 153
Constitution (of Canada), 9, 22, 29, 31, 32, 41, 43, 48–50, 55, 73, 75, 123–124
Cook, James, 16, 35
Cooke, Mike, 198

Co-operative Commonwealth Federation
(CCF), 36
Cossette Média, 131
Crenshaw, Ben, 196
Criminal Code of Canada, 129, 132, 133,
143
CRTC, 130–133, 142
CTV, 137
Cullen, Jack, 214
Curtis, Dean George, 246
Curtis, Hugh, 75
Cuthand, Doug, 138
Czechoslovakia, 91, 216, 255
d'Estaing, Valéry Giscard, 85, 90
Davey Report, 139
Davey, Keith, 140
David Spencer's Limited, 164
De Cosmos, Amor (William Smith), 17
de Gaulle, Charles, 42, 88
de Valera, Éamon, 28
defamation, 133, 143
Democrats, 148, 149
Denmark, 81, 85, 90, 93, 255, 269, 275
depression, 10, 55–61
Depression, see Great Depression
Des Groseilliers, Médard Chouart, 16
Diamond, Neil, 34
Diefenbaker, John, 21, 36
Doman, Herb, 77
Domet, Stephanie, 138
Dorsey, Tommy, 211, 216
Douglas, Tommy, 24
Downtown Eastside, 75
Dr. Strangelove, 107–108
Drake, Sir Francis, 182
Dreyfus, Alfred, 254
Drillon, Gordie, 18
Duplessis, Maurice, 156
Duval, David, 194
Dvorak, 216–217
Eaton's, 164–165, 172
Economic Development Committee, 76
Economic Times, 108
Edmonton, 21
Edward VIII, 250
Egypt, 101, 103, 109
Eisenhower, Dwight, 148, 149
El Salvador, 156
Ellington, Duke, 215
Elm Street magazine, 10
Els, Ernie, 194
Environmental and Land Use Committee
(ELUC), 71
Equity magazine, 197–198

Erskine, Steuart, 183
Ethelred the Unready, 242
European Atomic Energy Community
(EURATOM), 84
European Coal and Steel Community
(ECSC), 84
European Community, 81–93, 94
European Economic Community (EEC),
see European Community
European Union (EU), 42–43, 45, 85,
87–88, 95
Exchange Rate Mechanism (ERM), 45, 92
Expo 86, 77, 243
Fair, 135
Falwell, Jerry, 130, 149
Ferber, Edna, 264
Filmon, Gary, 50
Fina, Jack, 217
Finland, 85, 100
First Ministers Constitutional Conference,
55
First Nations, 27
fish farming, 124, 127, 236
Fitzgerald, Ella, 219
Forsey, Eugene, 49
Foster, Stephen, 219
Fox News, 133
France, 33, 42, 43, 45, 81–85, 87–88, 90–91,
93, 94–95, 114, 239, 250–252, 254
Fraser Institute, 235
Fraser, Alex, 71
Fraser, John, 20, 63, 210
Fraser, Russ and Jone, 289
Fraser, Simon, 17
Friedman, Milton, 234
Friedman, Thomas L., 45, 237, 247
G8 (Group of Eight), 46
Galbraith, John Kenneth, 234
Gallipoli, 250
Gardom, Garde, 73
General Motors, 40
George, David Lloyd, 225, 226
Georgia, 96
Georgia Straight, 197–198
Georgia Strait Alliance, 209
Germany, 33, 42, 82–85, 87, 90, 91, 97, 99,
110, 114, 116, 135, 141, 223, 249, 251,
254, 268
Gershwin, George, 219
Ghad (Tomorrow) Party, 103
Gibson, Gordon, 29, 49, 198
Gierach, John, 210
Gilbert, Sir Martin, 250
Gingrich, Arthur, 210

Giuliani, Mayor Rudolph W., 267
Global TV, 137
Global/BCTV, 135, 137
Globe and Mail, 66, 131, 137, 138
Gloucester land group, 71–72
Goethe, 254
Gomery Commission, 62–69
Gomery, Justice John H., 63, 64, 69
Goodman, Benny, 216
Google, 17
Gorbachev, Mikhail, 99
Gordon, Pete and Stella, 270
Graham, Billy, 149
Great Depression, 224, 226
Greece, 84, 85
Green Party, 12
Greenspon, Edward, 66
Griffiths family, 127
Gullane Manor, 75
Gzowski, Peter, 10
Hagen, Walter, 195
Haig-Brown, Roderick, 210
Haliburton, Thomas Chandler, 36
Halifax Daily News, 138
Hampton, Lionel, 216
Happy Gang, The, 17
Hargrave, Denis, 181–182
Harker, John, 16
Harlequin, 137
Harmon, Butch, 195
Harper, Elijah, 50
Harris, Hugh, 74
Harvard, 238, 245, 246
Hatfield, Dr. Bill, 183
Hatfield, Lois, 183
Heath, Edward, 86, 88
Heifetz, Jascha, 219
Hewitt, Foster, 18
Hill & Knowlton, 236
Hinduism, 151, 250
Hiroshima, 106–107, 108–109
Hitler, Adolf, 90–91, 97, 98, 106, 249–250,
    251, 253–256
Hockey Night in Canada, 18
Hogan, Ben, 194–196
Hogan, Paul, 167
Hogarth, Dr. Teresa, 57
Hollinger, 136
Hong Kong, 86, 259
Horton, Johnny, 35
House of Commons, 63, 123, 152, 210
Hudson's Bay Company, 163, 165
Hughes, Dave, 210
Huron, 16

Hybertsson, Henrik, 276
IBM, 238
Imperial Oil, 21
India, 44, 236, 237–238, 239, 250
IRA, 118
Iran, 31, 101, 102, 113, 148
Iraq, 36, 41, 44, 96, 101, 102, 104, 111,
    113–114, 148
Ireland, 28, 85, 268, 269
Iroquois, 16
Irving, David, 249
Islam, 45, 94–95, 100, 102, 103, 105, 109,
    110, 111–114, 118, 132, 147–148, 151,
    250
Ismaili, 112
Israel, 27, 101–103, 113, 118, 133–135, 138,
    147–148
Italian Broadcasting Act of 1990, 141
Italy, 84, 85, 215, 249
James, Harry, 211, 216
James Inglis Reid, 165
Japan, 73, 97, 99, 106, 107, 109, 110, 116,
    257, 259, 270–271
Japanese Canadians, 258–259
Johnson, Lyndon, 36, 149
Johnson, Samuel, 37
Jones, Bobby, 194, 195, 196
Judaism, 27, 82, 110, 132, 133, 134, 135,
    147, 148, 151, 249, 253–256, 259, 286
Kaiser, 90
Kamloops, 12, 21, 73, 186–188, 197
Kansas City Star, 157
Kansas, 19
Katayama, Michiko, 258
Kaufman, George S., 264
Kemano Completion Project, 124
Kennan, George, 97
Kennedy, John, 36, 149
Kennedy, Robert, 149
Kennedy, Ted "Teeder," 18
Kent Commission, 139
Kent, Tom, 140
Keynes, Maynard, 234
Khrushchev, Nikita, 97
Kimber, Stephen, 138
King FM, 205
King George VI, 125–126
Kingston Trio, 245
King, William Lyon Mackenzie, 21, 36, 258
Kirby Commission on Mental Health, 55–61
Kirby, Michael, 55, 75
Kissinger, Henry, 36, 46
Kitchener, Lord, 250
KLM, 268

Kogawa, Joy, 257–260
L'Academie Francaise, 202
Laine, Frankie, 214
Lalonde, Marc, 32
Lamont, Norman, 92
Lang, Michelle, 138
Langer, Bernhard, 196
Laos, 107
Lapointe, Jerry, 164
Le Pen, Jean-Marie, 95
League of Nations, 82
Leigh, Sir Percival, 11
LeMay, General Curtis, 107, 108, 109
Lemieux, Pierre, 130–133
Lesage, Premier Jean, 156
Lévesque, Rene, 21, 50
Liberal Party, 23, 29, 32, 36, 49, 51, 62, 68, 126, 128, 137, 138
Liebling, A.J., 129
Lincoln, Abraham, 148, 153
Lind, Jenny, 219
Lions Bay, 166–167, 190, 191, 296
Lithuania, 97
London, 111–113, 115–118, 165, 213–215, 263, 265, 268, 272, 275–277, 279–281
Lougheed, Peter, 21, 31
Louis XIV, 90
Louisiana Purchase, 41
Love, Davis III, 194
Luxembourg, 84, 85
MacArthur, General, 271
Macdonald, Jane, 11, 16
Macdonald, Sir John A., 31
MacIntosh, Andrew, 128
Mackay, Mrs. Constance, 19, 211, 213, 217
Mackay, Pierre, 19
Mackenzie, Alexander, 17
Maclean-Hunter, 67
MacMillan Bloedel, 44, 46
MacMillan, Harold, 88
Macmillan, Sir Ernest, 19
Maillardville, 20
Mair, Elizabeth, 11–12
Mair, Eve, 185, 186, 188
Mair, Gilbert II, 11
Mair, Gilbert, 11–12
Mair, Karen, 187
Mair, Ken, 185
Mair, Patti, 189, 274
Mair, Shawn, 185, 188, 295
Mair, Wendy, 9, 12, 115, 116, 118, 122, 165, 167, 190–193, 207, 213–216, 218, 238, 251, 263–266, 270, 272, 274, 276, 279–281, 289, 294, 296

Major, John, 85, 92
Maloney, Mick, 198–199
Mamas & the Papas, 214–215
Manhattan Transfer, 213
Manitoba, 22, 23, 25, 31, 49, 50, 137
Manning, Ernest, 23
Manning, Preston, 22
Mao Zedong, 253, 254
Maple Grove Elementary School, 19, 258
Marshall, T.H., 224
Martin, Freddy, 217
Martin, Lawrence, 137
Martin, Paul, 21, 62
Marx, Harpo, 264
Massachussetts Institute of Technology (MIT), 238
McCarthy, Grace, 72, 76, 197
McClane, Al, 210
McClelland, Bob, 71, 73
McCreight, John Foster, 17
McCubbin, Cam, 122
McNamara, Robert, 107, 108
McWhinney, Dr. Edward, 29
Meech Lake Accord, 29, 48–51, 67, 124
Meeker, Howie, 18
Meredith, James, 149
Mexico, 44, 187, 289
Michener Award, 12, 124
Mickelson, Phil, 194
Middle East, 42, 100, 101–104, 105, 111, 113, 114, 135, 148
Miller, Glenn, 211, 215
Mills, Russell, 198
Mississippi National Guard, 149
Monnet, Jean, 84
Montcalm, Louis-Joseph de, 16
Montgomerie, Colin, 194
Montreal Canadiens, 18
Moore, Terry, 132
Moral Majority, 149
Morocco, 111
Mosley, Sir Oswald, 254
Mozart, 219, 254
Mubarak, Hosni, 103
Muhammad, Omar Bakri, 111
Mulroney, Brian, 21, 29, 31, 48–51, 66
Munich Olympics, 110
Murdoch, Rupert, 135
Murphy, Dan, 197
Murray, Lowell, 51
Museveni, President Yoweri, 156
Musharraf, General Pervez, 102
Muslim. see Islam
Musqueam, 16

NAFTA (North American Free Trade
   Agreement), 40, 42, 44, 47, 238
Nagasaki, 106–107, 108, 109
Napoleon, 81, 90, 98, 273
Nash, Ogden, 264
Nathan, Susan, 133, 135
National Energy Program (NEP), 30–31,
   32, 46
National Front, 95
National Health Service, 225, 226
National Post, 130, 137, 198
Natives, 27, 28, 50, 51, 259, 286. *See also*
   First Nations
Nazis, 98, 105, 135, 249, 252, 253, 254
NDP, 36, 50, 126, 242, 258
Nearly Neil, 34
Nelson, Admiral Horatio, 275
Netherlands, 84, 85, 224
New Brunswick, 140
New York, 263–267, 296
New Yorker, 200, 207
New York Times, 143
New Zealand, 11–12, 16, 23, 139, 213, 214,
   224, 269–270, 275, 277, 293
Newfoundland, 26, 34, 48–51, 140
Newman, Peter C., 48, 51
Newspaper Guild of Canada, 136
Nicaragua, 155, 156
Nicklaus, Jack, 194–196
Nielsen, Jim, 72
9/11, 111, 113, 116, 117, 118
Nisga'a, 16
Nixon, Richard, 36, 148–149
Noranda, 44
Normandy, 106
North Vancouver, 55, 56, 166, 189, 274
North, Richard, 86, 88, 91
North-East Coal, 76
Northern Ireland, 268
Norway, 91
Nova Scotia, 16, 164
NOW newspapers, 198
O'Conner, Patricia T., 201
O'Connor, Rick, 198
O'Gorman, Dennis, 71
Ogden, Frank, 207
oil, 39–47, 103, 244, 250
Ontario, 17, 22, 24, 26, 30, 37, 46, 47, 49,
   50, 87
Oregon, 26
Ottawa, 17, 22, 23, 24, 25, 28, 31–32, 37, 65,
   75, 87, 131, 176, 248
Oxford University, 245
Pakistan, 102, 111

Palestine, 101, 103
Palmer, Arnold, 195
Parizeau, Jacques, 30
Parker, Dorothy, 264
Parti Québécois, 30
Patten, Chris, 86, 87
Pattison, Jimmy, 128, 239
Pax Britannica, 82
Peace River, 26, 40
Pearl Harbor, 257–258
Pearson, Lester, 21, 36
Peckford, Brian, 49
Perot, Ross, 44
Peter the Great, 97
Peterson, Oscar, 217
Phillips, Art, 26
Phillips, Don, 72, 76
Phillips, Kevin, 34
Pinochet, Augusto, 71
Plasteras, Tom, 121
Player, Gary, 195
Plecas, Bob, 74–75
Pol Pot, 253, 254
Poland, 82, 99, 157, 255
Pope John Paul II, 156–158
Porter, Cole, 219
Portugal, 85, 95
Prelypchan, Norman, 72
Prince Edward Island, 140
Prince George, 62, 243,
Prince of Wales Secondary School, 212
Prince Rupert, 40
Professional Golf Association (PGA), 194,
   195
Province, 198
Prussia, 99, 225
Puerto Rico, 263, 264, 266
Punch magazine, 11
Purdy's Chocolates, 165
Putin, Vladimir, 99, 100, 102
Python, Monty, 266
Quebec Federation of Professional
   Journalists (QFPJ), 136
Quebec, 16, 22, 24–29, 30, 32, 33, 35, 37,
   41, 46–47, 48–50, 87, 131, 137, 156
Quebecor, 137
Queen Charlotte Islands, 22, 40
Queen Elizabeth I, 150
Queen Elizabeth II, 126
Rachmaninoff, 217
Radisson, 16
Ransome, Arthur, 210
Rape of Nanking, 258
Rathenau, Walter, 82

RCMP, 67, 132, 258
Reform Party, *see* Canadian Alliance Party
Regina Leader-Post, 138
Republican Party (GOP), 34, 42, 133,
    147–149, 153
Rheaume, Marc, 18
Richard, Maurice, 18
Richardson, Sir Earl, 275
Rimsky-Korsakov, Nikolai, 217
Roberts, Paul, 39
Robertson, Pat, 130, 149, 151, 152
Robinson, Jackie, 110–111
Robinson, Red, 214
Rocky Mountaineer Railtours, 243
Rogers Communications, 137
Rogers, Will, 159
Romero, Archbishop Oscar, 156
Rooney, Andy, 199
Roosevelt, Franklin, 35, 36, 99, 107, 111
Ross Lake Dam, 124
Ross, Harold, 264
Rubinstein, Arthur, 219
Run Out Skagit Spoilers (ROSS)
    Committee, 124
Russia, 37, 43, 82, 88, 91, 96–100, 102, 109
Rutherford, Doug, 124, 127
Ryerson University School of Journalism,
    137
Safe Streets Act, 60
Sage, Dr. Walter, 17
Salish, 16
Sandison, Bruce, 210
Saskatchewan, 22, 23, 25, 31, 140, 176, 265
Saturday Night, 17
Saudi Arabia, 31, 39, 101–103, 113
Scandinavia, 223
Schneidereit, Paul, 136
Schreiber, Karl-Heinz, 66
Schuman, Robert, 84
Seattle Light and Power, 124
separatism, 22–25, 30, 32
September 11 *see* 9/11
Shakespeare, 202, 266
Shaw, Jack, 210
Shevardnadze, Eduard, 96
Siemens, Gerry, 127, 128
Simmons, Matthew R., 31
Simon and Garfunkel, 213
Sinatra, Frank, 215–216
Singh, Vijay, 194, 196
600AM, 122, 127–128
Skagit River, 124
Smetana, Bedrich, 216–217
Smith, Adam, 241

Smith, Brian, 72
Smith, Charlie, 197
Smith, Mel, 29, 49
Smythe, Conn, 18
Social Credit Party, 12, 23–24
softwood lumber dispute, 36, 37, 42, 47
Somerled, 11
Soros, George, 45
South Africa, 126, 156
Southam, 136, 137, 138, 198
South-West Coal, 76
Soviet Union *see* USSR
Spain, 85, 89, 95, 113
sponsorship scandal, 62, 63, 68, 128
Springer, 141
St. George's School for Boys, 16
St. Laurent, Louis, 21
Stalin, Joseph, 35, 96, 97, 98, 99, 253, 254
Stanfield, Robert, 21
Stanford University, 238
Starbucks, 207, 280–281
Stordahl, Alex, 216
Strauss, Johann I and Johann II, 212, 219
Stravinsky, Igor, 219
Sun newspapers, 137. *See also Vancouver
    Sun*
Suzuki, Dr. David, 257–260
Sweden, 91, 97, 141, 224, 275
Sympatico, 137
Syria, 101, 102
Taliban, 102
Taylor, Austin Sr., 183
Taylor, Carole, 26
Taylor, General Maxwell, 107
Tchaikovsky, 217, 218
Telus, 142, 143
Ten Commandments, 152–153, 159–160
Terasen, 44
Terkel, Studs, 266
terrorism, 105–118
Thailand, 44, 237, 238
Thatcher, Margaret, 88, 92
32 Books Company, 166
Thirty Years War, 95
Thompson & Page, 212
Thompson, David, 17
Thompson, Joey, 198
Thurber, James, 264
Time magazine, 118
Tobin, Shiral, 122
Tokyo, 106, 107, 270–271
Toronto, 16–19, 24, 26, 34, 137, 138, 164,
    184, 278
Toronto Conservatory of Music, 19

Toronto Maple Leafs, 18
Toronto Star, 17, *137, 138*
Toronto Sun, 137
Torstar Corporation, 137
Tovey, Bramwell, 219
Travers, Robert, 210
Treaties of Rome, 84
Treaty of Maastricht, 84–85
Treaty of Versailles, 81, 82
Treaty of Waitangi, 12
Treaty of Westphalia, 81, 95
Trentadue, Mary, 166
Trevino, Lee, 195
Trudeau, Pierre, 21, 30, 32, 36, 66, 73
Truman, Harry, 83, 107, 109, 251
Turkey, 95, 98
TV3, 139
TVA network, 137
Twain, Mark, 191
Tyee (website), 143, 198
Uganda, 156
UK (United Kingdom), 35, 40, 41, 42, 43,
    45, 83, 85, 88, 89, 90, 92, 93, 101, 102,
    103, 225, 239, 249, 288
Ukraine, 96, 98, 99
Ullman, Harlan, 108
Union Carbide, 236
United Arab Emirates, 25
United Church, 112, 130
United Kingdom, *see* UK
United Nations, 35, 253, 265
United States, 26, 33–47, 82, 83, 88, 90, 96,
    97, 98, 100, 102, 103, 106, 107, 113–114,
    148, 156, 184, 223, 226, 238, 239, 242,
    246, 257, 259, 265, 286
University of British Columbia (UBC), 17,
    20, 164, 184, 185, 245, 246
University of Mississippi, 149
University of Pennsylvania, 184
University of Toronto, 184
US Air Force, 107
USSR, 35, 96–99, 102, 226, 249, 250, 272
Vancouver, 12, 16, 20, 26, 60, 75, 115, 135,
    165, 166, 172, 174, 182, 230, 237, 243,
    275, 277, 278, 286
Vancouver Canucks, 127
Vancouver Club, 177, 263, 286
Vancouver Courier, 198
Vancouver Public Library, 207
Vancouver Sun, 198
Vancouver Symphony Orchestra, 219

Vancouver, George, 16, 35
Vander Zalm, Bill, 71, 242
Victoria, 12, 49, 75, 132, 278
Victoria Times-Colonist, 17
Vietnam, Vietnam War, 107–108, 114 ;
    North Vietnam, 108, 113
Viorst, Milton, 94
Wagner, Richard, 254
Wahhabi, 103
Walker, Dr. Michael, 235–236
Wallace, George, 186
Walls, Doug, 62–63
Wal-Mart, 46
War of 1812, 35
Washington Post, 137, 138
Washington state, 20, 26
Washington, George, 34
Waterland, Tom, 71
Watson, Tom, 195
Webster, Jack Jr., 122
Webster, Jack, 74, 121, 123, 128
Weisel, Elie, 253, 255
Wells, Clyde, 48–51
Weyerhaeuser, 44
Williams, Allan, 76
Wilson, Gordon, 49
Wilson, Harold, 86, 88
Winch, Ernest, 258
Winch, Harold, 258
Windsor Star, 137
Winnipeg, 136, 138, 278
Winter, James, 135–137
Wolfe, 16
Woods, Tiger, 194–196
Woodward, Charles, 165
Woodward's, 165
Woolcott, Alexander, 115
World War I, 82, 225, 226, 250, 256, 259
World War II, 16, 18, 19, 34, 35, 82, 97, 98,
    105, 106, 110, 116, 147, 157, 200, 224,
    225, 249, 286
Worthington, Peter, 137
Wotherspoon, Denis, 182
WTO, 238
Yalta Agreement, 35, 98, 109
Yeltsin, 99
Young, Hugo, 86
Young, Lester, 217
Yugoslavia, 82, 99
Zuckert, Eugene, 107
Zundel, Ernst, 129